D0962075

PRAISE

"*Stealing* is a must-read for music fans of all varieties, for it's much more than a book about The Clash. With a captivating narrative and well-written prose, *Stealing* makes sense of what happened to free-form radio and the DIY ethic of punk, and deftly connects that history to the era of file-sharing and satellite radio. Don't miss this book. Steal it if you must!"

—Michael Roberts, author of *Tell Tchaikovsky the News: Rock 'n' Roll, the Labor Question, and the Musicians' Union, 1942–1968*

"Randal Doane's *Stealing All Transmissions: A Secret History of The Clash* is not the story I was expecting from the title. Thankfully. We have all read those books about artists of all stripes (and zippers), from which we learn only about misery, malfeasance, and bad behavior. But this is not that book. The Clash is at the center of the story, but the heart of it belongs to other players. People drawn into the orbit who cared, who pushed both themselves and the band forward, who took risks because they felt and knew they were seeing and hearing a revolution. The people who were excited and inspired by the catalysts (The Clash), whose stories are integral to the core of the band's American journey, and fascinating to finally read about, all in one place.

I loved (and envied) The Clash—the gang of four who dressed better, who wore their hearts and mistakes on their zippered sleeves, and played songs with the force of racehorses bursting from the gate. A good number of people got it from the outset—and because of them as much as the band themselves, an even greater number eventually 'got it.' And they are still getting it.

A large and raucous cheer to Randal Doane for choosing the near-mythical Baker to write the foreword. We are treated to nearly two books in one! Ladies and gentlemen, please raise your glasses and cans to Messrs. Doane and Auguste. A triumphant work from this unlikely Gang of Two."

—Hugo Burnham, founder and drummer, Gang of Four, associate professor, New England Institute of Art

"Paul Simonon was the handsomest boy I'd ever seen in my life."

—Susan Blond, former VP of Epic Records, founder and president of Susan Blond, Inc.

STEALING ALL TRANSMISSIONS
A SECRET HISTORY OF THE CLASH

Randal Doane
Foreword by Barry "The Baker" Auguste

Stealing All Transmissions: A Secret History of The Clash
Randal Doane © 2014
This edition published in 2014 by PM Press

ISBN: 978-1-62963-029-8
Library of Congress Control Number: 2014908059

Cover: John Yates/Stealworks.com
Cover photo: © Pennie Smith. Palladium, New York, September 1979
Layout: Jonathan Rowland

PM Press
P.O. Box 23912
Oakland, CA 94623

10 9 8 7 6 5 4 3 2 1

Printed in the USA by the Employee Owners of Thomson-Shore in Dexter, Michigan
www.thomsonshore.com

CONTENTS

For all that is solid:
Rebecca and Katherine

The world is before you, and you need not take it or leave it as it was when you came in.

—James Baldwin

I can't see anybody playing Clash records on the radio.

—Joe Strummer

Acknowledgments

L ike so many good things, this book began as a conversation—a conversation with Gregg Wirth, to whom I am especially grateful. His wordsmithing superpowers are evident in the best parts of this book. Thanks to Pam Donovan and Erich and Lisa G. Stonestreet for their unflagging encouragement. Joshua Davidson performed valiantly as my research assistant, and Paul Schick and Harley Foos offered insightful feedback on different drafts of this tale. Thanks, too, to the wonderful reference librarians at Oberlin College, the OHIOLINK staff, and Dianna Ford and Jennie Thomas of the Rock and Roll Hall of Fame Library and Archives. Craig O'Hara, Gregory Nipper, assorted comrades at PM Press, and Melanie Hegge offered an abundance of kindness and decency.

A special measure of gratitude goes to Barry "The Baker" Auguste, a veteran of multiple tours of duty with The Clash, for taking an early interest in this project, and for his words and generosity. To Dan Beck, Susan Blond, Robert Christgau, Caroline Coon, Yale Evelev, Wayne Forte, Chris Frantz, Meg Griffin, Bob Gruen, Ivan Kral, Harvey Leeds, the very Handsome Dick Manitoba, Ron McCarrell, Pam Merly, Barry "DJ Scratchy" Myers, Rick Neblung, Richard Neer, Joe Piasek, Pennie Smith, and Roy Trakin: many thanks for taking the time to speak and correspond with me. I hope the account that follows does justice to your tales of joy and glory. Joe Streno also shared his tales of glory, and allowed me to include images from his impressive portfolio in these pages, and for that I am immeasurably grateful. Thanks to Will Keller for sharing his ideas and research (get that book together, Will!), and to Dave Marin for sharing the missing tracks of on-air chatter from *The Guns of Brixton* bootleg. Much gratitude is due to my mentors, Bob Alford (I still miss you something fierce), Stanley Aronowitz, Steve Brier, Patricia Clough, Douglas Daniels, and Kathryn Stuart.

Discretion prevents me from naming key figures whose work behind the scenes made this project possible; you know who you are.

I burned many an hour listening to rock'n'roll with the following characters, to whom I owe much knowledge and grace: John Bagley, Sam Binkley, John Bouchard, Matt Flynn, George Kostopoulos, Eric Lauerwald, Tom Lewis, Shon Martin, Pete Naegele, Ron Nerio, Jon Niefeld, James Nolan, Jerry Olivera, Charles Peterson, Nick Petzak, Dan Pipal, Jeff Shannon, Bryan Stubbs, Suzanne Korock Trickey, Nikki Melvin Vitale, and Betsy Wissinger. Thanks to Brooks Dees, Brian Gifford, and Armen Markarian—you have picked up the tab for an undue share of first rounds, for so many years. Our friendship lends a rock-steady cadence to my world. Kudos to Casey Curtis and Katie Dyer—keep burning brightly. Seamus, my man, you may have fleas, but you can crash on the couch with me anytime. Much gratitude, of course, is due to Messrs. Strummer (rest in rock-steady peace), Jones, Simonon, Headon, and Chimes: thank you for making thoughtful dance music for rebels (and dance music for thoughtful rebels). I might not have made it through adolescence without you.

The greatest thanks is due to my father, the first rock'n'roller I ever met; my mother, who taught me an appreciation for (ahem) the finer things in life; my sister, Stacey, whose camaraderie I cherish; and my wife, Rebecca, and my daughter, Katherine O., a real rock'n'rolla, to whom this book is dedicated. Life with you is a double LP of joy and love and wonder.

Foreword
Everybody Hold on Tight!

When beggars die there are no comets seen; the heavens themselves blaze forth the death of princes.
—William Shakespeare, *Julius Caesar*

It was the epoch of belief, it was the epoch of incredulity . . .
—Charles Dickens, *A Tale of Two Cities*

Every nerve-wrenching night, every frenzied stage invasion, every sweat-soaked guitar riff and every gob-covered drum beat—night after night, the essential ingredients braided together to form the intricate legacy of The Clash. For our seven-year convulsion of raw intensity and outrageous audacity, there was no script, no master plan. Sheer bluster and guts sustained our momentum. Every gig was a street-fight, every tour was a war, and we played the hand we were dealt at every show, like a tightrope walker with a death-wish, willing himself from beginning to end, treacherous winds be damned. The Clash's journey from English High Street clubs to American sports stadiums was a visceral story of adrenaline-fueled bravado: rare in their sensitivity, rash in their violence, but ultimately dazzling in the reactive chemistry with which they seared the musical landscape.

For my part, as backline roadie, loyal foot-soldier, and éminence grise, I weathered every night and day of the seven-year mission and, when it ended for me, in 1983, I never sought another gig. Dozens more travelled portions of that voyage with them—unsung heroes and shameless villains alike. Some treated this gig like any other gig. Others went all-in, and their lives changed irrevocably. By 1979, Strummer/Jones/Simonon/Headon were not regular folk, but they knew damn well what it was like to be bored, on the dole, youth without future. If you worked for The Clash, you inexorably became swept up in the tide of fervor and adulation that surrounded and reflected off them. For better or worse—and in war, it's often the worse—you became part of the insanity of those times. As Randal Doane notes in the pages that follow, in the war waged on mediocrity, against "that safe, soapy slush [coming] out of the radio," the stakes were high.

Within "Clashworld," even the most innocent features of everyday life could turn into a nightmare, unbidden. For those of us on the crew, touring entailed a daily descent into hell, a Kafkaesque rush of sense-distorting highs and lows, blurring the lines between fact and fiction. Several times a day, we flipped from combat-stance to stand-down: adrenaline on, adrenaline off! There were no weekdays or weekends, no bank holidays or Easters. Both crew and band, in our insulated time-capsule, careened from one gig to the next, and sometimes we had a moment to visit with friends in New York and elsewhere. Just as often, though, life was gig-to-gig-to-gig: the calendar proved irrelevant, and weeks and months slid past unnoticed, the regions and seasons making themselves known only by changing temperatures.

Days commenced with a bleary-eyed stagger from the crew bus onto yet another empty stage, in some nameless city, and a tally of the carnage from the previous night. For hours, we changed drum skins, re-soldered jack-plugs, replaced amplifier valves, and jerry-rigged broken flightcase wheels. And the gob! Gob removal was a constant ritual and, unless performed daily, it would accumulate and spread, like some insidious alien virus. Daily music-store runs were a necessity too. Like hit-and-run missions, we snagged parts, supplies, and gaffa tape, especially. It was the currency of the day. If we hit lucky, we bought the store's entire stock.

As the backline was setup, tuned, and taped, the anticipation rose for the night before us. We had only a short time to get it right because once the band bounded into the hall, with all manner of "friends" (ha!), journalists, and photographers in tow, all hell broke loose! If the day's interviews and photo sessions had gone well, if the hall had good, dry acoustics, and if the electrical supply was well-grounded, we had a chance of a decent soundcheck. If not, feedback rang-out unchecked, leads buzzed like chainsaws, and tempers flared. ("Like trousers like brain!" Joe quipped early on.)

If the mood was good, there was ample time for wind-ups between the band and crew at soundcheck. One of my favorites was to fill Topper's stick bag with warped drumsticks that broke within a matter of minutes. With a straight face, I assured him that a new batch were due to arrive on a late train from London— and, while he was 99 percent sure I was winding him up, that 1 percent doubt haunted him nonetheless. There's also the time the crew explained to Paul and Mick that, "due to the hall's acoustics," Paul would be on Joe's right, and Mick would be on Joe's left. They stamped, cussed, and even threatened to cancel the gig! We broke into laughter, of course, and that night—like so many nights— they evened the score. Too often, for my own nerves, soundchecks turned into impromptu rehearsal sessions, and it was up to the crew to physically drag the band offstage.

With the soundcheck complete, we eased up on the adrenal throttle, straightened out problems, and taped and tightened everything once again. For the soundcheck for the support bands (The Specials and The Undertones were among our favorites), I took pride in helping The Slits, The Lous, and The B-Girls inflict their feminist punk rock savvy onto the audiences.

Backstage, as the band's pre-gig sacraments commenced, the adrenaline ramped up to DEFCON-3. Like warrior tribesmen from ancient history, each band member practiced his own talismanic order. To assuage his nerves, Mick turned chatty (unusual). Like a samurai contemplating hara-kiri, Joe turned quiet (unusual). With his repertoire of practical jokes and occasional measure of Remy Martin, Paul tried to relax (with limited success). Topper keyed himself up like a boxer before the opening bell, and his preparations fell to me. Like a trainer for Henry Cooper, I applied tape, Band-Aids, gloves, wristbands, ice-spray, and glucose tablets—along with a neck massage to loosen him up. If any of the crew or band needed, um, special supplements to get ready, that's the time they took them.

After one last check of everything onstage, I raised the all-ready signal, the lights went down, and the crowd united in their anticipatory roar. For the next few minutes, we hunkered down in the dark, like troops in the trenches, with butterflies in stomach, waiting to go over the top.

Once the band hit the stage, another jolt of adrenaline heightened the senses and awareness. Each gig was a blur of color and light, sweat and sound. Most nights, it was white-hot chaos, with clamorous noise to match. Time sped-up like a street-fight: hesitate, and you were done for. When strings broke, drum skins split, and mike stands toppled, we leapt from the dark for a quick repair. It was all coded nods for band and crew—or, for Johnny Green that night at the Palladium, while trying to fix Joe's wrist-guard of gaffa tape, a sing-song, dressing-down at the microphone: "You're always too late, Johnny!"

Amid the panic, the exhilaration, the brilliance, and the fuck-ups, we lived right behind our eyes, performing as one and desperately trying to cover each other's backs. Joe loved the fuck-ups and purposely collided with equipment, knocking things about. Joe, Mick, and Paul ran back and forth throughout the show, purposely tangling the guitar leads and had a laugh while we scrambled to untangle the growing ball of spaghetti. Countless times I was summoned onstage by an apparently irate Joe, only to have him burst into a big grin and a wink. "Bastard!" I muttered, as I sprinted back into the wings. Stage invasions, fights onstage and off, and unconscious fans, bottles, cans, and gob all rained down upon us. It was a hair's breadth from mayhem on a dangerous scale.

And then, after the last glorious encore, it was over—a pressure drop indeed. Adrenaline levels returned to equilibrium, and reality seeped back into consciousness. Most nights, in that moment, I took stock of my own condition: was I drenched in sweat, or gob, or both? Was that blood? Was it mine? And that was it: we exhaled, inhaled a second wind, then tore down the stage. With our ears ringing, we packed up the gear, crunching beneath our boots the detritus of another battle. By the time the truck doors closed, the hall was silent once again.

I always savored the surreality of striding across an empty stage, where just hours before such passion, emotion, and frightening intensity had played out. The dreams and memories burned upon hundreds of retinae and ear drums were now just ghostly echoes in a lifeless arena.

If we were in town for the night, we returned to the hotel, and band and crew recounted the highlights of the day. In the early days, especially, more riotous hijinks commenced. How a drunken Mick ended up hanging by his jacket from a chandelier in the hotel bar, I'll never know—but I bet Robin Banks does. One night in Bournemouth, Topper and his girlfriend decided to go skinny-dipping and, after emerging from the frigid Atlantic, opted not to get dressed, and paraded their wares before the hotel staff and a gaggle of journalists, traipsing through the hotel lobby and into the elevator. Later the police raided the hotel in their customary manner—I'm sure Bournemouth had never seen such scenes! If we were moving on that night, we climbed back onto the crew bus and hit the road hard, fuelled by Heinekens and exhaustion-defying high spirits. The next morning, we did it all over again.

By the Take the Fifth tour, I was mostly numbed to the rigors and trauma inflicted by this so-called lifestyle. Today, each of us bears the physical and psychological wounds of that improbable saga: Paul's hip, Topper's back, and of course Joe's mortality. No one escaped without injury.

The music stopped long ago and in the intervening thirty-three years, just haphazard scenes and random images remain in my memory. The minutiae of each gig is now the property of not only the journalists and photographers who chronicled the events but, more importantly, of the fans who were there each night, who made such memories possible, and who remember it incident-by-incident. Every one of them also had a part to play in the journey.

Of course, the other two-thirds of the journey were spent rehearsing, recording, and playing football, but that's a story for another day.

This story, the one in your hands, comes as a delightful surprise, thirty-five years after that legendary night at the Palladium. After reading this tale, I stand corrected: I only thought I knew where the bodies were buried. *Stealing All Transmissions: A Secret History of The Clash* is the first history of The Clash by an American, and it lovingly documents—as Doane notes—how "The Clash fell in love with America, and how America loved them back." It's unlike anything else you've ever read about The Clash. Where band biographies and oral histories have focused their attention mostly on the band, its inner circle, and its occasional spat with CBS, *Stealing* recounts that history, situates it amid larger cultural and economic forces in the U.S., and takes stock of the will of key players to refuse the terms of mediocrity, determined to revive the righteous fury of rock'n'roll.

When we arrived in the states in February 1979, the magic just seemed to happen, like a fairy tale. For their debut concert in Berkeley, California, The Clash played to a raucous sold-out crowd of three thousand or so, and we thought, "Bloody hell—they get it!" It was only upon reading *Stealing* that I realized that nothing happens in a vacuum: many people were tilling the soil to make America a fertile environment for the arrival of "the only English band that mattered."

If you have ever considered how The Clash became the most talked about live act from England in the space of less than eighteen months, then look no further. In *Stealing*, Doane peels back the layers of a previously unknown history and documents how the band's meteoric rise in the U.S. was as much about the valiant efforts of those figures who laid the groundwork for The Clash to break America, as it was about the four musicians themselves. Sure there were a couple good eggs at Epic, but The Clash's stateside success was largely the result of writers in the alternative press, the bands at CBGB and elsewhere and, most importantly, deejays like Meg Griffin, Pam Merly, and Jane Hamburger. While we in the UK flirted with pirate radio as an alternative to the somnambulist offerings of the BBC, U.S. radio was in the midst of a cultural revolution. Unbeknownst to us at the time, they helped foster the initial audience for The Clash, and helped ensure their continued success.

Stealing, of course, takes its title from the 1981 single "Radio Clash," and it's a story of secrets and betrayals, plotting and intrigues, and includes original interviews with crucial figures in radio, music journalism, and the record industry—Griffin, writer Robert Christgau, photographer Bob Gruen, Epic's Susan Blond, and Talking Heads' Chris Frantz, to name a few. The book transports you on a very different journey than any previous punk history or band bio: Doane weaves together strands from the histories of American FM radio, the rise of serious rock journalism, the biography of The Clash, and his own coming-of-age story into a tale of epic proportions.

This is the main reason why *Stealing* represents a critical addition to The Clash canon—and there are five other reasons, too. First, *Stealing* does not assume the weight of being the definitive tale of one band, one man, or even one album, and is thereby free to rise above the gossip-y sordidness of many previous biographies. Second, like the best songs of '77, Doane packs a wide-ranging story into a refreshingly tight 130 pages. He takes us through the hell-raising antics of free-form deejays, who streaked through competitors' stations to prank on-air arrests for marijuana possession, to station takeovers complete with hunting knives and ransom demands. He outlines how Griffin and Hamburger solidified the fan base for punk and new wave by spinning discs at Hurrah's, where Sid Vicious smashed a bottle over the head of Todd Smith (Patti's brother), and landed himself at Rikers Island. The book is full of casual asides with unpredictable tangents and the author pierces the heart of the culture and the industry that surrounded it.

Third, his analysis of the New York punk scene is critical and sympathetic, and Doane's division of the U.S. bands into the camps of art-punk, garage-punk, and pop-punk captures punk as a dynamic force, and characterizes how bands are like sharks—they move and thereby change, or they risk death by self-parody—and he thereby skewers the usual orthodoxies about who qualifies as "punk." Fourth, his spirited play-by-play account of that epic night at the Palladium brings the reader as close as possible to the orchestra pit of a Clash show, and his challenge to the history of the greatest photo in rock'n'roll must be reckoned with. Fifth, he also offers a fully original take on the *London Calling* LP, which captures the band's affection for New York and London, past and present, and rightly recalls Paul's description of the album as "Cinemascope sound."

This intelligent and refreshing interpretation of that history also fully explores the band's disenchantment with the British music press backlash (which I remember well). "London calls and New York answers," Doane cleverly comments! While Lester Bangs was penning a landmark multi-thousand-word endorsement of the band, and singing the praises of *Give 'Em Enough Rope* and singles such as "White Man in Hammersmith Palais," the British press was at full tilt, pronouncing the irrelevance of the band. *NME*'s Ian Penman pronounced, "The Clash is a dying myth"; *Melody Maker*'s Jon Savage lamented, "so do they squander their greatness." In the U.S., though, Doane notes, "the myth not only endured, it flourished." By the time The Clash returned to New York's Palladium Theatre in September 1979, the entire music scene was primed and pumped, which led to the show being broadcast live on WNEW.

• • •

Over the years, I have been asked many things about The Clash, from the sublime to the ridiculous. As the backline roadie, I was uniquely placed to be witness to (and be a small part of) their development from the spearhead of the fledgling punk rock movement, to the unstoppable force that gave hope to a young generation and, in the end, could not prevent their own implosion. Thirty years later, then, why should we care about The Clash? Do they still matter?

With the benefit of hindsight, it is clear to see that the band had transcended their own cultural reference point, rising far above their squalid punk rock beginnings. They were free enough inside themselves to recognize their collective uniqueness, to live within their own reference system and at a level above and beyond the culture they were raised in.

Now, I'm not so daft as to imagine that a couple hundred words from my pen—okay, *machine*—are going to inspire more action than the best tunes on *Sandinista!* Still, their importance and influence over today's music and fashion cannot be overstated. Taking a relatively simple style of music, infusing it with hard-hitting politics while staying dynamic, vital, and danceable, they demonstrated that anyone willing to work hard can make great music. "Just do it!" Joe would always say, if someone asked him whether he should do such-and-such.

The Clash inspired young people to pick up guitars and books. The Clash taught us all that it was alright to give a shit. And The Clash dared to question the so-called facts of life: Why should you work in a boring factory and waste your life toiling to make profit for a rich corporation? Why should you die in a war under the illusion of fighting for peace and democracy? And why should you continue to accept totalitarian jack-boot brutality and injustice from the *very regimes* you vote for and place in power?

And they served up a cautionary warning—a warning of a world where individuality and legitimate choice are lost, a society that creates machines that act like men and men that act like machines: the world we find ourselves in now! From the 100 Club Punk Festival in 1976 to the US Festival in 1983, they never wavered in their stance against authoritarian injustice, political corruption, and social inequality. That The Clash were able to stick to such principles while laboring under the burdens of record company pressure and commercial constraints is a testament to their commitment to at least *try* to make a difference. Their stance in word and deed sought to renew our faith in rock'n'roll and our commitment to each other and this planet.

Doane's riff on Marx in the book's dedication echoes the forces amassing in the 1970s against labor in general, and the labor of free-form deejays especially. In tracing the history of commercial free-form radio, Doane examines how the emergence of a countercultural spirit was nearly decimated by industry automation. (And it only got worse.) He notes that in the U.S., "by the mid-seventies, one in seven FM stations had been automated." The music being played at most of these programmed stations sounded programmed too, and it's no accident that the counter-insurgency of the early New York punk scene arrived in its wake.

The attack upon a fluid, listener-directed media was at the heart of all The Clash railed against. It is no coincidence that the band fell victim to the same forces that inevitably drove the individualistic, deejay-inspired format from the airwaves of the U.S. And with the eventual arrival of MTV, digital audio, and more recently satellite and Internet radio, the days of real connections between entertainer and listener were doomed to the pages of history. We have lost the likes of The Clash now, maybe never to be repeated, just as we have lost the wonderful experiment in human contact and communication that was free-form radio. As Joe Strummer knew and patently stated later in life, "When you take people out of the equation, you're nowhere." Truer words were never spoken.

The Baker, in 1978, outside Rehearsal Rehearsals, with his Renault, official vehicle of Clashworld (Barry Auguste, personal collection).

Only by the conscious act of rejecting the rubbish thrust at us by corporate consumerism and by thinking about and choosing our own destiny can we make the world a better, saner, caring world. This was the message The Clash gave the world, and this message resonates throughout the pages of *Stealing*, which concludes with an analysis of how we listen to music today and its impact on the written word. Randal Doane asks (and answers) the important question, "Could a band like The Clash emerge today?" He recalls the pleasures of LP listening, and reading ten-thousand-word profiles in *Rolling Stone*, both of which required "a depth and devotion of attention rarely nurtured in the digital age." The advent of digital music technology and its transmission have rendered FM radio all but obsolete:

"the magical romance mediated by the analog transmission of a regional deejay at two turntables and a microphone, constructing a community among punks, freaks, and geeks about the sublime power of The Clash" is a thing of the past. Moreover, he speculates that "the pasts of many great bands of the present era, will not be written at length, if at all." I'm convinced he's right, but let's hope he's wrong and that future authors assemble tales from the history of rock'n'roll as compelling as this one.

—Barry "The Baker" Auguste

Prelude
Paul Simonon Wields a Mighty Ax

With her Pentax camera in hand, Pennie Smith stepped onto the left wing of the stage of the Palladium, just behind the curtain, and waited for The Clash to return for their encore. It was September 21, 1979, the second of a two-night stint for The Clash in New York City. WNEW-FM, the album-oriented rock station that had recently found felicity in punk and new wave, supplied a live simulcast for the tri-state region. On the opposite stage wing, Richard Neer, the on-air host, gushed, "If you've never seen The Clash it's an experience, I'll tell you that. I was out front for a bit and it's so loud. I'm used to loud music but it is loud to the point of real distortion, and the people are just totally enveloped in the music. . . . They're dancing, they're jumping up and down and they are just totally into it!" Back onstage, The Clash offered the audience a respite from their collective fury with "Armagideon Time," a 1978 reggae tune by Willi Williams. "Armagideon" was a new addition to the band's live repertoire and, with its walking bass line and adagio pacing, it confirmed over a leisurely five minutes that The Clash were not prisoners to the sonic parameters of punk.[1]

Following "Armagideon," lead guitarist and vocalist Mick Jones shouted "1-2-3-4!" and the band launched into the snarling "Career Opportunities." Without pause, The Clash blasted through "What's My Name" and the incendiary "White Riot." Over the last few bars, lead vocalist and rhythm guitarist Joe Strummer offered a final, exhausted, melismatic "whi-ite rii-ot," as bassist Paul Simonon and drummer Topper Headon thumped ahead to the cadence. "White Riot" was a band favorite for closing encores, as it stoked the frenzy of a crowd delighted by The Clash and agitated by everything else. The three songs were done in five short minutes.

On this night, The Clash were aware that they stood at the crossroads of rock history. The band had just laid down the final tracks for *London Calling*, a double album they had put together largely on their own. Brimming with confidence, The Clash drew on their advance to finance the tour, despite the fact that *Give 'Em Enough Rope*, their second album, had failed to crack the U.S. *Billboard* Top 100. The Clash were nearly $100,000 in arrears and in a week would run out of money.[2]

Still, the Epic promoter who deemed The Clash "the only band that matters" appeared to be onto something. Their chief UK rivals, The Sex Pistols, broke up in January 1978, on the last night of a nearly aborted tour of the United States. Sid Vicious, the twenty-one-year-old bass player for the Pistols, died in February 1979, on the first night of his latest parole, of a heroin overdose. The live-fast, die-young ethos had its adherents among the rock elite, too—those who, given enough rope, would hang themselves. Keith Moon of The Who, in September 1978, suffered a fatal overdose of Heminevrin, the sedative prescribed to alleviate his alcohol withdrawal symptoms. Within the year, Bob Dylan would enter a born-again stupor, and John Bonham of Led Zeppelin would enter a vodka-induced stupor and never awaken.[3]

As Strummer, Jones, and Headon left the stage, a young woman dashed across front-stage right, with a bouncer in close pursuit. Simonon, alone, remained onstage and stepped toward the stage left exit. After two weeks on the road with The Clash, Smith told me, "I was shooting very little live stuff. . . . It was only when Paul started looking really fed up that I thought something peculiar might be about to happen." On this tour, Simonon had been using a variety of basses, "cheap Fenders from CBS," he recalled, but that night he played an older Fender Precision, which retailed for $350. Simonon turned to his left, spread his feet wide, and gripped his Fender by the neck. Smith stepped forward from the wing and pressed her eye to the viewfinder. "I was very close to him, using a wide-angle lens," she said. "He was almost three feet away and heading in my direction, so I was backing off." Simonon lifted the Fender past his left ear, folded his frame at the waist, and drove the instrument like an ax toward the floor. As it arced toward her, Smith stepped backward, clicked, advanced the film, clicked twice again, and dove out of the way.[4]

Clash fans at the Palladium had little idea how prescient it was for The Clash to close with "White Riot" and a bass-smashing coda—for upon their return to

New York City, in May 1981, The Clash would inspire a riot of their own. The thousands of Clash fans who caught the shows at the Palladium in 1979, and the thousands more who descended upon Times Square for their residency at Bond International Casino, came together as a result of the determination of punk aficionados on the airwaves and in print in New York City.

Thirty-five years hence, it's evident that The Clash—more so than other bands of that moment—were aided en route to pop stardom by free-form FM radio and long-form rock journalism: two media mechanisms that would, in the ensuing years, follow the eight-track cartridge, the seven-inch single, and the televised teen-dance show into the dustbin of rock history. The agents behind these forces helped construct the initial audience for The Clash and, in turn, helped ensure their success—and the success of dozens of other post-punk and new wave bands—through the 1980s. Beginning in 1976, select deejays and rock journalists championed punk and new wave bands and, with punk bravado, sought to consummate a desire articulated by Strummer himself: "All we want to achieve is an atmosphere where things can happen. We want to keep the spirit of the free world. We want to keep out that safe, soapy slush that comes out of the radio." Amid the skirmishes between deejays and management, the former held sway, if only temporarily, to help The Clash secure a shot at superstardom.[5]

This is the story of how The Clash loved America, and how America loved them back. It's the story of the deejays and rock journalists who constructed the New York audience for The Clash and their musical brethren. This story chronicles the antecedent events of their appearances at the Palladium in September 1979, and it explores the beautiful ferocity of their September 21 performance. It offers a new genealogy of the greatest photograph in rock history, and it takes stock of The Clash's sustained glory, which allowed deejays across the country, night after night, to save the lives of American youth, including my own.[6]

CALIFORNIA DREAMIN'

In September 1978, Jones and Strummer were mixing tracks for The Clash's second LP, *Give 'Em Enough Rope*, in San Francisco, just sixty miles from my new hometown. My family had moved from Sacramento to Stockton, California, that summer. I was nine years old, entering fifth grade, and I had no friends. My father signed me up for the local youth soccer league and, as luck would have it, my new teammates had something I could never claim: cool older brothers who dictated their musical tastes. For my tenth birthday, I received Styx's *Pieces of Eight* and Cheap Trick's *Heaven Tonight*. I dug Styx's "Renegade" and "Blue Collar Man," and had little idea that the lyrics for "Blue" captured a slice-of-life known well by my own grandfather. Still, the fey harmonies and ersatz prog-rock elements prevented me from becoming a Styx devotee. Cheap Trick, though, were something else. The following year, I bought *Live at Budokan*, and began to navigate the shadowy terrain of crushes and secret admirers. I listened closely to "Need Your Love" and "I Want You to Want Me," mining the lyrics for clues regarding the curse of unrequited desire. I saved my car-washing and lawn-mowing earnings and, over the next three years, I bought Cheap Trick's *In Color*, *Dream Police*, and *All Shook Up*. When Cheap Trick came to Stockton's Fox Theater, in December 1982, I was there, in the front row of the balcony. The night proved bittersweet, though, as my attendance was akin to a wake: I was there in tribute to the person I once was, and not as the person I was determined to become. The previous summer, I had toured England and Europe with the Boy Scouts of America, and returned home a devotee of punk and new wave.

My host family in Coventry, England, occupied a modest, turn-of-the-century flat in the district of Little Heath. Their family name escapes me, but I remember Paul, the elder of two boys, who made me my first mix tape, which included songs by dozens of bands I had never heard before: The Specials, Captain Sensible, Madness, Kid Creole and the Coconuts, Fun Boy Three, The Selecter, Echo and the Bunnymen, and The Clash. The tape was a hissy TDK C-90, but it hardly mattered. Side A opened with "London Calling," and I wore the iron oxide of its first three-and-a-half minutes brittle and thin.

Soon thereafter, I quit the Boy Scouts. Despite the allure of ski outings in the nearby Sierra Nevada Mountains, I knew that the top-down ethos of the Boy Scouts contradicted the do-it-yourself (DIY) spirit of punk and new wave. At my high school, though, taking sartorial cues from punk and new wave entailed serious health risks. At the time, population-wise, Stockton was among the largest dozen cities in California. Culture-wise, it resembled the Mayfield of *Leave It to Beaver*, circa 1958. The cheerleaders donned uniforms of pleated skirts and matching sweaters the Friday morning of every home football game. Muscle cars were the objects of choice in triangles of well-repressed homosocial desire. Young men parted their hair down the middle and feathered it back across the ears. Led Zeppelin and Van Halen dominated the after-market speakers of Chevy Camaros and El Caminos.

By the summer of 1983, though, Stockton had nearly caught up to history. Every so often, when the barometric pressure reached a certain point, and I angled my monophonic radio just so, I picked up the signal of KQAK, "the Quake," out of San Francisco, which kept—among others—The Jam, Heaven 17, The Pretenders, and Wall of Voodoo in heavy rotation. MTV offered the occasional nod toward English synth pop, and I accumulated a wardrobe of second-hand gabardine pants, perm-a-press shirts, Ray-Ban Wayfarers, and glacier blue Top-Siders. (In the San Joaquin Valley, mod attire was an odd amalgamation, and the androgyny of blue shoes far outweighed the class implications of regatta-appropriate footwear.) By Labor Day, I parted my hair on the side.

A few knuckleheads at my high school policed the boundary of normativity, and interpreted the changes in sartorial parlance in stark terms: you are different. You are not one of us. We shall kill you. That difference coalesced around "faggot" as an all-purpose epithet, which gained symbolic value as the peril of HIV and AIDS began to register in our collective conscience. The town motto, "Stockton, Someplace Special," was plastered in eight-foot-high letters on a water tank along Interstate 5 and, with its whispery alliteration, it struck me and my closest friends as menacing, almost insidious. We planned hasty exits upon graduation and, until then, we sought redemption in our friendships and our music. Over the years, we drifted apart, replaced dropout-plagued tapes with compact discs and mp3s, and the parents among us now impart to our children the righteous sounds of punk, post-punk, and new wave.[7]

WHAT'S MY NAME

The key lesson to be gleaned by the commemorations of "'80s music" on VH1 and elsewhere is fairly clear: in the battle for historical memory, The Clash beat Van Halen, Duran Duran trumped Bon Jovi, and even Kajagoogoo trounced Poison. Put another way: punk, post-punk, and new wave hold victorious sway. It may be silly, even petty, to think in these terms, but it is useful, too, to survey the wreckage of music history to improve our understanding of the materiality of popular music and the production of taste. Technological advances, including the programmable keyboard and drum pad, allowed music makers to emphasize composition—in other words, "putting together"—over virtuosity. These technologies shaped the emergence of dozens of musical genres, from hip-hop to drum'n'bass, house, techno, and more. The microchips that powered drum machines and synthesizers, though, also powered the algorithm-driven playlists of Clear Channel and Radio One, which rent asunder the regional variation of American radio, and effectively eliminated the craft labor of the professional deejay. The advent of the Intel-driven, disenchanted playlist did not, however, resolve the contradiction between art and commerce, labor and management in the world of radio. *Stealing All Transmissions* explores these contradictions, and outlines the connections between deejay pioneer Alan Freed, The Beatles, the birth of free-form FM radio, The Ramones, the movie *Grease*, and the volatile stock price of Sirius XM Radio, where the problems of free-form radio in the 1970s continued through 2013 in nearly unabated form.

KEYWORDS

On the use of "punk," "new wave," and "free-form": derogatory use of "punk" begins in the sixteenth century, and is used as a synonym for "prostitute" in Shakespeare's *Measure for Measure* (1623): "She may be a Puncke: for many of them, are neither Maid, Widow, nor Wife." Its use became elastic enough to include "male homosexual," "contemptible person," "weakling," "amateur," and "male companion of a tramp," by the pen of Jack London, in 1907: "A boy on The Road . . . is a road-kid or a 'punk.'" In *V.* (1963), Thomas Pynchon employs "punk" with a neutered connotation: "There was nothing so special about the gang, punks are punks."[8]

The etymology of punk as "punk rock" begins with the garage bands of the late 1960s. The philosophy and aesthetic of punk were originally articulated by Lester Bangs in the pages of *Who Put the Bomp*, a rock fanzine, and *Creem*, the irreverent rock magazine out of Detroit. For Bangs, punk was a stripped-down affair. Sonically, it embraced democratic principles (rather than long-hair virtuosity), and its practitioners sought to discomfit the sensibilities of their audience. Early exemplars included ? and the Mysterians, The Velvet Underground, and Iggy and the Stooges.[9]

The yang to punk's yin, then, included gravitas and complexity (the mystical escapism of prog-rock), musical and largely masculine virtuosity ("brutally precise" guitar solos played at "hypersonic speed"), and the self-distancing aesthetic of seriousness: music to confirm the listener's middle-brow sensibility (Yes's *Tales from Topographic Oceans*), rather than set it upon its head (Lou Reed's *Metal Machine Music*). As Robert Christgau, music editor for the *Village Voice*, wrote in 1977, "Not many music execs like the stuff [i.e., punk], which is designed to blast away every 'artistic' standard they hold dear." Bangs and his brigade were alienated in equal measure from contemporary AM hits and progressive FM radio, and were "forced to position themselves as a 'popist' avant-garde or underground." Punk discourse and music emerged from the productive tension of the art/pop dialectic, and The Clash (and The Sex Pistols) were no exception. Not all writers, though, embraced these distinctions: see, for example, the *New York Times* arts and leisure guide for the weekend of March 5, 1978: "Meat Loaf—A large rock singer who calls himself and his band by this name; the music is a sometimes hysterical extension of Bruce Springsteen's Baroque-punk rhetoric."[10]

The articulation of gender, power, and aesthetics also informs critic Carola Dibbell's rich conceptualization of punk. "Amid the terrors of feminism and the sexual revolution," Dibbell writes, "punk rallied a youth culture that had a problem with drum solos, showmanship, professionalism, chops and pretending to be black, not to mention hippie vagueness. . . . Punk just didn't like bullshit." Bullshit, though, is not the same as artifice, which is necessary to any expressive endeavor. For Dibbell, the punk archetype deployed artifice buoyantly and strategically at the table of rock'n'roll: "[He] acted tougher than he was, couldn't necessarily deliver on his boasts, but had to be reckoned with because you never knew." On occasion, he was actually a she, and took great pains (and pleasure) taking the piss out of the distinctions between the two.[11]

Punk, too, is irreducible to the downstroke guitar style of Johnny Ramone, or the stylized dishevelment of Richard Hell. As I explore below, the anxiety of influence of the British invaders loomed large in the imaginations of Joe Strummer, Johnny Ramone, and Chris Frantz of Talking Heads. Their respective, retaliatory gestures in song and stagecraft chartered radically different territories, but members of the punk brigade drew upon the same resources, with analogous inspirations. Punk, then, was not merely sonic or sartorial, but constituted by gestures of humor and earnestness, pecuniary aspirations and political resistance, mockery and homages, and an amalgam of do-it-yourself practices—from Paul Simonon's learning the bass on the fly, to Mark Perry's xeroxed fanzine *Sniffin'*

Glue, to Ivan Kral's *The Blank Generation*, his 1976 celluloid homage to his comrades-in-sound.

For "new wave," Heylin offers a serviceable starting point in *From the Velvets to the Voidoids*: "New wave is . . . what punk became as influences became more disparate, musicianship improved . . . and record labels realized that punk was unmarketable." New wave included new forms of artifice, too, as more arty, less aggressive bands "committed to minimalist, speedy music" cut tracks and took the stage. UK rock critic Nick Kent, among others, were using the term in the mid-1970s, and "new wave" established real purchase in the marketplace of ideas and commodities once deployed by Seymour Stein, of Sire Records. In October 1977, in service to its fall catalog, Sire decreed, "Don't Call It Punk," in order to reassure FM program directors and parents alike that Sire-sponsored vinyl was full of mainstream wholesome goodness.[12]

DON'T TOUCH THAT DIAL. JUST LEAVE IT IN THE OFF POSITION, PLEASE.

For decades, radio was the only game in town. From the rise of rock'n'roll to the premiere of MTV™ in August 1981, radio constituted the sonic fabric of American youth culture. With radios in nearly every home and automobile, and the disposable income of American youth on the rise, rock'n'roll deejays played a critical role in shaping popular culture. AM radio was unabashedly commercial and included a relentless cycle of ad spots and jingles between nearly every song. In the late 1960s, with the rise of FM radio, the hysterical deejay yielded to the free-form FM deejay, and he—and the deejay was nearly always a he—added commentary to between-song "raps" on culture, politics, and Schedule I substances. On television, Dick Clark of *American Bandstand* (1952–89) and Don Cornelius of *Soul Train* (1971–93) tarried largely in the domains of pop and dance music, and left rock-as-art (and punk and new wave) to their FM comrades. Free-form deejays played songs by the set, sequenced commercials in blocks and, by concluding such blocks before the opening passages of the songs, policed the boundaries between the sacred (music) and the profane (commerce). The treatment of music as art, and the composition of a sequence of segues, became its own creative domain. The ethic was simple: foster freedom, aesthetic education, corporeal exploration, and political liberation. Free-form deejays took their aesthetic cues from the artists they played, who in turn took their cues from previous generations of vanguard artists. As The Beatles' George Harrison told a *Life* reporter prior to the release of *Sgt. Pepper's Lonely Hearts Club Band*, "It's all right to dislike us, just don't deny us."[13]

In the mid- to late 1970s, and even into the 1980s, a handful of FM stations still imagined they could pay the rent while relying on deejays—rather than consultants—to determine the station's market segment. As a result, goths, geeks, and freaks turned to deejays for hope: these cultural intermediaries established bonds between punk and new wave artists and the fans otherwise starved by the anemic offerings of contemporary hits and album-oriented radio. In this period, a handful of determined individuals mustered significant agency, found the gems among the pabulum of popular culture, and thereby allowed a growing fan base to celebrate semipopular music.

Through a flurry of mergers and acquisitions in the late 1990s and early 2000s, Clear Channel, Cumulus, and CBS Radio established a near oligopoly on the FM airwaves. Their 2012 holdings included 850, 570, and 130 stations, respectively—all of which have been focus-group-tested-and-liberated from the possibility (or responsibility) of community, serendipity, or the sublime.

The Clash understood well the power of media, penned narratives starring culture-jamming heroes, and cast themselves in leading roles. The hip-hop track "Radio Clash/This Is Radio Clash" (1981) reflects their populist standpoint, and provides the inspiration for this book's title:

This is Radio Clash / Stealing all transmissions /
Beaming from the mountaintop / Using aural ammunition.

When The Clash recorded this track, they stood within sight of the mountaintop of popular music, aided along the way by their love affair with New York City and its ardent fans. *Stealing All Transmissions* recounts how select deejays and journalists embraced their roles (and responsibilities) with considerable verve, and played a key part in The Clash's stateside success. (To keep the narrative tidy, I have noted parallel activities and developments by deejays and rock journalists in San Francisco, Boston, and Los Angeles primarily in the footnotes.) *Stealing* confirms the prediction of Pat Wadsley of the *Soho Weekly News*, in advance of the Easter Rock Festival at Max's Kansas City, in April 1976, which

The resurrection of rock'n'roll at Max's Kansas City, 1976.

included performances by The Ramones, Cleveland's Pere Ubu, and Blondie: "This rock scene isn't staying underground for long. The talent of the individual performers, composers and musicians and the support of the artists, writers and friends in the underground society insure emergence into the above ground rock scene."[14]

Likewise, this book culminates with a detailed account of the iconic concert dubbed *The Guns of Brixton* bootleg. It focuses primarily on the events leading up to Simonon's impersonation of Paul Bunyan, but the story ranges from the rise of FM radio, in the 1960s, to the contemporary crisis in revenue at Sirius XM Radio. This story covers a key chapter in the struggle for the spirit of rock'n'roll, and includes cameos by William Bennett, Bo Diddley, Andy Warhol, Murray the K., John Cale, Bootsy Collins, Howard Stern, Bruce Springsteen, and a Yale law student named Hillary Rodham.

REMAKE/REMODEL

In 2012, a book was released under this title, credited to yours truly. I liken the relation between that book and the book in your hands to the relation between The Clash's *Vanilla Tapes* and *London Calling*, respectively. The germ of the project is visible in the thirty-thousand-word 2012 version, but more fully realized in the much lengthier PM edition. Still, this version of *Stealing* strives in terms of concision to be the literary analog to *The Clash*, their thirty-five minute debut, rather than *Sandinista!*, their acclaimed triple-LP. Like the earlier version, the tale jumps around a bit time-wise, and follows the narrative threads of characters and key actions more than chronology.

Chapter One, "Revolt into Style," covers the formation of the original Clash line-up, their aesthetics and politics, and the New York punk contingent co-alescing at Max's and CBGB. Chapter Two, "From *Sgt. Pepper's* to *Born to Run*," documents the emergence of free-form radio, provides a genealogy of the New York concerts broadcast live on WNEW from the mid- to late 1970s, and charts the rise of Bruce Springsteen. Chapter Three, "1977: Clamor, Exposure, and Camaraderie," covers the emergence of The Ramones, the evangelical music press, and the production and reception of The Clash's debut album. In Chapter Four, "The Good, the Bad, and the Ugly," deejays Meg Griffin and Joe Piasek enter the story from stage left, and ensure the inclusion of punk and new wave on play-lists at WNEW and WPIX. Chapter Five, "Rebel Waltz with the General, and Free-Form in Freefall," tracks the military precision of Sandy Pearlman in the production of the *Give 'Em Enough Rope* LP, which coincided with a key moment in the long demise of free-form radio. Chapter Six, "London Calls, New York Answers," details the recording of *London Calling*, presents an alternate history to the night in question at the Palladium, and offers an interpretation of *London Calling* inspired by Simonon's description of the album as "Cinemascope sound." In Chapter Seven, "Clash in Hitsville / WPIX's Train in Vain," The Clash's return to New York for a final date at the Palladium in 1980 coincides with the demise of WPIX. In "Afterword: All That Is Solid Melts into Air," I survey what remains for popular music fanatics, following the death of the long-playing record, free-form radio, and long-form rock journalism, and the impact of their demise on our collective attention span and future histories of rock'n'roll.[15]

This story is, then, a love story, a secret history, and a thank-you note.

1:
Revolt into Style: New Sounds in New York and London

L ike Pete Townshend of The Who, Keith Richards of The Rolling Stones, and Ray Davies of The Kinks, Paul Simonon and Mick Jones transposed their art school aspirations into musical aspirations. Art schools on both sides of the Atlantic offered their students loosely structured days informed by lessons in theory, craft, and creativity. The exigency of creativity inspired students with musical talent to pursue muses in the visual and sonic arts and, in turn, to paint by day and play house parties at night. These schools, then, served as incubators for the protagonists of the British Invasion of the 1960s and the emergence of punk (and new wave) in the 1970s. The punk circles of downtown Manhattan also included organic punk intellectuals, whose interlocutors included Andy Warhol, French poets, and *Mad* magazine's Alfred E. Neuman.

TODAY YOUR LOVES, TOMORROW THE WORLD

Simonon was born in 1955, and grew up in Brixton, in inner-south London. When he was eight years old, his mother and father separated and, seven years later, Simonon moved in with his father. A mishmash of pages from art history books adorned the walls of their apartment, and Antony Simonon encouraged his son to sketch masterworks by Johannes Vermeer and Vincent Van Gogh. Between the sketching and, at the behest of his father, leafleting for the Communist Party, Simonon found the time instructive. "Being with my father made me self-sufficient," he recalled. "It was tough but I needed it. I learned the value of hard work." Simonon's work ethic served him well during basic training on the bass, led initially by Jones and, in 1978, by producer Sandy Pearlman.[1]

Simonon's diligence reaped rewards, to begin, in the form of a scholarship to the Byam Shaw Art School. From 1974 to 1976, he later remembered, "The other students thought my pictures were great but the teachers used to take the piss out of me." Simonon's strength was figurative art, but the lessons of his instructors, who fancied American abstract art, eventually found expression in his low couture and stage backdrops for The Clash. If there was no future for Simonon at Byam Shaw, he did have the good fortune of good looks and good timing.[2]

Jones, like Simonon, was twenty years old in 1975, a fellow Brixtonite, and an art student. Unlike Simonon, Jones had homely hair, an imperial overbite, and could actually play guitar. Jones lived with his grandmother on the eighteenth floor of Wilmcote House, an exemplar of Le Corbusier's machines-for-modern-living, which provided the backdrop for Clash treatises on chronic boredom ("London's Burning") and youth-on-youth violence ("Last Gang in Town"). In his teens, Jones staved off boredom by following the Queen's Park Rangers Football Club and tuning into deejay John Peel on Radio London, a pirate station afloat the MV *Galaxy*, off the coast of Essex. Jones read the music weeklies, bought the latest LPs, and attended Hyde Park concerts by Traffic and The Rolling Stones. (Jones also pored over copies of *Creem* and *Rock Scene* sent from Minneapolis by his mother.) At sixteen, Jones was a self-starter on stylophone (a stylus-operated keyboard) and, in fairly quick succession, drums, bass, and guitar. With fellow Mott the Hoople devotees, Jones played in Schoolgirl, and eagerly solicited technical tips from the older kids. In their eyes, his hunger appeared "embarrassingly naïve," Jones recalled. "I was always asking how they did it. I think they couldn't understand where this kid was coming from. 'Why can't he just be a lot cooler?'"[3]

After a stint in 1974 with The Delinquents, a glam-rock outfit, Jones teamed up with bassist Tony James to place a classified ad in a July 1975 issue of *Melody Maker*, a rock'n'roll weekly: "Lead guitarist and drums to join bass-player and guitarist/singer, influenced by Stones, NY Dolls, Mott, etc. Must have great rock'n'roll image." That October, though, Jones hedged his bets on a future with James, and attended an audition on Denmark Street, London's version of Tin Pan Alley. The fledgling band was impressed with Jones's guitar skills, but their follow-up efforts ended in vain. When Glen Matlock and Malcolm McLaren arrived at Jones's address, his housemate grew suspicious, turned them out, and never reported the inquiry of the founding members of The Sex Pistols.[4]

In January 1976, Jones and James hired Bernie Rhodes as their manager, continued to audition drummers and, in archetypal punk effrontery, settled upon London SS as their appellation. By all accounts, Rhodes's back-story before the late 1960s is difficult to discern. His mother, pregnant with Bernie, arrived in London at the close of World War II. She worked as a seamstress in the 1950s, and Rhodes spent the early 1960s allegedly sharing ideas about rock, art, and fame with Marc Bolan, of T. Rex, Townshend, and Mick Jagger. Rhodes mash-mixed these ideas with agit-prop slogans from the Situationist International, including "Be reasonable, demand the impossible" and "The arts of the future can be nothing less than disruptions of situations." In 1974, Rhodes began working at Sex, the shock-and-awe clothing boutique owned by McLaren and Vivienne Westwood. A fall collaboration between McLaren and Rhodes gave rise to their first manifesto T-shirt, with its challenge to each passerby noted in large, bold script just below the collar: "You're going to wake up one morning and know what side of the bed you've been lying on!" In smaller typeface below, the shirt compiled the "hates" ("YES [the band] ... synthetic food ... David Hockney and Victorianism") and the "loves" ("Archie Shepp Muhammad Ali Bob Marley Jimi Hendrix ... Kutie Jones and HIS SEX PISTOLS ... Guy Stevens records").[5]

In this text lay the germ cell of the London punk scene. Rhodes's study of Marxist political theory left him well-versed in the importance of cultural revolutionaries, and the shirt reflected his fascination with avant-garde musical figures from the black Atlantic. Steve "Kutie" Jones, petty thief and eventual guitarist for the Pistols, had been hanging around McLaren's shop for years, hounding the aspiring impresario to support his musical aspirations. Guy Stevens possessed an encyclopedic understanding of black music, worked for Island Records, and produced a handful of albums for Mott the Hoople—a band that loomed large in the imaginations of Strummer and Mick Jones.

Within the logic of loves and hates, a number of paths could have been forged. The two that would come to dominate UK punk in the late 1970s dovetail nicely with the political maxim often attributed to Antonio Gramsci, the cofounder of the Italian Communist Party: "The socialist conception of the revolutionary process has two characteristic marks which Romain Rolland has encapsulated in his watchword: pessimism of the intelligence, optimism of the will." (Rolland was a French dramatist, recipient of the Nobel Prize for Literature, and pen pal of Sigmund Freud.) The intellect compiles facts and renders judgment. The will drives the subject onward, regardless of the odds. From his damp prison cell, on the Mediterranean island of Ustica, Gramsci had every reason to despair. Still, he wrote on, hopeful that his words might inspire his comrades and their progeny. In the UK conception of punk, McLaren and the Pistols would select the path of pessimism, dwell long in the negative ("God Save the Queen," "Pretty Vacant"), and dismiss the counterbalance of possibility. The Clash would take the alternate route, embrace the contradictions endemic to politics, art, and commerce, and ensure Stevens one more collaboration worthy of commercial and critical celebration.[6]

Rhodes's first steps along that path entailed the managerial and propaganda duties for London SS. For his audition, drummer Roland Hot arrived with Simonon in tow. After Hot's turn, Simonon recalled, "Mick said to me, 'Are you a singer? . . . Do you want to have a go?' and I said, 'Yeah, why not?'" Simonon's performance of "Roadrunner," by The Modern Lovers, inspired Jones and James to continue to look for bandmates, until Jones met Simonon again in south London. Jones reported the encounter to Rhodes, who recalled Simonon's angled countenance and cool demeanor—which, in 2014, still recalled Marlon Brando's dreamy sidekicks in *The Wild One*. "Forget Tony James," Rhodes said, "start a band with that bloke."[7]

That April, Jones and Simonon spent hours together in Jones's flat in west London. They borrowed a bass from James who, seven months later, with William Broad (a.k.a. Billy Idol), formed Generation X. Simonon painted the notes on the fret board, and Jones took painstaking efforts to help Simonon learn the rudiments of rhythm. "I remember Mick introducing me to all his mates," Simonon said. "'This is my new bass guitarist, Paul. He can't play but he's a painter.'" New bandmates included Chrissie Hynde, who in 1978 would form The Pretenders; and Keith Levene, a self-taught guitarist who idolized Steve Howe of Yes and, in 1978 with John Lydon, would cofound Public Image Ltd.[8]

On April 23, Jones, Simonon, and Levene attended a gig at the Nashville Room. The headliners were pub-rock favorites The 101'ers, with Joe Strummer on vocals and, as his moniker suggests, rhythm guitar exclusively. Then in their third year on the pub-rock circuit, The 101'ers had just completed the recording of their first single, "Keys to Your Heart," and had rough cuts of a handful of other originals ready for post-production. According to Nick Kent, of *New Music Express* (NME), Strummer was "the snaggle-toothed troubadour of the capital's new bohemian squatocracy," and the 101'ers' sound shared more with The Hollies—of "Long Cool Woman in a Black Dress" fame—than the night's opening act, The Sex Pistols.[9]

Despite six months of rehearsing and gigging in England and France, the Pistols onstage remained a shabby lot. Their musical shortcomings, though, were eclipsed by Rotten's I-don't-give-a-toss nihilism, and their bad-lad behavior. As an opening act on February 12 for Eddie and the Hot Rods, they made their mark by trashing Eddie's gear, and codified the transgression in Situationist terms: "We're not into music," Steve Jones blurted. "We're into chaos." On April 23, at the front of the stage, Westwood ached with boredom and, for inspiration's sake, slapped an unsuspecting concertgoer. The victim's boyfriend sprang to the offense, grabbed Westwood, and started smacking her. McLaren joined the fray, as did Rotten. The chaos the Pistols had fabricated for interviews spilled onto the stage and, subsequently, was splashed across the headlines of *NME* and *Melody Maker*. Lydon's "I'm-sick-of-being-boring!" aesthetic resonated with writers at *NME*, who were critical of "lumbering progressive rock acts" and advocated for a renewed alliance between rock'n'roll, rebellion, and fun.[10]

Another audience member was able to look beyond the melee, and liked what he saw. "After I saw The Sex Pistols," Strummer noted, "I realized we were yesterday's papers." Luckily for Strummer, Jones and Simonon and Levene were ready to court a new front man to make their own headlines.[11]

URBAN MUSIC GOURMANDIZERS

At the terminus point of Bleecker Street, beneath the most famous awning in Western history, the Bowery contingent gathered to give shape to their own variety of rock'n'roll, joy, and outrageousness. Hilly Kristal opened CBGB OMFUG in December 1973, banking on a country music renaissance and, to keep his options open, devised an acronymic moniker with catholic principles: Country, Bluegrass, Blues and Other Music for Urban Gourmandizers. Previously known as Hilly's on the Bowery, the club occupied the bottom floor of a flophouse, and its clientele lined the street at eight a.m., eager to be indoors for the next round of drinks.

In spring 1976, on the same weekend that Jones and company identified their muse, New York's protagonists of the new rock'n'roll filled CBGB to celebrate their appearance in *The Blank Generation*, the scene's first representation on celluloid. From April 22 to 24, the film was the opening act for The Heartbreakers, in Richard Hell's last appearance as a sideman. Over the previous two years, Ivan Kral, of the Patti Smith Group, had recorded 16mm footage of Talking Heads (as a trio), Blondie, The Ramones, Television, The Heartbreakers, The Patti Smith Group, The Shirts, Harry Toledo, The Marbles, The Miamis, Wayne County, and The Tuff Darts, onstage at Max's Kansas City, the Bottom Line, and CBGB, for posterity, not publicity. "I picked up this Bolex camera at a midtown pawnshop, and started filming," Kral told me. "I filmed the subway, I filmed the ocean. I filmed people on 5th Avenue. And once I knew everyone around Max's and CB's, I took my camera in there with me." The film, he figured, would be the equivalent of a do-it-yourself video diary: "Like a slideshow for my parents!" he said, laughing. While filming Talking Heads onstage, Kral recalled, "I had my light in one hand, and the camera in the other, and I couldn't see through the viewfinder, so I was filming David Byrne's molars, and Tina [Weymouth] was shy, so she often backed away." To get a well-lit shot of drummer Chris Frantz, for example, Kral had little choice but to wriggle his way from stage left to the vicinity of the bass drum. "It was the first time we'd ever been filmed," Frantz recalled. "It was really fun, and Ivan was somebody we really liked."

In a single day, Kral edited the nearly sixty-minute film and, for the audio track, synched bands' home and demo recordings to the video footage. The black-and-white film is an endearing collage of live footage, candid offstage shots, and audio with varying levels of synchronization. Close-ups of lead singers dominate, and the camera is kind to Debbie Harry's radiant cheeks, Wayne County's lovely legs, and Richard Hell's blankly perfect pout. "We were all there because everyone was excited to see themselves on 'the big screen' [laughs]. It was a fun event. We thought of it . . . like one of Andy Warhol's underground films," Frantz recalled. "We knew it wasn't going to be a Hollywood movie or anything, or have any appeal to mainstream rock audiences, but we thought it was a pretty cool record of what was going on at CBGB and Max's."

In the six-season span that bookends the premiere of *The Blank Generation*, the New York punk scene produced an impressive record of vinyl, too. Patti Smith's *Horses* appeared on the shelves of Bleecker Bob's (and elsewhere) in

November 1975. The following spring, critic Lester Bangs had *The Ramones* (April 23) in heavy rotation and, by summer's end, blessed Blondie's "X Offender," their debut single, with buoying rapture: "[It] contains the best roller rink organ since the Sir Douglas Quintet [and] the best surf guitar since [The Velvet's] 'I'm Set Free.'" That autumn, Smith and comrades added *Radio Ethiopia* to the mix, and Blondie's debut album led all releases in 1977. In February, Television's legendary *Marquee Moon* represented the fifth full-length release from the Bowery camp ahead of the first British punk LP, The Damned's *Damned Damned Damned*.[12]

PUNK THEORY: AN INTERLUDE

At the time, "punk" as a catch-all had yet to take hold. The experimental duo Suicide promised "punk music" in a 1970 flyer, and added an eschatological twist by hosting a "punk music mass" in 1972, at the Mercer Arts Center. Three years later, while *Voice* scribes increased the use of punk and "punkdom," the respective organizers of the Christmas Festival at CBGB in 1975, and the Easter Rock Festival at Max's in April 1976, passed on "punk" to describe the new rock underground. (Our Jewish, club-owning protagonists loved their Christian holidays, and admired one another, too. An early April concert listing for CBGB noted, "C.B.G.B. Salutes Max's Kansas City Great Easter Rock Festival."[13]) Once it gained

"Punk Music Mass" by Suicide, with Reverends Martin Rev and Alan Vega presiding, 1972.

greater currency, the designation "punk" glossed over the differences in the pop-punk, garage-punk, and art-punk musical camps pitched around the Bowery. The differences are considerable, but the musical and performative codes shared by these bands were significant, especially in terms of their adversaries.

Around CBGB and Max's, the protagonists of the new sound drew inspiration, in various combinations, from a host of forebears and New York institutions. The Velvet Underground, to begin, offered a compelling, alternative vision of the holy trinity of sex, drugs, and rock'n'roll. On their debut album (*Velvet Underground and Nico*, 1967), they countered the hippies' insipid, consonant visions of amorous utopias with gritty, drone-laden tales of sex and humiliation ("Venus in Furs"), drugs and humiliation ("I'm Waiting for the Man"), and rock'n'roll and humility ("Run Run Run," "There She Goes Again")—with the first two offering homage to the minimalism of LaMonte Young, more so than the blues aesthetic of saxophonist Lester Young. On the virtue of simplicity, The Velvet's Lou Reed noted, "One chord is fine.... Two chords are pushing it. Three chords and you're into jazz." The New York Dolls modeled a lack of gentility for subsequent punks, but they dressed it up in chiffon, boas, and androgyny (rather than misogyny), and affirmed a life Eros and humanism unrivaled by their patchouli-scented counterparts. Detroit's Iggy and the Stooges peddled passion rather than perfection, and Iggy's situationist-style engagement with the audience served as a model for punks onstage: "How can I make them hear me?" versus "How can I make them like me?"[14]

In addition, punks rejected the serious approach to music embraced by the art rockers and, in their lyrical depictions of taboo subjects, drew inspiration, too, from the Theater of the Ridiculous. The Theater rejected the naturalist aesthetic, employed cross-gender casting and nonprofessional actors (including Patti Smith), in order to send-up straight culture and explore so-called sexual deviancy in a ridiculously amusing forum. The Theater grew out of Warhol's camp, and staged productions at La MaMa Experimental Theatre Club and Bouwerie Lane Theatre—both stood within a stiletto's throw of CBGB.

A host of stylistic developments emerged in service to the renaissance of rock'n'roll, rebellion, and fun. As a rule, the Bowery bands drew upon a combination of the principles outlined above in the production of punk. Here, "punk" is used provisionally, to identify gestures, practices, or as a basis for cultural politics or negative self-definition ("let's not sound like that"), rather than as a conceptual box in which to secure The Ramones, or exclude Talking Heads, for instance. The categories pop-punk, garage-punk, and art-punk highlight a tendency of a given group, since most of the bands who endured expanded their musical visions from album to album. Punk, to begin, binds these bands around a common disdain for the musical order of things in the mid-1970s. "We did share an aesthetic with the punks," Frantz told me. "The pop radio stations were getting pretty [pause], well, [pause] we had the same things then that we have now: we have The Eagles, Elton John, and Tony Orlando and Dawn [laughs]. We were reacting against that, and we thought we could make music that we would like better than this stuff."

In service to this vision, and to counter the gravitas of rock-as-art (and conceptually related movements), bands emphasized passion over virtuosity in short, punchy, sometimes aggressive, tunes. The virtue of getting on-stage supplanted the (self-) righteousness of virtuosity, and The Ramones and Blondie did a lot of learning in front of perplexed audiences. Even their first manager (and eventual drummer) Tommy Erdelyi counted himself initially among the confounded: "To me, [The Ramones] was an avant-garde thing. Then we started getting really good and I said 'This isn't avant-garde this is commercial!'" Likewise, punks rent asunder the privilege of composition over interpretation, by way of cover tunes— see Patti Smith's "Gloria," The Ramones' "Let's Dance," and The Dictators' "I Got You Babe." For original compositions, practitioners of the New York sound penned lyrics about novel and often taboo subjects. In the opening stanzas of the vinyl noted above, with varying levels of irony, protagonists deny the Christian ideal of atonement (*Horses*), stand in awe of a Third Reich–inspired dance craze (*Ramones*), and celebrate sexual taboos ("X Offender"). The vocal styles, too, often came from beyond the history of the blues tradition. David Byrne of Talking Heads, Alan Vega of Suicide, and even Joey Ramone and Richard Hell introduced vocal phrasing, timbres, and attacks that owed more to the experimental works at La MaMa Theatre than the oeuvre of Big Mama Thornton. "We deliberately avoided blues progressions, and the standard blues formats," Chris Frantz told me. "I loved the blues, but that was a Rolling Stones thing and a Led Zeppelin thing. And we knew we couldn't compete with them at that game." On this question (and little else), Johnny Ramone shared Frantz's sentiments and, upon joining The Ramones, forswore his youthful aspiration to become the next Jimi Hendrix. The new goal? "Pure, white rock'n'roll, with no blues influence," Johnny surmised. "I wanted our sound to be as original as possible." If the notion of "white rock'n'roll" was a misnomer, a historical impossibility, even, many punk bands avoided blues scales, 12- and 32-bar blues formats, Stax- or Motown-style horn sections, and archetypal blues vocal styles—be it rhythm and blues (Jackie

Wilson), gospel (Aretha Franklin), or soul (Marvin Gaye). More consciously than not, New York rockers understood the genealogy of their disdain. The musical touchstones of the British invaders were Black and American and, from The Beatles to Led Zeppelin, they drew heavily from the musical—and sometimes corporeal—codes of blues, soul, and rhythm and blues.[15]

The black rebel archetype loomed large in the Black Atlantic imagination, too, especially on American shores. In the twenty years between Norman Mailer's "The White Negro" (1957) and The Clash's "White Riot," white fantasies of the black rebel informed the narratives and aesthetic choices of beatniks, rock'n'rollers, and punks alike. Mailer's puritan sexual hang-ups led him, per usual, well over the top in his much-maligned essay, but his fantasy here is social, rather than personal:

> The unstated essence of Hip, its psychopathic brilliance, quivers with the knowledge that new kinds of victories increase one's power for new kinds of perception . . . one is a rebel or one conforms, one is a frontiersman in the Wild West of American night life, or else a Square . . .
>
> A totalitarian society makes enormous demands on the courage of men . . . Indeed if one is to be a man, almost any kind of unconventional action often takes disproportionate courage. So it is no accident that the source of Hip is the Negro for he has been living on the margin between totalitarianism and democracy for two centuries.

Mailer's depiction of the hipster's sexual potency deserved the ire of cultural critic Albert Murray, as noted in a letter to Ralph Ellison: "Man, where did Norman Mailer . . . get that shit from"? Still, Murray and Ellison shared Mailer's interest in the durable centrality of black aesthetics to American cultural rebels, for those aesthetics served as a steady resource for refusals through the twentieth century—if in highly tempered form, during the emergence of punk.[16]

The poaching and remixing of codes, in whole or in part, drives innovation in art in general, and popular music in particular. The innovation of The Beatles, to begin, operated at sonic and formal levels. With the healthy songwriting co-operation (and competition) of Lennon and McCartney, the band grew restless as interpreters and constructed new codes (and new understandings) of how any sound—from sitar to mellotron—could be identified as rock and art. Beginning with "Love Me Do," The Beatles tweaked phrase lengths derived from the blues to great effect: see, too, the varying phrase lengths of the verses and the three-bar chorus of "I Am the Walrus."

At historical and aesthetic impasses, the avant-garde is often keenly aware of the sins of their forebears and the forces that begat their fall from grace. By the 1970s, the innovations of musical forms and virtuosity soon yielded to (ludicrous) narratives of mystical fantasy (e.g., Emerson, Lake & Palmer's *Tarkus*) and inimitable guitar solos of inexcusable duration (e.g., Led Zeppelin's "Dazed and Confused," live version, 26:53). The celebration of narcissistic virtuosity and, ostensibly, art for art's sake, set the terms for punk backlash. The negation comprised new ranks of auteurs, seeking their way in a world without future, ready to remix existing codes for expressive joy and musical rebellion. That joy, on occasion, in its rejection of the African-American roots of their archrivals, assumed unsavory forms—"death to disco"—and extended the history of the myth of black sexuality, as well as (middle-class) white anxiety over the pleasures of the body. See punk dance forms, for instance: the pogo allowed members of the audience better, if fleeting, sight lines of the stage, while freeing the dancer from keeping to the beat, or the responsibility of finding a partner. Slam-dancing and the mosh pit also entailed equally arrhythmic action, and slam dancers derived pleasure from risk and pain, rather than Eros. The mosh pit did not lend itself to foreplay.[17]

In the U.S. in particular, the blues tradition cast an expansive shadow across the history of popular music—one that proved difficult to escape, as punks sought to assemble codes commensurate with their musical proficiency and cultural politics. For some of the bands in the pop-punk and art-punk brigades, respectively, and for Talking Heads in particular, their critical end-around of the blues aesthetic reflected a similar move by Kraftwerk, whose album *Autobahn* (1974) reached number five on *Billboard's* Top 200 LPs. Bands in the U.S. and UK owed a profound debt to the Düsseldorf combo for their reimagining of the first principles of popular music. Rather than "in blues, in wood, in anger, in lust, in sexual frenzy, in poverty," Paul Morley writes, "What if [popular music] began in the avant-garde, in metal, in celebration, in abstract art, in universal awe, in modern comfort laced with psychological anxiety?" The punk singers noted above, along with Mark Mothersbaugh of Devo (est. 1972), David Thomas of Pere Ubu (est. 1975), and Andy Gill of Gang of Four (est. 1977), offered compelling answers to this possibility.[18]

Sound-wise, image-wise, and sales-wise, Blondie represented the most successful band of the pop-punk brigade (see also: Mink DeVille, The Marbles, The Miamis, and The Shirts). With her credentials as a former go-go dancer and Playboy bunny, lead singer Debbie Harry offered an alluring mash-up of (bottle-) blonde beauty and gritty, brazen desire—way more Mae West than Grace Kelly. Blondie songs were short, sharp, and ambivalently sweet, and owed much to the Phil Spector-produced girl groups of the 1960s.

The Ramones, The Dictators, The Tuff Darts, and The Heartbreakers comprised the core of the garage-punk brigade—artifice with neither poetry nor pretension. The Ramones excepted, these bands embraced more elements of the blues tradition than their counterparts. The Heartbreakers' Johnny Thunders, to begin, drew upon the blues by way of the behind-the-beat (and biochemical) legacy of Keith Richards. With her mascara, wigs, and garbage-strewn couture, Wayne-to-Jayne County defied easy categorization, and with punchy numbers like "Rock'n'roll Enema" (often performed with plunger in hand) drew directly upon the twelve-bar blues form. "Out of all the bands in that scene, Wayne County's was the best," Ivan Kral told me. "She had the best band of rock'n'rollers." Maximal brashness—and minimal use of keyboard and horns—united their affront upon clean living, good taste, and the ennui of contemporary radio.

The premier students of the art-punk school included The Patti Smith Group and Television, both of whom poached inspiration from the poets of old, and French poets in particular. Smith dedicated *Radio Ethiopia* to Rimbaud. Television's lead singer, Tom Verlaine (né Miller), nicked a last name. Suicide's challenge to pop sensibility commenced in 1970, and their lengthy, minimalist compositions—as well as their Brechtian, occasionally blood-splattered performances—represented a radical departure for (not nearly) popular music. Likewise, Smith and Verlaine, with poetry solos and guitar solos, respectively, sought to extend the formal parameters of rock, rather than revive its danceable brevity.[19]

In fact, prior to the export trade of British pogoing, few New Yorkers danced to punk. Arturo Vega, the artistic director for The Ramones, believed the factors were threefold: a Ramones show was, circa 1975, "too fast for anything. The crowds weren't that young. People saw them as some kind of minimalist artists."[20] Kral reported, "Nobody danced at CBGB. We'd nod our heads along to Television"—and there were certainly aerobic prohibitions to pogoing along to a live version of the thirteen-minute-long "Marquee Moon." At Max's, the Warhol denizens had long-abandoned the esteemed back room at Park Avenue and 17th Street—a void filled largely by young, carousing punks crossing bridges and traversing tunnels. Alan Vega of Suicide recalled, "CB's drew more of the art crowd, the intellectual crowd, without a doubt. Max's drew more of the Brooklyn kids." Critics, too, imagined The Ramones owed some debt to Warhol's tweaking of art, pop, and self-representation: in a concert announcement in the *Village Voice*, from April 1976, Christgau wrote, "Hard, loud, fast, and tuff, this is the most cleanly conceptualized New York rock show there is to see, and the last time I caught them I walked home high."[21]

The parameters of the concept, though, took time to coalesce. In August 1974, for their debut gig at CBGB, The Ramones' stage persona owed a clear debt to the Dolls' androgyny: lead vocalist Joey Ramone donned leather pants, flopped to his knees during "I Don't Wanna Go Down to the Basement," and regarded the crowd over the tops of his shades, with his right elbow cocked queerly akimbo. (Even a shirtless Johnny, in a leopard-print-lined leather jacket, with the cuffs rolled back and the collar popped, looked ready to hustle up to 53rd and 3rd alongside bassist Dee Dee Ramone, to secure some sweetness and some pocket cash.) By 1976, though, anxiety (and dread) over disco—and the spectacle of nimble bodies gay, black, and gay and black—resonated in the sartorial and musical aesthetics of the CBGB stalwarts. At that time, The Ramones were better conceptualized (and more definitively masculine and heterosexual), with their enduring regiment of sneakers, T-shirts, jeans, and leather jackets. Joey now placed his left foot forward, bent at the knees, gripped the mic in his left hand, and stood nearly stock still. "We at CBGBs—and then everybody who knew The Ramones—loved their whole *schtick*," Frantz recalled.

While Blondie and Talking Heads drew upon musical codes of disco, the analogous corporeal codes were largely eschewed, especially at CBGB. Much to the chagrin of his bandmates in Blondie, bassist Gary Valentine pogoed about onstage, and even heckled his fellow, less animate bass players with compassion:

Tina [Weymouth] never cracked a smile on stage, which I thought was a shame. I liked Talking Heads, especially "Psycho Killer" and "Warning Sign." But like Verlaine they seemed a bit detached, involved in the non-image they were non-presenting. . . . During one set at CBGB, when David Byrne was scratching away in some extended funk instrumental and Tina was nervously keeping time, I called out "Shake your booty, Tina!" She couldn't keep a straight face and laughed, and the audience did too.

Their laughter arose from the effort it took for Weymouth and the audience to sustain their claims of cool credibility: dancing was fine in other clubs, for the more colorful crowds in midtown and the West Village, especially, but not before discriminating music gourmandizers at Hilly's (punk) music gallery. This paradox resonated most with Talking Heads, and drummer Chris Frantz, especially. "I'd describe [our] sound as very clear," Frantz noted, in 1977. "It's very urban, but it's definitely white music."

Frantz imagined, too, how the sound of Talking Heads was shaped in part by the art school ethic, and by their effort to distinguish themselves from rock on the radio. In his final year at the Rhode Island School of Design (RISD), in a course on conceptual art with Alan Sondheim, Frantz bore witness to the creative lunacy of conceptual artist Dennis Oppenheim, experimental writer Kathy Acker, and minimalist composer Steve Reich. Their work and the ensuing conversations, Frantz noted, "It showed us that contemporary music, art, dance, writing—all this stuff was somehow connected, and it also showed us that the place we wanted to be when we got out of school was New York City, because that's where all these super-talented and sometimes crazy people were living and doing their work. Not LA [laughs]!"

In pressed slacks and buttoned polo shirts, Byrne, Weymouth, and Frantz rebelled sartorially against the aggressive dress and demeanor of the garage-punks, and drew upon their lessons at RISD to forge an aesthetic in accordance with their instrumental proficiency. Frantz recalled, haltingly, "We went into a more minimalist [pause], minimalist sort of [pause], it wasn't jazz either . . . Sorry [pause]. It was a very premeditated artful posture that we took, and we often said to each other what we didn't want to do, more than what we did want to do." David Byrne, too, in fits, ticks, and spasms, exemplified the ill-at-ease body of the white middle class and, along with their "angular sound," helped the band secure one foot in the bucket of art punk. "We weren't following any rock stereotype," Byrne later noted. "We were discovering our own stereotype that we could fall into."[22]

With the addition of Jerry Harrison on keyboards and guitar, and the brightly pop aspirations of producer Tony Bongiovi, *Talking Heads: 77* cracked the top 100 *Billboard* albums. In the next few years, though, Talking Heads' venture beyond their "nerd rock" aesthetic was heralded by their rendition of Al Green's "Take Me to the River," which represented an anomalous nod toward Black American music aesthetics en route to an allegedly African aesthetic. "I Zimbra," the opening track on *Fear of Music* (1979) (and the irrepressibly danceable A-side of *Remain in Light*), reflects the debt owed to Kraftwerk noted above, and heralded the cosmopolitan character of The Clash's *London Calling*.[23]

As a rule, between-band camaraderie eclipsed hostilities, and the ill-defined rubric of punk served them well in terms of domestic and overseas appearances. In early 1977, their connection via CBGB earned The Ramones the opening slot on a February 4 gig with Patti Smith and headliner Blue Öyster Cult at the Nassau Coliseum. That spring, The Ramones and Talking Heads set off for a six-week tour of Europe and England, and Television and Blondie soon followed. The days of winos and roses, though, did have their thorns, and Smith was among the sharpest. Blondie's Debbie Harry noted, "Basically, [Patti] told me that there wasn't room for two women in the CBGB's scene and that I should leave the business 'cause I didn't stand a chance against her!" Blondie's pop aspirations, and their initially modest chops, drew the visible ire of the art-punk aesthetes. "I may be paranoid," Harry noted, "but I think that whole clique wanted to destroy us." She wasn't, and they did. To straddle the divides between the various camps took real dexterity, which even Richard Hell was unable to muster. Verlaine drove him out of Television because Hell's tastes (and songs) were too prosaic. Later, Thunders and Jerry Nolan drove him out of The Heartbreakers because Hell's aesthetics (and antics) were too pretentious.[24]

The matters of art and artifice in rock culture, from 1967 through 1977, and the influence of Western art principles on rock musicians and rock deejays was profound. As rock-as-art took shape in the mid-1960s, and FM radio and home audio technology allowed listeners at home a more robust sonic experience, the deejays constructed their own aesthetic and politic. As George Harrison refused to be denied in 1967, so did the deejays of free-form FM radio, many of whom rose to prominence in the late 1960s as curators of musical arts on WNEW-FM, in New York City.

2.

From *Sgt. Pepper's* to *Born to Run:*
The Rise of Free-Form Radio

n 1967, with the release of Jefferson Airplane's *Surrealistic Pillow*, Jimi Hendrix's *Are You Experienced?*, and The Beatles' *Sgt. Pepper's Lonely Hearts Club Band*, the market was in ascendance for album-oriented rock, rather than singles-oriented rock'n'roll. That April, at KMPX, an FM station in San Francisco, Larry Miller and Tom "Big Daddy" Donahue forged the template for free-form FM radio by adopting the album as the *objet d'art*, rather than the hit single. Donahue also punctuated his departure from AM radio that November by penning "AM Radio Is Dead and Its Rotting Corpse Is Stinking Up the Airwaves," for the second issue of *Rolling Stone*.

For FM converts, the bane of AM radio included the antics of the hysterical deejay and the constant intrusion of the marketplace. "The tempo is Go! Go! Go!" Donahue lamented. "The air is replete with such blather as, 'Here comes another twin spin sound sandwich.'" A "twin spin"—two songs in a row—was an aberration in a format that was largely song, commercial, deejay doggerel (repeat), which ensured that every song in the all-hits format of AM radio was adjacent to a commercial, deejay banter, or both. Miller and Donahue forged the template for free-form radio in accordance with the contrarian and mellower cadences of the counterculture. They played songs by the set and "double-spotted" the commercials in blocks of two to four in order to minimize the exposure of art to contiguous, commercial contamination. Donahue's staff, too, dabbled in pop musicology, providing listeners with running commentary about the songs in the previous set. These commentaries unfolded without reference to the clock, and the left-leaning, conversational approach to political music readily modulated to "raps" about power and politics.[1]

Across the United States, FM deejays forged a vanguard alliance against the commercialism of AM radio, inspired by musical artists who refused to release singles from their albums. "There's no point putting out a single when the album is the statement by the band," noted Robert Plant of Led Zeppelin. By the mid-1970s, though, members of the vanguard had turned rearguard. The free-form gospel of "rock is art" and "anything but disco" eventually excluded punk and new wave, too. This decree, though, rang false with key figures in the subsequent generation of deejays and, at New York's WNEW, the rebellion arose from within. Led by Meg Griffin, and aided by WNEW's concert series from the Bottom Line in Greenwich Village, select deejays at WNEW overcame the punk-phobia of their peers to forge an expansive fan base that reached from Fairfield, Connecticut, to Philadelphia.[2]

WITH A LITTLE HELP FROM MY FRIENDS

In 1967, in New York City, the deejays at WOR-FM included "Murray the K" Kaufman, Bill "Rosko" Mercer, and Scott Muni. Kaufman previously played second fiddle at WINS-AM to "Moondog" Alan Freed, who promoted racial integration among American youth through the popularization of rock'n'roll. Like Freed, Kaufman assumed a key role in shaping radio and popular music tastes among youth in New York and, in 1962, during his seven to eleven p.m. time slot at WINS-AM, he developed many of the stylistic techniques that earned him the sobriquet of the original hysterical deejay. In 1964, Kaufman ingratiated himself with The Beatles, and on a trip to Miami even shared a hotel room with George Harrison. He also kept closely attuned to the artistic turn of The Beatles' music and, as The Beatles made new demands on the attention span of their fans, Kaufman followed suit.[3]

For the first four studio LPs by The Beatles, the average length was 32:31. For their next four LPs, the average length jumped by 10 percent, and the number of tracks stayed the same. By *A Hard Day's Night*, their third album for Parlophone, their days as three-minute heroes were numbered. With *Rubber Soul*, especially, The Beatles treated the LP, rather than the single, as the unit of composition. In the summer of love, during his evening shift at WOR, Kaufman played full-album sides without interruption. Muni affirmed Kaufman's heterodoxy, breaking ground on the East Coast by playing songs in sets. WOR's 1967 flirtation with free-form proved short-lived and, in October, the station switched formats to adult top 40.[4]

Nonetheless, the failed experiment at WOR piqued the interest of George Duncan, the general manager of cross-town rival WNEW. In 1966, WNEW entered the FM province with an all-female cast of deejays. The June press release touted the acting credentials of new hire Alison Steele, who previously starred in her own television show, "You and Your Figure." The music director boasted credentials from Yale and Julliard, and the station emphasized contemporary music, "familiar standards performed by recognized artists." A playlist that fall included Oscar Peterson's "Serenade in Blue," Barbra Streisand's "I've Got No Strings," and Sammy Kaye's "Spanish Eyes." In October, Duncan added Bill "Rosko" Mercer to the seven-to-midnight slot and, by December, Rosko, Muni, and Jonathan Schwartz were the leading voices of a mostly male, free-form rock station.[5]

To create his "audio pictures," Rosko assembled collages of jazz, rock, and spoken-word performances: he segued from John Coltrane to Shel Silverstein, from Jimi Hendrix to Khalil Gibran, and he courted left-leaning listeners through his open opposition to the Vietnam War. The sales of commercial spots during Rosko's initial run impressed Duncan, and inspired him to adopt a policy structured around good taste and "meaningful music": "We will not tell a deejay not to play a Frank Sinatra record," Duncan said, "because there are some Sinatra performances that may fit into this format." Schwartz's decision to play Peggy Lee's "Sing a Rainbow," though, merited scrutiny. "Did he play it because he liked it," Duncan noted rhetorically, "or because he wanted to construct or demonstrate something?" Duncan wanted to construct a college-aged audience and, to demonstrate WNEW's commitment to the evolution of rock music, he placed station ads in the *Village Voice*, and accompanied Rosko on speaking gigs to Queen College and Columbia University. "It was a hell of an experience," Duncan said. "Exhilarating. Two to three hundred students firing questions at us."[6]

In July 1968, Rosko's break from the gate continued apace: his show ranked number two in the New York market among the eighteen-to-thirty-five demographic. Muni created a persona known for knowing everyone in rock, hosting on-air interviews with The Who, The Grateful Dead, and Elton John. Steele moved from days to the graveyard shift and, with her newly affected sultry voice and her penchant for the string-heavy tracks of Genesis and The Moody Blues, seduced listeners for the next ten years as "the Nightbird."[7]

Richard Neer joined WNEW in 1971. Before spinning discs on his two-to six-a.m. shift, Neer often accompanied Matty Matthews of Columbia Records to Max's Kansas City. Max's opened in 1965 and, in short order, became the preferred social venue for painters such as Robert Rauschenberg and Larry Rivers. In the early 1970s, Max's hosted concerts by David Bowie, Lou Reed, and Iggy Pop, and Andy Warhol and his entourage frequented the über-hip back room. Warhol regarded Max's as the place where "Pop Art and Pop Life came together in the sixties—teenyboppers and sculptors, rock stars and poets from St. Mark's Place, Hollywood actors checking out what the underground actors were all about . . . everybody went to Max's."[8]

"I would go to Max's to see the Columbia artists play," Neer told me. "And Bruce [Springsteen] was a guy I went to see fifteen times." In 1974, Springsteen had one album left on his three-record deal. His first two albums, *Greetings from Asbury Park, N.J.* (1973) and *The Wild, the Innocent & the E Street Shuffle* (1973), had garnered critical acclaim, but limited commercial success. (Of the seven tracks on *Shuffle*, four were over seven minutes long, and not one was released as a single.) Neer put tracks from *Shuffle* into heavy rotation, as did deejays at WMMR in Philadelphia and WMMS in Cleveland. Like *Greetings*, though, *Shuffle* received scant attention elsewhere, and failed to crack the charts upon its release. Springsteen, though, had his devotees. In Christgau's "Consumer Guide" in the *Voice*, *Greetings* received an A−. In *Rolling Stone*, Ken Emerson lauded the sound and the "punk savvy" of the lyrics. And, in a concert review in Boston's *Real Paper*, Jon Landau penned the oft-quoted line: "I saw rock and roll's future, and its name is Bruce Springsteen." Devotees also included Allan Pepper and Stanley Snadowsky, owners of the Bottom Line—though their devotion was, at the time, considerably more tempered. In summer 1974, "The shows were interminably long," Pepper remembered. "He didn't really have it together, but you saw he had a *vision*. It wasn't quite there yet. He was just reaching."[9]

The year 1974 represented the half-life of commercial free-form radio. By that time, the casualties included WABX in Detroit, WNCR in Cleveland, and WCBS in New York City. By September, no fewer than eighteen automated services were plying prepackaged radio programs, with minimal assembly required. In order to reduce the length of disk jockey shifts, local insertions such as weather, public service announcements, and time of day could be recorded in a single session. One station executive found that, for an automated format, a deejay could produce enough snippets in forty-five minutes to cover four hours of air time. Less skilled hands stitched together the snippets and the playlists, and Rosko-esque "raps" were thereby eliminated. Sales proved brisk and, at the time, up to eight hundred stations in the United States offered "virtually live" programming and—of particular interest to owners and managers—savings in labor costs and exasperation. "I got good and tired of trying to ride herd on a gang of woolly-headed jocks," noted one convert. By the mid-1970s, one in seven FM stations had been automated. The November issue of *Broadcasting*, the weekly trade journal for radio and television managers, highlighted the gap between the FM segment of the radio audience, which was 33 percent, and the FM segment of revenue, which was 14 percent. The following month, *Broadcasting* registered the rise in the "study of [FM] audience tastes as measured by sales and requests." Beginning with tightened playlists, the narrow strictures of the AM format were gaining headway on FM radio. WNEW remained immune to such strictures for the moment, and its deejays took great pride in their stake as sentient, cultural arbiters. "We were always on the cutting edge," Neer told me. "For a while it was singer-songwriters, then folk rock and country rock. We played R&B, we played The Mahavishnu Orchestra." Muni held the coveted afternoon slot on WNEW and, through the 1970s, his "Things from England" segment introduced new bands to WNEW listeners.[10]

In fall 1974, Neer's brother obtained a bootleg copy of the title track of *Born to Run*, and Neer included the track on his show. Requests for the song soon lit up the board, and WNEW deejays, many of whom initially balked at Columbia's hard sell of "the next Bob Dylan," added the track to their playlists. By 1975, Pepper and Snadowsky figured that Springsteen's grasp had equaled his reach, and scheduled a five-night, ten-show residency in August for Springsteen and his band. Neer lobbied Mel Karmazin, general manager of WNEW, to showcase one Springsteen show for a live broadcast from the Bottom Line. "The record companies would try to get the band at the Bottom Line," Neer said, "[as] the Bottom Line was the premier showcase for new bands." In effect, Neer was asking Karmazin to forego two hours' worth of scheduled revenue in favor of the prestige that follows the first principle of rock music aficionados: we were into this band before anybody. (The second principle is, of course, to be into, and then done with, a given band before anybody.)[11]

After months of recording and mixing the forthcoming LP, Springsteen returned to the stage with joyful earnestness. For the early show on August 15, Springsteen opened with "Tenth Avenue Freeze Out" and, in the middle of the set, the band romped through "She's the One," "Born to Run," and "Thunder Road." During his residency, Springsteen danced on the table tops and held the crowd rapt with stories about first encounters with saxophonist Clarence Clemons and guitarist Steven Van Zandt. He closed sets with covers of "Quarter to Three" and "Twist and Shout."[12]

The show was simulcast by WMMR in Philadelphia, and reached listeners from southern Connecticut to eastern Pennsylvania. The *Born to Run* LP hit record shelves by the end of the month and, in October, Springsteen appeared on the covers of *Time* and *Newsweek* simultaneously. *Born to Run* stayed on *Billboard*'s album chart for two years, peaking at number three. Springsteen's newfound national fame benefited from the marketing muscle of Columbia Records, and from Springsteen's willingness to drop by a handful of radio stations to chat and spin discs with his favorite deejays. Most importantly, the live broadcast represented the cultural sway held by WNEW deejays long after the appearance of the first wave of obituaries for free-form radio. As early as 1971, in an article in the *Village Voice*, deejay Dave Herman lamented the demise of New York's WPLJ-FM in particular, and free-form radio in general: "Commercial radio all across the country has become as much a wasteland as TV. All I know is radio. It's all I've ever done. I love radio. But only when it's real, spontaneous, and creative. Only when it serves people's needs, and is a vital communication medium." He also noted the reported losses at seven of ABC's FM stations the previous year: $2.5 million, which he understood was unsustainable.[13]

In 1976, thirteen WNEW broadcasts from the Bottom Line included performances by Billy Joel, Donovan, Leo Sayer, and Don McLean. In 1977, most of the broadcasts logged equally safe territory, with a June performance by Southside Johnny and the Asbury Jukes, and an October performance by Nils Lofgren. The riskier broadcasts that year included Jesse Winchester, following President Carter's grant of amnesty to draft resisters, and Jerry Jeff Walker, an Austin-based country-rock artist touring to support the rerelease of his 1969 hit, "Mr. Bojangles."[14]

For WNEW, the risks paid tribute to discerning audiences and dividends, too: that June, *Billboard* hailed WNEW as "the most profitable [station] in FM radio." Springsteen's post-broadcast triumph solidified WNEW's commitment to the live simulcast and, over the next two years, WNEW aired live concerts by The Tom Robinson Band, The Police, and Joe Jackson—UK bands attuned to the music of the New York punk scene coalescing at CBGB and harnessing anger as an energy. According to Tony James, the band that mattered most to the UK punk groups was The Ramones.[15]

3.
1977: Clamor, Exposure, and Camaraderie

The Ramones' debut gig at the Performance Studio in New York City on March 30, 1974, proved memorable, if for all the wrong reasons. "We were terrible," Johnny Ramone recalled. "Dee Dee was so nervous he stepped on his guitar and broke its neck." After four months of rehearsals, The Ramones returned to the stage, this time at CBGB. Their performance was still a shambles, but endearing enough for Hilly Kristal to bring them back again and again.[1]

Writers at the *Village Voice* frequented CBGB for a variety of reasons. Music critic Richard Goldstein took great delight in the camaraderie between writers and musicians, if less so the odd affections of writers for each other: one night, while seated near the stage, he received a (love?) bite on the leg from *Punk* reporter Eddie "Legs" McNeil. Christgau, too, accompanied by his wife, confidant, and fellow scribe Carola Dibbell, stopped by for the music and the occasional chat with Kristal. "It was an important place, a place I cared about," Christgau told me. "And it was because of Hilly."[2]

By 1975, the regulars also included photographer-manager Leee Black Childers and Wayne County, who graced the stage with various ensembles, including the original Backstreet Boys. After seeing The Ramones for the first time, Childers gushed, "I knew that I was home and happy and secure and free and rock'n'roll." Shortly after his first live Ramones' experience, Danny Fields introduced himself to the band. "I want to manage you," he professed. "You've changed my life." Early Ramones' performances offered (illusory) evidence that anyone could play rock'n'roll, and writers at *Rock Scene* and *Creem* wrote warm-and-fuzzy reviews of their shows. Before long, writers at *NME* and *Melody Maker* joined the choir. The Ramones signed to Sire Records, recorded their debut album in seven days in the winter of 1976, and waited for the world to catch on.[3]

The formula proved infectious: start a band, learn to play (but not too well), and rely upon critics and audiences hungry for the sonic alternative to "the ruling coalition of 10cc/Queen/the Stylistics/Stevie Wonder/Boz Scaggs adult-orien-tated rock medicine shows." As one writer expectantly noted, "The ideology of the garage band is an attack on the star system." That ideology reflected the DIY spirit, which inspired deejay Pam Merly's quest for sonic justice at FM stations in Connecticut and New York. It inspired the publishers of *Trouser Press*, *Punk*, *New York Rocker*, and *Sniffin' Glue*, respectively, to foment the death of somnam-bulant rock and document the glories of punk. And it inspired Joe Strummer to join The Clash, pen a host of great tunes with Mick Jones, and to assemble one of the best debut albums since the demise of the Roman Empire. (St. Augustine's *Confessions* is right up there, too.) In downtown Manhattan, reporters on the rock'n'roll beat expanded in terms of numbers, tastes, and literacy, and contrib-uted to the steady transmission of print (and vinyl) between New York and London (and back again). If year zero for punk was 1976, it secured a critical rate of exposure, in clubs and in record shops, in print and on the airwaves, in 1977.[4]

THE BLITZKRIEG BOP

The Ramones hit record shelves on both sides of the Atlantic on April 23, 1976—the same day as the second 101'ers/Sex Pistols billing at the Nashville Room, and the same weekend as the premiere of *The Blank Generation*. In Tony James's esti-mation, "The Ramones were the single most important group that changed punk rock. When their album came out, all the English groups tripled speed overnight. Two-minute-long songs, very fast." Captain Sensible of The Damned agreed. "I don't know what the British punk scene would've been like if the Ramones hadn't come over in '76 . . . We took their influence when we recorded *Damned Damned Damned*—we deliberately under-produced it to keep it energetic and not over-glossy."[5]

The courtship of Joe Strummer for the not-yet-named successor to London SS was equally frenzied. On May 25, 1976, Strummer and Bernie Rhodes attended The Sex Pistols' performance at the 100 Club and, after the show, Rhodes invited Strummer to meet the members of the band he assembled to rival the Pistols. The following Friday, Levene and Rhodes pulled Strummer aside after a 101'ers gig and gave him forty-eight hours to decide. On Sunday, outside of a rehearsal space in Acton, Strummer stepped out of Rhodes's car, made his way over to Jones and Simonon, and asked, "So you got a few tunes then?" Strummer's last gig with The 101'ers took place the following weekend.[6]

For the previous six years, the nickname of Joe Strummer (né John Mellor) had been "Woody." His moniker had morphed from "Ollie," to "Woolly," to "Woody," and it established a fortuitous link to Woody Guthrie, with whom he shared a background of modest privilege, and the childhood loss of a sibling. Charley Guthrie was a prosperous real-estate speculator in oil-rich Okemah, Oklahoma, whose eldest daughter Clara died in a coal-oil fire. Ronald Mellor was a British foreign-service diplomat, whose eldest son David died at his own hand, at age nineteen, a victim apparently of undiagnosed depression.[7]

With the hire of drummer Terry Chimes, The Clash were complete. Chimes turned twenty in 1976 and, like Ringo Starr, imagined that rock'n'roll might provide a nice diversion before embarking on a more stable vocation—in Starr's case, as a flower shop proprietor; in Chimes's case, as a doctor. In June, Jones, Simonon, Levene, Strummer, and Chimes began playing at Rehearsal Rehearsals studio, sometimes seven days a week. On July 4, The Clash and The Ramones made their UK debuts: The Clash at Sheffield's Black Swan nightclub, and The Ramones in London's Roundhouse, to an audience of two thousand. At Dingwalls the next night, members of Clash-de-camp joined members of the Pistols to check out The Ramones. "In England we were treated like stars," recalled drummer Tommy Ramone (né Erdelyi). "It was very exciting—meeting the up-and-coming English punk bands that came to our soundcheck."[8]

After dabbling with different band names, including The Psychotic Negatives and The Weak Heartdrops, they settled upon Simonon's suggestion of The Clash, which was a popular phrase in London's *Evening Standard* and fit the ethos of the group. Rhodes delighted in the moniker, and took particular joy in testing the band members' individual mettle. "Are you here for a goal or are you here just eating a cucumber sandwich?" Rhodes would sneer, according to Chimes. "He had a way of wording things to make you feel stupid, and get you to do things his way." Rhodes's freedom from sentimentality resonated with his charges. Within a week of Strummer's suggestion that Levene be sacked, The Clash became a quartet.[9]

With Jones providing the arrangements and Strummer providing most of the lyrics, The Clash recorded their eponymous debut. Realist depictions of acne-cream promises and footwear envy reflected Rhodes's directive to Jones and Strummer: "Don't write about love, write about what's affecting you, what's important." Four tracks clock in under two minutes. Five other tracks take just shy of thirty seconds more. All but one of the songs end at full volume: the punk aesthetic had little patience for the ignominy of the fade-out at the cadence.[10]

Their embrace of that aesthetic, though, was tempered. Rather than the wall-of-sound bellicosity of The Sex Pistols' first single, "Anarchy in the UK" (1976), eight of the fourteen songs on *The Clash* balance passages of the full ensemble with short bursts of unaccompanied drumming or strumming. "Janie Jones," for example, begins with a lone snare drum and is joined, respectively, by Strummer's guitar, his voice, his voice and guitar, and the voices of Strummer, Jones, and Simonon and the ensemble of instruments.

As Pat Gilbert observes in *Passion Is a Fashion: The Real Story of The Clash*, the thirteen original compositions slated for *The Clash* comprised but twenty-eight minutes of material, at a time when albums were typically forty minutes in length. With the inclusion of "Police and Thieves," by Junior Murvin and Lee "Scratch" Perry, The Clash offered a seemingly aberrant, six-minute homage to their fascination with the rock-steady reverb of reggae and dub. From the falsetto "oh yeahs" of the chorus to the sparse instrumentation skipping between the stereo channels, the arrangement embraced the affirmative aesthetic outlined in the T-shirt manifesto noted above.[11]

The joyful noise of "London's Burning" and "Thieves" conveyed The Clash's sense of humor in their lyrics, their arrangements, and their musical attack. "It must be said that Mick Jones is a brilliant arranger," Strummer later recalled. "Any other group would've played on the off-beat [on 'Thieves'], trying to assimilate reggae, but we had one guitar on the on, the other the off. I mean, he really set it up. He's a genius." With a balance of ire and joy, frustration and catharsis, The Clash drew upon the principles of Caribbean popular music. Punk embodied white (male) anxiety and rage, as a rule, and reflexively distanced itself from the chic sensuality of the blackness of rhythm and blues, funk, and disco.

The arrangement for "Thieves" provided a delightful respite from the elated fury of the other tunes—a respite that never comes on the Pistols' *Never Mind the Bollocks* (October 1977).[12]

BACK IN THE U.S. OF A.

In 1977, the expanding popularity of punk beyond the Bowery depended in part upon rock scribes at the *Voice*, the freewheeling promotional guys at the distributor Jem Records and, in turn, punk-o-philes at independent record shops, within and beyond Manhattan. Deejay Pam Merly established her deejay credentials in the free-form format and, by 1977, ensured that listeners in the metropolitan region could find another ally on the airwaves.

The Clash was released in April 1977 in the UK only, as CBS deemed the sound quality to be too low for American radio. Christgau read about *The Clash* in *NME* and *Sniffin' Glue*, a punk fanzine established in 1976, and he made his way to Bleecker Bob's in Greenwich Village. "I was with [fellow *Voice* writer] Richard Goldstein at the time," he recalled. "We had been reading about it, and went to Bleecker Bob's and bought it and we both said, 'This is fucking great!'" Christgau deemed *The Clash* to be "notoriously underproduced," but still anointed it his favorite punk LP from the UK. He directed his readers to Bleecker Bob's to acquire the import pressing, musing that the album may never be released in the States.[13]

That same week, *Billboard* reported that the following LPs were in heavy rotation on FM stations in the northeast: Emerson, Lake & Palmer's *Works, v. 1*, Supertramp's *Even in the Quietest Moments*, and Fleetwood Mac's *Rumours*. The chart-dominant *Rumours* secured a top-five position in both "The 1977 Pazz & Jop Critics Poll," the annual survey in the *Village Voice*, and Christgau's Pazz & Jop ballot. On both lists, the top five LPs also included Television's *Marquee Moon*, The Ramones' *Rocket to Russia*, and The Sex Pistols' *Never Mind the Bollocks, Here's the Sex Pistols*. The adoration of punk by Christgau and his colleagues inspired some of Christgau's most earnest prose in 1977. "I'm buying records, calling people up to announce finds, playing the Vibrators and the Radiators from Space for everyone who walks in the door," Christgau professed. "First it was isolated artists, then a vanguard, but now it looks like a movement ... ready to make exciting noises of its own."[14]

The distributor Jem Records also claimed an early stake in the virtues of punk, and they supplied domestic and import vinyl to Bleecker Bob's, Sounds, and the libraries of metropolitan radio stations. When it came to punk and new wave releases, WNEW's Richard Neer recalled, "The Jem promo guys were telling us about this stuff, six months to a year beforehand, which would upset the release schedules of the domestic labels and really piss them off." In 1977, Pam Merly included a smattering of punk and new wave discs on her show at WLIR, a free-form station on Long Island, and she was a quick convert to Jem's promotional strategies. "Oh my god! You should see the records that I would get," Merly told me. "I would get tons and tons of records! They would meet you in the stairwell before your show, and help your mood a little bit. It was the good old days."[15]

SEGUES AND SERENDIPITY

Merly grew up in Bridgeport, Connecticut, an hour north of New York City, entering her teens the same year as The Beatles' debut on the *Ed Sullivan Show*. Merly's mother kept the kitchen radio tuned to top 40, and Merly recalled listening to the likes of Murray the K, Cousin Brucie, and Dandy Dan Daniel. Merly attended college at the University of Bridgeport, where she began her career in radio.

As a first-year student, Merly accompanied a friend for his show at WPKN, the campus radio station. "I watched him doing segues, and all I could think of was I wanted to get my hands on those records and those turntables," she told me. "I wanted to put music together and be able to create moods and be able to entertain people by using other people's music. I was sort of a frustrated musician myself." Her interest in coursework waned almost immediately. "Once I discovered the college radio station, it was pretty much all over," she confessed. In order to maintain her status as a student, and thereby remain eligible to work at the station, Merly enrolled in the occasional class, including the history of jazz, and pronunciation and articulation, in accordance with her plan to become a professional deejay in free-form radio.

From May to August 1973, Merly's daytime show often comprised little more than managing the live feed from the chamber of the U.S. Senate. "I would just come in and monitor the board while the Watergate hearings were on. It was pretty amazing." When she had the opportunity to play music, Merly had few constraints at WPKN. The station was "completely free-form," she recalled, "so it was a great groundwork for learning all kinds of music and progressive radio." After years of knocking on doors, Merly landed her first professional gig at WHCN in Hartford, Connecticut, another free-form station. On Sunday mornings, Merly was responsible for running "the God Squad tapes," which ranged from lessons in fire-and-brimstone Christianity to the Zen teachings of Alan Watts.[16]

In 1976, Merly became the only female deejay on full-time at WLIR. WLIR's signal reached the New York metropolitan region, but was not considered a rival to either WNEW or WPLJ, a (largely) progressive rock station. The staff at WLIR included Earle Bailey and Ray White, and the musical guidelines were simple: anything but disco. Joni Mitchell segued into Chick Corea's Return to Forever, and discs by Nick Drake, Herbie Hancock, and Led Zeppelin were regulars in the mix. The WLIR audience was partial to "dirt bands" and, according to Merly, the deejays obliged with plenty of air time for The Outlaws and The Grateful Dead.

Jerry Garcia, lead singer for The Grateful Dead, appreciated the support and appeared one day at the studio to do an on-air interview with White. "Jerry Garcia had this little bottle of white powder that he kept taking out of his pocket," Merly recalled. "When Ray would play a record, Jerry would say, 'Excuse me,' and would take out his little vial, and snort a little bit. He wasn't offering it around or anything, it was just his *medication*." By 1977, Merly and a few others ensured that the boundaries of free-form were increasingly elastic. She reported playing Black Sabbath, Ray Charles, and Johnny Cash alongside tracks by Television, The Clash, and The Ramones. Around that time, Frantz told me, "When I wanted to hear punk and/or new wave, I would listen to WLIR, because they were really good to Talking Heads, and they played our friends like The B-52's." In April 1978, on successive Tuesdays, WLIR exemplified the range of radio's possibilities, with live performances by Emerson, Lake & Palmer, Elvis Costello, and The Doobie Brothers.[17]

COMPLETE CONTROL

In signing with CBS, The Clash expected that major label support would deliver them from the Wilmcote House to the world, and to a U.S. audience in particular. In doing so, in the eyes of some chroniclers, The Clash had forsaken the DIY ethic of the punk scene. According to one critic, "Punk died the day The Clash signed to CBS." In DIY culture, agents assumed the responsibility of producing their own culture, by starting record labels, creating a network of venues for live performance, and publishing fanzines—independent of corporate overlords such as CBS. The DIY ethic was manifest in nascent fanzines on both sides of the Atlantic, and The Clash loomed large in the imaginations of Mark Perry of London's *Sniffin' Glue*, and Ira Robbins and Karen Rose of New York's *Trouser Press*.[18]

Perry was the primary writer, head xeroxer, and thereby publisher of *Sniffin' Glue*, which he established in June 1976 to honor his muse, Joey Ramone, and year zero of anarchic joy in the UK. Perry was a dedicated reader of *NME* and, when Nick Kent praised The Ramones' debut, Perry bought an import copy. "One time I was at [the record shop] Rock On, trying to find out if there were any magazines I could read about these bands in," Perry recalled. "There weren't, so the people behind the counter suggested flippantly that I should go and start my own. So I did." The subjects of Perry's hand-scrawled musings in *Glue*'s debut included Eddie and the Hot Rods and Blue Öyster Cult. By issue three, he had narrowed the editorial focus to *punkier* punk groups. In June 1977, Perry's laudatory essay on *The Clash* lamented at length his previous life as a bank clerk in which, like millions of others in the UK, he had only the weekends to look forward to. The review reproduced the lyrics to "London's Burning" and, in all-caps earnestness, Perry proclaimed, "THE CLASH ALBUM IS LIKE A MIRROR. IT REFLECTS ALL THE SHIT. IT SHOWS US THE TRUTH. TO ME, IT IS THE MOST IMPORTANT ALBUM EVER RELEASED." Perry's anti-star-studded readership included members of The Damned, The Sex Pistols, and The Clash. "John Lydon had it, Strummer had it, Rat Scabies had it," Perry reported. "I thought, 'If I say this in the *Glue*, it's going to happen.' I knew that, and that's what fueled me, knowing that it was being taken seriously."[19]

Robbins and Rose, with mentor Dave Schulps, founded *Trans-oceanic Trouser Press* (*TOTP*) in 1974. In its opening editorial, *TOTP* set out to be "the first consumer-orientated, (inter)national rock fanzine," in order to help readers "decide if your pennies are better off in the piggy bank, or if, indeed, a given double-album English import is worth goin' without food for a month." Todd Rundgren excepted, the editors identified themselves as "severe Anglophiliacs," and were well-aware of the perks of running a music magazine. In the thank-you section of the opening editorial, they included "*The Record Industry*—for the gifts we are about to receive" (emphasis in original). The twenty-four pages of crude photography and Courier typeset ended with the classifieds, in which Robbins himself—to help finance the venture—listed collectible 45s, including The Beatles' "Sie Liebt Dich/Komm, Gib Mir Deine Hand." Articles over the next three years lavished attention on the British rock triumvirate—The Beatles, The Who, and The Rolling Stones. If Anglophilia still steered the editorial course of "America's Only British Rock Magazine," the April–May 1976 issue included "NYC Notes . . . and NO DISCO!!," which covered the Bowery beat. The subsequent issue represented the first with the tidy moniker of *Trouser Press* and, by 1977, it provided its readers with some of the definitive coverage of the New York and London punk scenes. In his September 1977 review of *The Clash*, Robbins celebrated the group's horrible singing and its "wild-eyed hate of every-thing stupid." The *Trouser Press* cover in February 1978 juxtaposed two pressing questions: "The Clash: England's Best Band?" and "Cheap Trick: America's Best Band?" By the time The Clash made their New York debut in February 1979, *Trouser Press* had published three more stories on The Clash, two in excess of three thousand words. *Rolling Stone*, in turn, did not see fit to review it at all. According to Bob Gruen, rock photographer extraordinaire, "*Rolling Stone* wasn't interested in anything that didn't have a record company behind it . . . they didn't want to put bands in the paper that people couldn't get at their local record shops."[20]

Danny Fields, rock impresario and long-time manager of The Ramones, confirmed the coincidentally timorous character of American radio and the sala-cious character of American television. On the terminal tour of The Sex Pistols, in January 1978, Vicious's auto-aggression provided fodder aplenty for fear-mon-gering news anchors, in Atlanta and San Antonio, especially. "Whatever chance The Ramones had to get on the radio based on the merit of the music was then wiped out by The Sex Pistols because [punk] became too hot to handle," Fields lamented. "American radio, then as now, doesn't like to participate in anything that is dangerous."[21]

In the mid-1970s, though, the future was yet to be written, and anything was possible. Alan Betrock, a music writer for the *Soho Weekly News*, invited Blondie into the studio in spring 1975. Blondie had just established its original line-up as a quartet (having parted ways with a conga player and a flautist), when they recorded four originals, including "The Disco Song"—a beta version of "Heart of Glass." While still in his mid-twenties, Betrock was already a veteran DIY trooper, having served as the publisher of *JAMZ*, an early fanzine, and *Rock Marketplace*, a favorite of record collectors in search of obscure recordings. Betrock's interest in Blondie reflected his obsession with girl groups and his growing stake in the cultural significance of the downtown scene. He was assembling his own rock periodical, in fact, when the first issue of *Punk* hit local newsstands, in January 1976.[22]

John Holmstrom, a recent drop-out of the School of the Visual Arts in Manhattan, combined resources with Ged Dunn and Legs McNeil to found *Punk* magazine, in the roles of editor, publisher, and "resident punk," respectively. The editorial vision entailed a grand refusal of the soft rock clogging the airwaves. "I hated most rock and roll, because it was about lame hippie stuff," McNeil recalled. "There really wasn't anyone describing our lives—which was McDonald's, beer, and TV reruns. Then John found The Dictators, and we all got excited that something was happening." Exemplars also included the Stooges and The Ramones, who—after a late 1975 performance at CBGB that McNeil considered "the best eighteen minutes of rock & roll that I had ever heard"—agreed to an interview with *Punk*. "They were like us," McNeil remembered. "They talked about comic books and sixties bubble-gum music and were really deadpan and sarcastic."[23]

The first three issues of *Punk* included features on Lou Reed, Patti Smith, and The Ramones, respectively. Headlines and articles were handwritten and, in the opening editorial-as-manifesto, Holmstrom offered stark counsel to *Punk*'s readership: "Kill yourself. Jump off a fuckin' cliff. Drive nails into your head. Become a robot and join the staff at Disneyland. OD. Anything. Just don't listen to discoshit. I've seen that canned crap take real live people and turn them into dogs! And vice versa. The epitome of all that's wrong with Western civilization is disco. Eddjicate yourself. Get into it. Read *Punk*."

The counsel of self-destruction, rather than, say, start your own band, reflected the aggressive, editorial imagination of *Punk*. The first article in the first issue, Joe Koch's "Marlon Brando: The Original Punk," cited the mumbled improvisations of the leather-clad leader of *The Wild One*, along with the fidgetiness of Terry Malloy in *On the Waterfront*, as the archetypical images of punk.

Punk defined punk negatively, too, through Robert Romagoli's "Do It Yourself Sixties Protest Song." For the opening stanza, the reader is spotted "Well the," and could choose protagonists from "brothers and daughters"; "poets and the preachers"; or "ad-men and the beggars"—who, in turn, are either "fucking up my mind"; "eating out the moon"; or "watching *Adam 12*."[24] *Punk* itself, in its style and its selection of subjects, celebrated the strategic aggression of the pugilist and the barbed wit of the satirist. In turn, as they documented punk, Holmstrom and McNeil enacted an occasionally right-wing, largely homophobic masculinity in their representation of punk-ness. "*Punk* specialized in a fanatically narrow canon of hard core punk bands," noted Blondie's Gary Valentine. "The Ramones, Richard Hell, The Dead Boys and The Dictators." If *Punk* was not as editorially narrow as Valentine recalled, its sensibility comprised traces of the vicious and the vainglorious. In an early piece on Talking Heads, *Punk* reporters noted, "Musically they take up where Lou Reed left off when he packed up his guitar to pursue a career in self-parody: skeletal and hypnotic, tormented yet restrained."[25]

In February 1976, with the debut issue of *New York Rocker*, Betrock offered a different vision for the new rockers of New York: he sought to introduce the Bowery bands to the world. "His motivation for putting out *New York Rocker* was, I think, love," Valentine remembered. "I'm not sure he ever made a dime from it." The debut issue included features on Talking Heads and The Ramones, as well as articles on The Miamis by Blondie's Debbie Harry, and on Blondie by The Miamis' Tommy and Jimmy Wyndbrandt. *Rocker*'s debut issue lacked a direction-defining editorial, and reflected Betrock's ill-defined role with *Rocker* itself: in successive mastheads, Betrock was listed as "editor," "cover designer" and "creative consultant" and, by issue four, "senior editor," with publishing duties credited to Guillemette Barbet, a contributing photographer for *Punk*. In these various roles, Betrock secured and maintained a solid respect from his staff. "One of the things I loved about Alan was whenever the *Rocker* came out, I would get a copy of the magazine and a check in the mail," writer Roy Trakin told me. "I wouldn't have to ask."[26]

By the third issue, though, the emergent reputation of *New York Rocker* weighed on Betrock, and he engineered a lengthy review essay on *The Ramones* for an assortment of ends: to disabuse readers of *Rocker*'s boosterism; to prevent volleys of slander between *Rocker* and *Punk*; and to articulate his politic for the not-quite-popular-downtown music—and how best to write about that music.

The essay offered, to begin, the expectant platitudes for one of most important LPs of the era. "[It's] a trendsetting blast of much needed energy . . . a must-buy for any rocker worth his salt . . . this album stands as one of the most energized, committed and relevant pieces of vinyl to come down the pike in a long time." Betrock's thoughts on the LP itself, though, follow a nearly five-hundred word meditation on the circulation of opinions "in a relatively small, insular scene like New York," and the difference between *Rocker's* policy to "nurture, support and spread the word about New York bands" and the economic tomfoolery of "unanimously favorable drivel." The prelude concludes on the value (and limits) of "one person's honest opinion," which leads into his critical assessment of the album's nearly live sound, which he identified as its aesthetic Achilles heel: "A recording studio offers the opportunity to make a great record; of getting a sound down; of experimenting and perfecting the song form; of creating sounds, moods, and blasts of energy different from live performance. Making a great record is as much of an art as being a great stage performer—but they're two distinct talents." Betrock concludes the paragraph with a chilling portent: "To underestimate the importance of one [of these talents] can only bog down an otherwise successful career."

Betrock's counsel reflects his aesthetics and his politics. First, his idea of what an album could be reflected his love for the girl groups' sound engineered by Phil Spector, the master of studio artifice, and eventual producer of The Ramones' *End of the Century* (1980). (*Century* was their highest charting LP, reaching #44 in the U.S., and #14 in the UK. The Ramones never had a top 40 single.) In Betrock's eyes, even the garage-punk bands needed to understand the essence of artifice when it came to assembling an album. Betrock's problem with *The Ramones* is that it is the sonic analog to the editorial vision of *Punk* (i.e., fuck art, let's mock), rather than *New York Rocker* (i.e., art's good, pop's good, and so is Abba. Betrock had a soft spot for Abba). In effect, Betrock (and *Rocker*) wanted the world for The Ramones. *Punk* wanted The Ramones for themselves.[27]

The *Rocker* sustained a lighter-hearted sense of humor, too, and took aim with soft artillery at the Goliaths of classic rock. In the second issue, readers were invited to match pictures of pets to budding stars: Weymouth and Thunders were the dog owners of Natasha and Wolf, respectively, while Puma the cat belonged to Television's Richard Lloyd. In Betrock's LP reviews, he offered a brief meditation on *Presence*, by Led Zeppelin: "These guys are the best at what they do, and well they should be since they've been doing it over and over since 1969." Lower on the page, below a promotional picture for The Rolling Stones' *Black and Blue*, the caption asked: "Have You Seen Your Grandmother, Baby, Standing in the Shadows?" Betrock also noted his fondness for Abba's latest offering, dismissing naysayers who translated the Abba acronym as "another banal band's ascent." Betrock dared to counter punk dogma, too. On the long-awaited debut LP of the Modern Lovers, produced by John Cale of The Velvet Underground, Betrock described the sound as "a bit dated."[28]

In 1977, the ninth issue of *New York Rocker* included cover prices for the U.S. and the UK, and followed select vinyl and issues of *Punk* into the New York-London pipeline of DIY cultural artifacts. "The first thing we heard from New York was the Television single, 'Little Johnny Jewel.' I remember listening to it and being blown away," recalled Rat Scabies, drummer for The Damned. With intermittent bits and pieces, Scabies and rival figures in the London punk scene were able to form only an impressionistic portrait of the Bowery's elect. "Our entire knowledge of the New York punk had come from *Punk* magazine," Scabies reported. "No one had seen the Heartbreakers live, but we thought they looked great. We had seen pictures of Television, Richard Hell and Blondie but nobody had heard anything. Because Danny Fields was involved with the MC5 we knew [The Ramones] had to be the right kind of thing." Once The Damned did listen to *The Ramones* and, in July 1976, saw them live at Dingwalls, the standard was set.[29]

Shortly after securing a UK readership, Betrock sold *Rocker* to a Minnesota émigré named Andy Schwartz. Schwartz's debut editorial in issue twelve praised and promised to honor Betrock's vision for *Rocker*, while tapping more explicitly the New York–London pipeline: the corresponding cover story on The Clash celebrated the UK release of their eponymous debut, and represented the first time a band graced the cover of *Rocker* prior to its appearance at a Bowery venue. Likewise, thanks to Jem Records, shops including Bleecker Bob's secured a steady stock of import pressings of *The Clash*. The October–November 1977 issue of *Punk* included a Clash feature by Anya Phillips and, in turn, reinforced the band's fascination with the Big Apple writ large.[30]

That fascination owed a great deal to the vibrant exploits of The New York Dolls. Strummer and Jones reported they were awestruck by the Dolls' performance in November 1973 on *The Old Grey Whistle Test*, a late night rock show on the BBC. The following summer, after acquiring both of the Dolls' LPs, Jones was mesmerized anew by their sound, their look, and their attitude. That attitude, Bob Gruen stressed, was not a drag queen attitude, but ends-oriented artifice: "People think [the Dolls] were in some way transvestites or kind of dressed like girls, but actually they dressed up like dolls because they wanted girls to play with them!" Jones, along with Tony James, wanted to play the role of guitarist Johnny Thunders to a yet-to-be-cast David Johansen type. Their March 1975 classified ad in *Melody Maker* sought a "DECADENT MALE VOCALIST. Must be exciting, pretty, and passionately committed to the rock'n'roll lifestyle." For Christgau, too, the Dolls' lead singer David Johansen fully embodied the ethics and aesthetics of rock'n'roll:

> Johansen's an exceptionally literate guy . . . and for the fact that he really was living a life more dissolute than I would have engaged in . . . it wasn't just for show. He was apparently doing a lot of really crazy things with his penis and probably taking some drugs.
>
> He had a humanistic side, which was always there. He was not a nihilist . . . and he was not into decadence, either. There was too much love in him—love was too much at the center of what he was talking about. It was quite clear that the homo-erotic part, or the omni-sexual part of it, was just an expression of Eros as a life principle.

Johansen's Eros belied an optimism that countered the destructive capacity of both nihilism and decadence. For Christgau, too, the Dolls adhered to the same upstanding principles embraced by The Clash. "They really liked fifties rock'n'roll, and they understood the best stuff of black music even though they were emphatically white. Johansen's a great melodist, and one of the greatest lyricists in the music's history. And they had a great beat!"[31]

The Eros of The Clash was less doggedly genital than Johansen's, and it took shape in their songbook, their performances, and their Platonic contact with their fans. "Not only was The Clash's musical aesthetic extraordinary, but every one of those songs is really singable," Christgau said. "And they had great politics, from beginning to end." The self-anointed dean of rock criticism continued, at length, channeling the sophism of Socrates:

> Were there contradictions there? Of course there were contra-
> dictions there. Did they find it too difficult to deal with? Yes.
> But if anybody wanted to talk to me about The Clash's being
> poseurs and that they didn't mean it, and that they weren't, well,
> [Marxist theorist Louis] Althusser [laughs], I just think that's
> so asinine that it's beneath contempt. These are rock'n'roll per-
> formers, not political science professors. They really figured out
> a way to make effective political art, which as we know is very
> difficult. It's very difficult. And what do I mean by effective? I
> don't mean it changed the world. I mean it was aesthetically
> effective.

The band's capacity to draw upon the traditions of rock'n'roll and black music, and to shape lyrical narratives in descriptive and imaginative ways, proved effective. With the help of devotees in *Punk*, *New York Rocker*, the *Village Voice*, *Trouser Press*, and on the airwaves, along with a steady supply of import vinyl at Bleecker Bob's, *The Clash* became the best-selling import LP to date in the United States. By 1978, tracks from *The Clash* were occupying more airwave transmissions than ever before, including the signal of one of the premier radio stations in New York City.[32]

4.
The Good, the Bad, and the Ugly

From the rise of rock'n'roll in the mid-1950s, through the rise of rock as art in the mid-1960s, New York City played host to some of the greatest AM deejays in the country. "In New York, AM radio was quite good, and Scott Muni, among others, were the deejays who took us all through the British Invasion," Meg Griffin told me. "It was really good AM radio that mixed everything from Motown to The Rolling Stones." With the spread of FM stations across the country, select deejays offered a sonic homology to the Civil Rights Movement and campus sit-ins, by offering dissenting opinions on sex, revolution, and the sexual revolution, and by introducing listeners to musicians such as Jimi Hendrix. "Hendrix was different and outrageous and pushing the boundaries and doing it for art and rebellion, and all of those things that separated us from them in those days," Griffin told me. "There was definitely a line—an us-and-them line—in the beginning days of FM radio. It was very clear what side that kind of radio was on."[1]

Muni knew which side of the line he occupied at WNEW and, ten years after Hendrix's debut album, he performed two heroic deeds. First, during his shift cut short by the blackout of July 13–14, 1977, Muni packed up a turntable, a microphone, and some LPs from the WNEW studio, walked thirteen blocks to the Empire State Building, and hooked up his hardware directly to the station's transmitter tower. With the connection established, Muni said, "I think it might be a nice idea to tell some of your friends, since we are sort of a family, if you would talk to your friends, give 'em a call since telephones are working, and say 'WNEW is back on the air.'" Second, he hired Griffin at WNEW, and thereby opened the door to a key voice determined to forge a real alternative to the star system dominating "rock medicine shows."[2]

Griffin, in turn, opened new opportunities for New Yorkers fond of punk and new wave to dance to it at the clubs and, with the help of Joe Piasek, to tune into a station programmed around her Elvis-to-Elvis, backbeat aesthetic. Other female deejays, including Pam Merly and Jane Hamburger, lent their voices to the cause, and ushered in the new order of things on the airwaves and the dance floor. Carol Miller, though, after brief stints at WNEW and WQIV, took the road more traveled at WPLJ, only to confront a few years down that road the logical limits of decisively commercial FM radio.

At WNEW, Griffin worked alongside some of the deejays who shaped her musical experience of the 1960s, few of whom offered punk a sympathetic ear. Griffin's charm and growing popularity allowed her to challenge her listeners (and her fellow deejays) to recognize the connection between rock, rebellion, and the sounds of the new wave. Scribes including Lester Bangs, Robert Christgau, and Nick Kent admired the musical virtue and populist vision of The Clash, and bolstered the rebel incursions on the airwaves with typeset sorties of their own.

I ♥ Rock'n'roll Radio

Griffin was born in 1953, and she grew up in Greenwich Village listening to top 40 radio. That experience, she recalled, "was very influential in my love of rock'n'roll and what I heard as kid was definitely influential in my love of the whole punk thing." She attended State University of New York, Cobleskill, in 1974, to study veterinary medicine, but changed her plans after a fortuitous pass by the campus radio station. "I looked through this glass studio window and I saw somebody that was in one of my classes in there," Griffin told me. "He was clearly on the air and I just remember thinking, 'Oh, god, if he can do that, I can do that!'"

The reigning campus soundtrack featured a heavy rotation of The Grateful Dead and The Allman Brothers. On her show, Griffin countered with tracks by Mott the Hoople and The New York Dolls, whom she had seen at Max's Kansas City. "At first, the kids weren't really crazy about it," she told me. Within a few weeks, Griffin reported, listeners were calling her at the station, asking, "Would you play that thing by the Stooges again?"

In 1975, Griffin joined WRNW, in Briarcliff Manor, an hour north of Manhattan, where she first encountered a young and gangly deejay from Queens named Howard Stern. The preferred discs were, once again, not to Griffin's liking. "When I got there it was very Seals and Crofts, Crosby, Stills & Nash," she lamented, "and things were starting to get very overproduced, with The Eagles, and Fleetwood Mac."[3]

Merly, too, when recalling that period, contrasted the punk aesthetic with the gentler, kinder sounds of country rock: "Punk was so passionate and raw, and wasn't polished and pretty and done up in a gorgeous package. It felt like, it felt like youthful angst. It felt real, and it felt like it was expressing something real, and that these were real people, that these were real musicians."

At the time, Griffin was dating Chris Kelly, who worked at Bleecker Bob's and Sounds, on St. Mark's Place. At both shops, which were just a short walk from CBGB, Kelly's responsibilities included stocking new titles. Griffin recalled, "All we ever did was go out and see bands and pore over catalogs and try to decide what he should order for those stores." Shortly thereafter, Griffin became romantically involved with Joe Piasek, and thereby forged an alliance for securing heavy rotation in the New York market for The Ramones, The Damned, and The Clash.

DEATH OR GLORY!

Piasek was born in Hartford, Connecticut in 1950, and assumed the on-air appellation of "Joe from Chicago" upon realizing that, in radio, "One needed to remain anonymous if one wanted to remain alive." Piasek attended college at Quinnipiac University, in Hamden, Connecticut, and worked at the campus radio station. To fulfill a requirement for a political science course, Piasek joined the campaign of Joe Duffey for U.S. Senate. On the campaign trail, construction workers toted signs that read "SDS [Students for a Democratic Society], Pot, and Duffey Go Together," and "A Vote for Duffey is a Vote for Khrushchev"—providing Piasek and Hillary Rodham, Duffey's campaign manager, with a key lesson in the rules of engagement in future skirmishes in the culture wars.[4]

Soon thereafter, Piasek split time between free-form stations WPLR in New Haven and WQIV in New York City. The original call letters for WQIV were WNCN, which began broadcasting round-the-clock classical music in 1957. In 1974, WNCN was acquired by the Starr Broadcasting Group, whose chairman was William F. Buckley, a key figure of contemporary American conservatism. Buckley was, of course, a staunch defender of the Western canon, but in this case his role entailed bidding only on behalf of the shareholders. It was Buckley, too, with his "preposterously mellifluous" accent, who announced the imminent replacement of the classical music format with four channels of free-form programming. For WQIV, "Q" stood for quadraphonic; "IV" stood for the four channels of sound (front left and right, rear left and right).[5]

On the sunny morning of November 7, 1974, the station engineer cued up the final track of WNCN programming, the "Kyrie" from Mozart's *Requiem*. At its conclusion, the new program director thanked the WNCN listening audience before bidding them *adieu*:

> And now by authority of the Federal Communications Commission, WNCN New York changes its call letters to WQIV-FM New York . . . WQIV-FM is broadcasting twenty-four hours a day in compatible quadraphonic sound, using the QS matrix system. We're going to do our best to reflect the contemporary realities of life in New York, its music, the people who perform it and listen to it, its news and the lifestyles we live. . . . Welcome to our alternative in New York: WQIV-FM.

The segue to the opening motif of Beethoven's *Symphony no. 5 in C minor* yielded to the leitmotif of Chuck Berry's "Roll Over Beethoven." The Velvet Underground's "Rock and Roll" followed. With the president of the Starr Broadcasting Group at his side, Buckley recorded the transition and wept. The program director was free-form pioneer Larry Miller, of KMPX and KSAN, where he, Tom Donahue, and Thom O'hair reigned among the eighteen-to-thirty-four demographic in the Bay Area. The original Quad Squad deejays included O'hair, Carol Miller (no relation), and Rosko, renewed from his exile in France, ready to spin discs and lengthy yarns about music, culture, and politics.[6]

Two months later, Larry Miller quit WQIV, citing "policy differences with the Starr Broadcasting Company," and O'hair was given the reins of program director. "These were West Coast guys coming to New York with their guns loaded, ready to do real progressive radio," Piasek recalled. "O'hair was really great, he was a total lunatic type, the kind that movies are made of. He hired people and made sure that they promised that they would do things that, well, couldn't be anticipated." At KSAN, such stunts included deejays streaking through competitor stations and on-air arrests for marijuana possession. Carol Miller, meanwhile, was more disgusted than amused. In her eyes, O'hair was a "rootin-tootin', sadly self-destructive, sex-and-drug-crazed hippie, [and] QIV was the devil's lair for any young woman on the premises." O'hair favored a life lived at 78rpm and, according to Miller, "There was constant pressure for sex; drugs and booze were around all the time." Shortly after Piasek joined O'hair's gang, station management determined that the Quad Squad's glories would be short-lived. WQIV was the radio equivalent of the *Vasa*, the sixteenth-century Swedish vessel that sank within minutes of leaving the dock.[7]

In the mid-1970s, the Federal Communications Commission was in its final years as an arbiter of both community service and programming, and thereby provided final approval of format changes. The WNCN faithful protested, and key allies supported the cause, including the editors of the *New York Times*: "Despite legal action taken to protest [WNCN's] change in format [to] another rock station, the Federal Communications Commission is dragging its affidavits." By August, the grand experiment in quadraphonia was over. Miller received the news while on vacation in Los Angeles and, shortly thereafter, entertained overtures from WPLJ, the key rival to WNEW. Piasek staffed the turntables at WQIV through the dog days of summer, before the station went temporarily silent. On August 25, 1975, to signify the resurrection of WNCN, the silence was broken by "Et resurrexit," from Bach's *Mass in B minor*, in stereophonic sound.[8]

With visions of decadence still aswirl in her head, Miller found comfort that September at WPLJ, where program director Larry Berger offered reassurance, rather than revolution. For Berger, the business of radio entailed the science of keeping listeners tuned in, by way of the proper format: "The music library of rock songs was subdivided into categories based on various criteria of popularity, time of release, and/or potential for popularity, and then further delineated by sonic characteristics such as tempo, and 'hardness.' The deejays would put together their shows by selecting music that fit these parameters according to a pattern sequence, which would vary for different times of the day." Taste confirmation supplanted "taste education" and, with the wide variety of rock LP releases each year, the return of AM techniques into FM studios scarcely raised an eyebrow. The format soon became known as album-oriented radio (AOR). At WPLJ, Berger sought to split the difference between the progressive ethos of WNEW and the top 40 programming of WXLO, with a twist of serendipity borrowed from the world of Western concert music.[9]

Since 1938, symphony and opera orchestras have typically tuned to a reference pitch of A at 440 hertz (i.e., on the piano, the A above middle C). The New York Philharmonic, during Zubin Mehta's reign as principal conductor (1978–1991), tuned to A at 442 hertz, as did his peers in Boston and Chicago. Tuning pegs in Berlin and Moscow, though, were stressed at 448 and 450 hertz, respectively, to appease listener demand, as advocates report that the higher tuning produces a more brilliant orchestral sound and, in turn, more patron excitement.[10]

A few years into his tenure at WPLJ, Berger learned that the studio turntables were spinning a hair's width shy of 34 rpm, rather than 33 1/3. Berger instructed the engineers to respect the status quo—which also included sound compression via the Dorrough processor, in order to "correct" (read: boost) low passages almost instantaneously. If the extra liveliness of the WPLJ sound offered a slight betrayal of the musicians' visions for their art, it proved distinctive and successful in the New York market.[11]

In adherence to the format, Miller opened her first shift with KC and the Sunshine Band's "Get Down Tonight" and a crisis of countercultural confidence. Miller imagined herself a rock connoisseur, not a purveyor of disco. The instant the request lines lit up with a host of enthusiastic calls, though, the crisis passed. By 1976, Miller was rubbing elbows with Paul McCartney and, soon thereafter, rubbing more than elbows with Steven Tyler of Aerosmith. For the next seven years at WPLJ, Miller established herself as the pin-up deejay of AOR in New York City. During that period, albeit with different formats, Miller, Griffin, Merly, and Hamburger demonstrated that women had a place at the banquet of rock'n'roll—even if each of them, in their own way, would be escorted from the table before the old guard served dessert.

CAREER OPPORTUNITIES

Across the Atlantic, after seven months of rehearsals and a handful of gigs, The Clash hit the road in December 1976 in support of The Sex Pistols. On the Anarchy tour, The Clash established and maintained close proximity to their fans in the UK. "We didn't really have that thing where, today, backstage is almost like a monastery, protected by rows of goons," Strummer said. "Because you could talk to the audience, and they could talk to you, it meant you kept your feet on the ground."[12]

Lester Bangs agreed. Bangs grew up in southern California and, in 1971, while in his early twenties, he moved to Detroit to work for *Creem* magazine. Five years later, he moved to New York, freelanced for the *Voice* and *Rolling Stone*, and, in 1977, toured the UK with The Clash on assignment for *NME*. The result was a landmark piece of rock journalism: sixteen thousand words on The Clash and sundry matters spread out over three issues. With characteristic flair, Bangs noted,

> If there's one thing I've learned to detest over the years it's sitting around some goddamn hotel lobby like a soggy douchebag parasite waiting for some lousy-high-and-mighty rock'n'roll band to *maybe deign* to put in an imperial appearance.
>
> But then a few minutes later The Clash came down and joined us and I realized that unlike most of the bands I'd ever met they weren't stuck up, weren't on a star trip, were in fact genuinely interested in meeting and getting acquainted with their fans on a one-to-one, noncondescending level.

Bangs's admiration was threefold. He loved their music, their energy, and the correspondence between the DIY ethos of the music and the populist ethos fostered by the band off-stage.[13]

That correspondence was sustained by the three British music weeklies, *NME*, *Sounds*, and *Melody Maker*, but not by *Rolling Stone*. The former needed to fill column inches on a regular basis for a British readership that resided within a day's drive of London. Weekly issues printed on Thursday were delivered overnight by train and lorry to newsstands across the country. The biweekly *Rolling Stone* lacked the luxury of proximity and, as a result, was simply unable to break hot stories. "We would find out things that happened in New York from *Melody Maker* and *NME*," Gruen recalled, "because they'd be reporting on it, and [the stories] wouldn't be out in *Rolling Stone* until a month and a half later." In turn, *Rolling Stone* embraced an editorial policy that privileged depth over timeliness, and the implications were pragmatic and political: first, as Gruen told me, "It was literally six weeks from deadline to newsstand." Second, *Rolling Stone*'s emphasis on human-interest stories, rather than reportage, helped sustain the artistic aura of rock musicians that Bangs and others found increasingly tedious. The London weeklies, though, according to Nick Kent of *NME*, were willing to "glom on to anything new and potentially provocative and splash it all over their pages." The interests of their retailers were paramount for *Rolling Stone*, and their editors focused indefatigably on musicians with records available at those retailers. Put another way: *Rolling Stone* played it safe. It's one of the key reason why punk exploded in the UK, but not in the U.S.[14]

In the first half of 1977, the weeklies teemed with interviews, concert reviews, and pop sociology, as music journalists codified punk on their own terms. *NME*, *Sounds*, and *Melody Maker* dispatched reporters for The Clash's March 11 gig at the Harlesden Coliseum in London. In *Sounds*, Vivien Goldman's report reflected the droll urgency of the times: "The Clash's visuals (couture be-zipped ensembles) are so hot that I can't make out which is a bigger plus, the music, the words, or the image (dare I say)." On the performance itself, she noted, "The energy roared like starved lions let loose at fat Christians." For *NME*, Kent satirized the punk ethos, yet found himself unable to resist the charms of Joe Strummer: "Strummer's stance sums up this band at its best, really: it's all to do with real 'punk' credentials—a Billy the Kid sense of tough tempered with an innate sense of humanity which involves possessing a sense of morality totally absent in the childish nihilism flaunted by Johnny Rotten and clownish co-conspirators." The compassionate demands The Clash made upon its audience resonated with Kent, and stood in stark contrast to the approach of other bands of the era.[15]

The do-it-yourself aesthetic of punk. Concert poster for The Clash, March 11, 1977.

Melody Maker's Caroline Coon seized on the matter of

camaraderie, too, in her 1977 manifesto on the punk scene. In *1988: The New Wave Punk Rock Explosion*, Coon articulated how, at the 100 Club Punk Rock Festival in 1976, with The Pistols and The Damned as headliners, "Most of the established musicians are encouraging friends to form bands of their own . . . 'Do it Yourself' could be the motto of the 100 Club. Everyone wants to get in on the act. Everyone can." Coon's book included a Clash profile, and she closed the final chapter with an audacious coda: "Whatever happens now, the force of punk rock will be felt in society at least until 1988."[16] Whoa.

LET THE DRUMMER HAVE . . . HIS WALKING PAPERS?

If The Clash distinguished themselves from aristo-rockers with convincing performances of authenticity, they still adhered to one of the key conventions for achieving rock stardom: sack your original drummer—see Pete Best of The Beatles, Doug Sandom of The Who (formerly The Detours) and, later, Chad Channing of Nirvana. Chimes's dreams of rock stardom and riches, including his open desire to own a Lamborghini, did not mesh well with the group's well-manicured ethos of rebellion.

Nicholas Headon was born in 1955, to Welsh parents, and was raised mostly in River, on the fringes of Dover. Headon's father worked as the headmaster for the local grammar school and, in his spare time, played the piano. Headon's sense of restlessness served him well behind the drums, where he emulated the strength and finesse of jazz greats Buddy Rich and Elvin Jones. Upon joining The Clash, Headon received the nickname "Topper," from Simonon, due to his likeness to Mickey the Monkey from the *Topper* comic. Headon debuted with The Clash on April 26, 1977, after submitting to a full makeover, with new hair, new clothes, and a new biography: in a band profile in *Melody Maker*, his middle-class roots and positive matrimonial status were keenly glossed over.[17]

The dividends were immediate, as Headon's second performance secured The Clash a *mea culpa* from Charles Shaar Murray of *NME*. In an earlier review of a Clash concert, Murray had concluded, "They are the kind of garage band who should be speedily returned to the garage, preferably with the motor running."[18] In response, Strummer and Jones penned "Garageland," a rollicking number on *The Clash* that articulated their suspicion of critics and middle management. "Garageland" represented the first in a series of songs—"Complete

Control," "Guns on the Roof," and "All the Young Punks" among them—in which The Clash embraced another key convention for achieving rock stardom: manneristic self-referentiality in song lyrics, à la The Rolling Stones, with "Torn and Frayed," Mott the Hoople, with "One of the Boys," and John Lennon, with "God," in which he offers the following theorem: Yoko + me = reality. As Rhodes rightly noted, the performance of authenticity entailed singing about a life the fans themselves might be living, rather than damning profiles of former bandmates (Lennon) or, in the case of "Garageland," a critic who dared to be critical. As the last track on the album, "Garageland" received scant attention in the nearly universal accolades of their self-titled debut, which was released on April 8, 1977.

The following month, The Clash played twenty-eight dates in thirty-one days and established themselves as the standard bearers of UK punk. The sets included covers of The Maytals' "Pressure Drop" and Junior Murvin's "Police and Thieves"—be it humble offerings or reflexive homages, The Clash lay claim to these reggae tunes to articulate the differences between key bands riding the new wave from the UK and their classic rock forebears. Their U.S.-based allies included Joe Piasek, whose first principles in the deejay booth also connected black aesthetics, rebellion, and humor.

USING AURAL AMMUNITION

Radio worth its frequencies was, in Piasek's estimation, constituted by the subtleties of the music mix and a bit of serendipity. "It had to do with the political sensibility, too, without necessarily being overtly political," Piasek said. "It had to do with humor, a great deal of humor, and not taking oneself too seriously. It had to do with mixing and matching the things that were meaningful to . . . our target audience."

For Piasek, too, it had to do with James Brown. Piasek saw James Brown with The Famous Flames in 1967, and the experience transformed his musical sensibility. "Without James Brown," Piasek told me, "I figured you couldn't get anywhere else." "Spunky James Brown" appeared in the loves column of Rhodes's cultural and sartorial manifesto, and Brown's significance carried equal resonance on American shores. If the segregation of public spaces was worthy of the attention of civil rights activists in the 1960s, so was the segregation of the airwaves by select deejays in the 1970s. With this in mind, Piasek took over as program director at WRNW.

Piasek and Griffin were unable, though, to convince Fred Schreier, WRNW station president, of the long-term merits of free-form, which produced negative financial returns for the station. Schreier decided to follow the advice of a radio consultant to adopt a tamer format—"not quite so hard rock," in Schreier's words—and thereby prompted the resignations of Piasek and Griffin. "Perhaps the approach at WRNW was too eclectic," Piasek conceded. "There were those outside the loop, like the sales department and management and ownership, especially when group ownership was coming in. It was very difficult for them to understand the subtleties of music mix . . . and the nuanced differences [among] the competition."[19]

Griffin's moonlighting assignment at WNEW became her primary gig in November 1977, which coincided with WNEW's celebration of its tenth anniversary as New York's "premier progressive radio station." The five-day commemoration included on-air interviews of Bruce Springsteen by Richard Neer, John Lennon by Dennis Elsas, and Elton John by Scott Muni, and broadcasts of concerts by Boz Scaggs, Yes, Billy Joel, and The Grateful Dead.[20]

"WNEW was one of the most important rock stations in America," according to Harvey Leeds, former director of national album promotion at Epic Records, The Clash's U.S. label. "It was one of the first free-form rock stations with important personalities who turned you on to great music." Upon Griffin's arrival, the personalities at WNEW also included Dave Herman, Thom Morrera, and Vin Scelsa—all proven veterans of the New York airwaves.[21]

With her first-hand knowledge of the burgeoning punk scene, and a steady supply of domestic-schedule-busting imports from her allies at Jem Records, Griffin spiced up overnights and fill-ins at WNEW. "That was the beauty of the station in those days," she said. "You could play what you wanted. Your show reflected you." Before her weekend shifts, especially, Griffin frequented CBGB and Max's Kansas City, watching the bands she kept in heavy rotation. Caller by caller, Griffin learned, her fellow clubgoers were tuning into her show. "What was great about it was that people who really liked this music, a lot of them were just getting back from the clubs right about the time my show started," Griffin told me. "And then I started to hear from people. I got tons and tons of letters." She also received regular phone calls from Robbins, of *Trouser Press*, and Schwartz, of *New York Rocker*. Week by week, her show gradually solidified the Gotham audience for punk and new wave. "I felt a deep loyalty from the people who called up and started to listen," Griffin said. "Not to me so much, per se, but to the music, and so we felt that here's a place where we can gather around it: the radio." A month after its October 1977 release, The Sex Pistols' *Never Mind the Bollocks* landed on *Billboard*'s "Album Radio Action" list as a top add-on in the northeast region. By mid-November, The Pistols' LP topped WNEW's playlist, which also included recent releases by Electric Light Orchestra, Boz Scaggs, and Genesis.[22]

Griffin played a key role in creating a place where punk loyalists could dance, too. In early 1978, she accepted an invitation to spin discs on Monday nights at Hurrah, a nightclub in the Theater District, at Broadway and 62nd Street. On the weekends, beginning that March, Hurrah hosted "The Neon Woman," starring John Waters's drag-queen muse Divine, which opened to spirited reviews, and sustained a long-standing connection between drag-queen culture and the new rock'n'roll. In 1969, Patti Smith took a small role in *Femme Fatale*, alongside Warhol doyen Jackie Curtis and Wayne County—both of whom roomed with Leee Black Childers, who became a key photographer of the punk scene.[23]

Word spread quickly among punk fans and punk icons. "I would look out on the floor, and I would see David Johansen, and I would see Lenny Kaye [of The Patti Smith Group], and I would see all the cool people coming to dance to *my* spinning, and I'd be like, 'Oh, I have hit it now!'" Griffin told me. "It just felt so exciting."

Griffin's comrades at *New York Rocker* were not so optimistic, and perhaps for good reason. Of the debut LPs of CBGB's favorite alumni, only *Talking Heads '77* cracked the *Billboard* Top 100 albums, peaking at ninety-seven. *The Ramones* reached one hundred and eleven. *Blondie*, Television's *Marquee Moon*, and Richard Hell and the Voidoids' *Blank Generation* failed to chart at all.[24] In response, the September issue of *New York Rocker* featured an indictment-cum-post-mortem of punk and new wave. Bangs decried the musical ethos as "anti-sexual, anti-emotional, and anti-feeling." Compared to their UK counterparts (e.g., Stiff and Rough Trade), American independent labels failed to flourish. Writers reserved their most scathing indictments for radio: "Most of the new wave records don't have a chance in hell of getting any radio play." Griffin, meanwhile, continued to bolster the tri-state market for new wave, on the dance floor and on the airwaves.[25]

With Griffin's help, Hurrah hosted live shows in 1978 by The B-52's, The Dead Boys, Suicide, and Skafish, for patrons of varying degrees of infamy. Sid

Vicious, free on bail and awaiting trial for the murder of Nancy Spungen, attended the Skafish gig on December 5. Vicious made unwanted advances toward the girlfriend of Skafish drummer Todd Smith, kid brother of Patti Smith. Todd intervened, Vicious picked up a Heineken bottle, smashed its end, lunged at Todd, and opened a wound above his eye that took five stitches to close. Vicious was arrested and remanded to Rikers Island, where he remained until February 1. The night of his release, at a party with friends and family, Vicious died of a heroin overdose.

Piasek also stopped by one Monday to check out Griffin's picks and segues on the wheels of steel. "This is the format for a radio station," he said to himself. By spring 1979, with the help of Jane Hamburger and Dan Neer (Richard's younger brother), Griffin and Piasek would remake WPIX in the sonic image of Griffin's backbeat aesthetic.[26]

Pretty Vacant

Meanwhile, at WNEW, Griffin's on-air affinity for The Dictators, The Ramones, Blondie, and The Clash proved nettlesome. The other deejays, Griffin said, "were threatened—or insulted is almost a better word—by what they thought punk was saying about them. They took it personally." They had good reason to take it personally. From Jagger's androgyny to Jimmy Page's climaxes of distortion, from Roger Daltrey's rippling biceps to Robert Plant's squeals of pleasure, rock had elevated one truth above all others: the joy of sex. The legislation of sexual congress had long been celebrated in country, bluegrass, and blues—and, in the late 1960s, sex was regarded as the principle tool to battle the one-dimensionality of the man in the grey flannel suit. Punks, though, were nonplussed by the promises of liberation through fornication. In the summer of 1976, Johnny Rotten noted, "By the time you're twenty you just think—yawn—just another squelch session." With their 1977 single "Oh Bondage, Up Yours!," X-Ray Spex suggested that even kinky fornication was hardly worth the bother.[27]

Likewise, in the formative days of punk, a notable refusal of traditional masculinity reigned, including its vision of romantic, artistic transcendence. Progressive rock embraced, first, the conception of the work of art *sui generis*, in which virtuosity and the organic whole was prized above all else: see, for example, The Beatles' *Sgt. Pepper's*, or The Who's *Quadrophenia*. Second, rock's claim to high art entailed a corresponding debasement of low commerce. No longer were rock artists treated like worker bees—expected, as The Beatles were, in 1964, to produce four singles and two albums per year. In turn, a rock artist followed his muse and, when called upon, delivered the album as a sacred text. In free-form radio, similar guidelines governed the separation of the sacred and the profane, as blocks of tracks protected as many songs as possible from commercial debasement.

Punk, in turn, celebrated the fragment and the conjuncture. Torn clothing, for example, reassembled with electrical tape, chains, or safety pins, privileged the collage, rather than the seamless whole. Contrary to the alleged timelessness of artistic truth, punks celebrated the ephemeral quality of the commodity. Contrary to the rectitude of virtuosity, punk bands openly flaunted their haphazard musical skills. Simonon noted, "I did a lot of learning in public. I just pretended I was Pete Townshend and jumped around a lot." The albums, with the inclusion of cover songs, celebrated enthusiasm and interpretation, rather than composition.[28]

As noted above, The Clash were keenly aware of how and why their musical forebears had gone sonically and morally bankrupt. The Stones and Led Zeppelin had exhausted the musical codes of the blues by 1975, but they continued to make newish records all the same. The Clash, in turn, sought interlocutors of black music closer to home. With the episodic clashes on Notting Hill and the deejay work of Don Letts on their minds, The Clash drew upon the musical codes and aesthetics of the Caribbean for inspiration.

As a result, *The Clash* possessed a nearly-anything-is-possible resonance, and demarcated the routes they would not tread. The Who's maxim of "Maximum R&B" was bankrupt; the promise of "Maximum Reggae" could not be fulfilled by white punk rockers, but still plenty of territory was left to explore. The lineage of the musical roots of The Clash, along with the full complexity of their reworking of musical codes, is only alluded to on *The Clash* and would be, temporarily, largely erased (repressed?) on *Give 'Em Enough Rope*.

THE POLITICS OF DANCING

Punk fixed its gaze upon the so-called counterculture, and declared it bloated, indulgent, even hegemonic. On their debut album, The Clash assured its listeners that, in 1977, the jig was up for Elvis, The Beatles, and The Rolling Stones. Poly Strene (née Marion Elliott), the lead singer for X-Ray Spex, noted, "Up until [1977] it had been aristo rock, and the only way to get into it if you were a girl was to become a groupie." Barbarous youth, male and female, readied themselves to rattle the gates of rock from their hinges.[29]

At WNEW, Griffin followed suit. When her fellow deejays dismissed new wave, Griffin realized that the gap in their respective tastes represented much more than differing conceptions about musicality: it represented their waning faith in popular music's capacity to disrupt the consonant, straight-laced sensibilities of *them*. Griffin, to her defense, made a sound case for The Clash to be included in her egalitarian notion of *us*. "I would try to say to some of the deejays that I worked with, 'Can't you draw a line of similarity with punk that can go right back to Buddy Holly?'" she told me. "This is just a continuation of rock'n'roll."

Of the veteran deejays, Vin Scelsa offered the most open ears for the new sound. Scelsa was born in Bayonne, New Jersey, in 1947, and attended Upsala College, the home of WFMU-FM. Under Scelsa's reign, WFMU departed from its six-hours, five-days-a-week format when he commandeered the studio on a Saturday night, in November 1967, for rock and roll and discussion. Likewise, WFMU did not play "hypes"—records promoted or hyped by the label—and Scelsa and his comrades admired New York's noncommercial WBAI, in terms of "musical taste . . . community action, political thought, [and] freedom of expression." In a 1969 article for The *Upsala Gazette*, Scelsa outlined his vision of the responsible deejay and his duty to the music and politics of the avant-garde. On MC5, the leftist dissidents from Detroit, Scelsa said, "Commercial stations won't play something until the public is ready for it. We feel that we should start playing it to make the public ready for it."[30]

Herman also warmed up to the new wave, Griffin recalled, but it was Scelsa who embraced the cause with contrarian ease. "Vin and I have always been in a brotherhood-sisterhood with this stuff," Griffin recalled. "Vin is a person who always listens." Scelsa, too, maintained a soft spot for fellow infidels and, in 1978, when a Situationist-inspired brigade from Red Star Records arrived at WNEW, Scelsa served as the station emissary.

Marty Thau, former manager of The New York Dolls, formed Red Star Records in 1977, and the label roster included Suicide, The Real Kids, and The Fleshtones. Roy Trakin penned articles and reviews for Soho Weekly News and

New York Rocker, and joined Red Star in 1978 as Minister of Information. In accordance with the spirit of the Chinese Cultural Revolution, the staff of Red Star organized the Spring Offensive, which included the "Take It to the Streets" raid of April 7, 1978, on figures they regarded as media stooges. Their polemic described the crisis of representation and demanded one thing: "fair exposure" of youth culture and rock'n'roll. The mobile political bloc included Martin Rev of Suicide, Chris Stamey of The dB's, Miram Linna of The Cramps, and Legs McNeil of *Punk* and *High Times*. The Red Star rebels opened their sortie at the *Village Voice*, "so-called arbiter of hip taste . . . to protest the pseudo-intellectual pretensions and condescension with which the paper covers the rock scene." Successive stops included the top 40 station WABC and WPLJ, in order to protest their "strait jacket approach of demographics-oriented radio with its slavish devotion to ratings." At WNEW, though, they offered a show of solidarity upon meeting Vin Scelsa, and expressed their delight for the support of new music shown by Scelsa and Griffin.[31]

Scelsa repaid the tribute at the turntables. Following the "Streets" rally, he decided that his afternoon audience was ready for music of the home-grown variety, and cued up Patti Smith's "Because the Night," which she penned atop a melody provided by Bruce Springsteen. "When the record came out," Lenny Kaye recalled, "[Arista] sent it to WNEW for the first time, and Vin Scelsa played it three times in a row." Calls from disapproving listeners lit up the switchboard, which Scelsa expected. He had knowingly exceeded the recommended dose of audio stimulation for the progressive radio audience. Punks took notice. In 1981, The Ramones offered Scelsa an affectionate namecheck on "It's Not My Place (in the 9-to-5 World)."[32]

Still, few of her colleagues shared Griffin's inclusive sensibility. By 1978, the vanguard deejays of the late 1960s had metastasized into a rear-guard defensive. These gatekeepers had long-lost sight of the fact that, since the release of *Sgt. Pepper's*, the aesthetics of rock had expansively embraced the organizing principles of the bourgeois art world: originality, virtuosity, and refinement—hence "classic rock." By way of Rhodes's affinity for Marxian dialectics, The Clash were well-attuned to such contradictions. If members of the rear guard might eventually hang themselves, Strummer and his mates would gladly provide the noose.[33]

5.
Rebel Waltz with the General, and Free-Form Faces the Music

I n 1978, Neil McIntyre, former program director at WNEW, needed a dee-jay at WPIX-FM, a metropolitan top 40 station. Like Muni, McIntyre was a free-form veteran and possessed a wickedly Irish sense of humor. He liked leisurely lunches at The Palm, a steakhouse in midtown renowned for its stand-ing invitation to dining cartoonists to "sing for a meal"—to add a caricature to the wall in order to settle a tab. McIntyre liked Piasek, gave him the job and, when McIntyre departed in the fall, Piasek became the acting program director. With James Brown, serendipity, and Griffin's Hurrah performance on his mind, Piasek readied for battle.

This installation of the struggle for the spirit of rock'n'roll was glorious, if short-lived, and The Clash were among the key beneficiaries. In spring 1978, The Clash combined forces with producer Sandy Pearlman and were subsequently reviled by critics in the UK, for daring to release a second album (and thereby risk their wrath), and beloved by critics in the United States, for daring to make rock'n'roll that mattered. On Manhattan isle, WNEW faced the pressures of increased reliance in the industry on Arbitron ratings, and the pressure of com-petition from the more conservative WPLJ and the more footloose WPIX. With Joe Piasek at the helm, WPIX deployed its "Elvis-to-Elvis" format, and the rock'n'roll ethos of the 'PIX staff stood in sharp contrast to the business-as-usual approach of WNEW and WPLJ. Local musicians took notice, including Velvet Underground alumni Lou Reed and John Cale, who joined forces as co-hosts in January 1979 on 'PIX's "Radio/Radio" show. With Griffin and Hamburger deejaying at WPIX and Hurrah, the audience for punk and new wave continued to expand. Concert promoter Wayne Forte knew full well which side of the bed he was on, and organized The Clash's debut tour in theaters (rather than clubs) in the United States and Canada and, in turn, compelled Epic brass to showcase the bankable pony in their stable.[1]

GARAGELAND NO MORE

For *Give 'Em Enough Rope*, their second LP, The Clash forged a sound considerably more rock than punk. CBS matched The Clash with producer Sandy Pearlman, renowned for his work with Blue Öyster Cult—if less so for producing two punk albums for The Dictators, including *Go Girl Crazy* (1977). Recording sessions from April to June 1978 took place in London, and the mixing of the album took place in San Francisco and New York—largely without Simonon and Headon. Strummer dubbed Pearlman and Corky Stasiak, the engineer, "general" and "captain," respectively, for their exacting method in the studio.

For *The Clash* sessions, which lasted short of three weeks, Simonon sat across from Jones, learned his bass parts phrase by phrase and, when the tapes rolled, banged them out as best he could. Pearlman was considerably less forgiving and, as the least virtuosic member of The Clash, Simonon chafed under these conditions. Twenty takes per song was not unusual and, at the end of the early sessions, Simonon could be found still practicing, learning by ear the bass lines arranged and performed by Jones. As Barry "The Baker" Auguste reported, "It was a very tense time. Paul had gone from doing the first album, which was basically single notes, and now we were working with these high-tech, American producers that wanted everything spot on." Simonon's diligence reflected his understanding that, at any moment, Jones could readily re-record his parts with equal or greater proficiency.[2]

At the mixing boards, Jones continued a tutorial begun at Richmond Studios, where The Clash recorded "Complete Control" and "White Man in Hammersmith Palais." Like Pearlman, Jones was fascinated with recording gadgetry and committed himself to the near perfection made possible by multitrack recording. In early August, Jones and Strummer flew to San Francisco to join Pearlman to mix the album. Three weeks of twelve-hour days allowed a smug

Pearlman to report, "There are more guitars per square inch on this record than in anything in the history of Western civilization."[3]

The Gibson-intensive topography of the album offered Simonon, Jones, and Strummer little consolation. For Simonon, "that album was a bloody nightmare to make." For Jones, recording under Pearlman was "a fucking misery. It was like 98 days in hell." For Strummer, the repeated takes and exacting overdubs "half killed us . . . We looked at each other and said, 'We don't ever want to go through that again.'" The album arose as a testament to The Clash as the last gang still standing. Yet the mix is not only less punk and more rock, it's missing that sense of gang solidarity—not so much The Clash, but Joe Strummer and his El Clash Combo.[4]

The final review of the mix took place at the Record Plant, in New York City, and Simonon and Headon flew over for a September reunion. Gruen joined the band at the midtown recording studio, and served as their late-night tour guide. "They were gassed out. They loved America," Gruen told me. "They felt like they were living in the *Taxi Driver* movie. That's why we went around trying to find steam." In Gruen's 1954 Buick Special, they toured the city in search of effusive manhole covers, for Gruen to capture the band and his car in a Manhattan tableau. In one portrait, Simonon, Headon, and Jones, in leather jackets and leather boots, strike nearly menacing poses and stare directly at the camera. Strummer sits astride a front fender and directs his gaze to the rooftops and beyond.[5]

For *Rope*, on side A especially, the nightmare is manifest in arrangements which curb The Clash's expressive camaraderie. The resolute "Safe European Home" and hard-charging "Tommy Gun" condemn romantic fantasies of Caribbean travel and Baader-Meinhof-inspired terrorism, respectively. Strummer takes lead vocals on nine of ten tracks, and the democratic harmony vocals of the debut album are stark in their infrequency. When Jones and Simonon were called upon for the rare supportive phrase or extraneous intensifier, it sounds as if their microphones were halfway across the studio, pushed low in the mix by Jones's power chords and Headon's rat-a-tat precision. The immediacy of *The Clash* and the sense of distance of *Rope* correspond with the proximity to the street of the respective studios used for the final mix for each album. *The Clash* was mixed on the ground floor of the CBS Studio. *Rope* was mixed at the Record Plant, ten floors above Times Square. Even with *The Clash*'s assortment of effects, including a smattering of overdubs, the album evoked the sound and fury of the band's live shows. With their debut, The Clash endeared themselves to dozens of British and American music critics by way of their amazing sound, righteous politics, and credible embrace of artifice.[6]

On *Rope*, things improve with side two, but Jones's only lead vocal, on the sentimental "Stay Free," casts him in the role of Strummer's vulnerable foil, rather than his equal comrade. Only on "Safe European Home" and "Julie's Been Working for the Drug Squad," and in fleeting phrases on "Drug Stabbing Time," do The Clash sound as if they were enjoying themselves. *Rope* leaves little doubt that The Clash still rocked, but where was their quirky ebullience?

The release of *Rope* coincided with the initial wave of Clash backlash in the UK. A reporter in the November 4 issue of *Melody Maker* lamented that a concert-going audience "got everything it expected but very little of what it deserved." The same day, an *NME* scribe concluded, "The Clash is a dying myth." Upon the album's release, the disenchantment spread. An LP review in *Melody Maker* concluded, "They sound as though they're writing about what they think is expected of them.... So do they squander their greatness." UK fans were undeterred, and lent credence to Epic's designation for The Clash: "the only English band that matters." The album entered the British charts at number twelve. It peaked at number two.[7]

In the United States, the myth not only endured, it flourished. In a nine-hundred-word salvo in the *Voice*, Bangs opened by characterizing *The Clash* as "barbed wire in lashing motion . . . brothers and sisters, that is rock'n'roll."[8] Likewise, in a single, tidy sentence, Bangs affirmed his own aesthetic standpoint, conceded Epic's nervy declaration, and praised the moral character of readers who, while shopping at Bleecker Bob's or Sounds, picked up the import version of *The Clash*: "So almost none but we the converted are going to know that *Rope*, though it sounds a bit overworked, contains more evidence that The Clash are the greatest rock'n'roll band left standing." While slightly chafed by Pearlman's overdubs, Bangs found redemption in the raw energy of the band's "deluges of molten noise," which extended the ethos of UK singles released between *The Clash* and *Rope*: "Complete Control," "Jail Guitar Doors," and "White Man in Hammersmith Palais." These singles exemplified the avant-popism Bangs championed, for these "panoramas of white fire . . . packed so many ideas . . . they began to seem like little symphonies."[9]

In the January 1979 issue of *Trouser Press*, Robbins deemed *Rope* "a great rock album," avowing that "The Clash do what few bands can do—make music that explodes with both fury and venom." The subsequent issue included a Robbins-penned feature about the making of the album, and previewed The Clash's nine-date North American tour, including their February 17 appearance in Manhattan. This time, *Rolling Stone* offered genuine cooperation, publishing Greil Marcus's laudatory review a week before their first North American appearance. For Marcus, *Rope* proved brilliant: "The tracks grow with each listening; after a week with the record, you only think you know what's on it."[10]

Griffin said, "I really just liked the boppin' roundness to the sound," and she and Merly highlighted "Julie's Been Working for the Drug Squad" as a favorite track. The album's popularity among New York musicians, however, was limited. Handsome Dick Manitoba, the lead singer for The Dictators, recalled that, among his friends—most of whom agreed upon the virtues of The Beach Boys' *Pet Sounds*, for example—there was little consensus about the virtues of *Rope*. Manitoba emphatically assured me, "*Rope* is no one's favorite Clash record."[11]

BARBARIANS AT THE GATE

In 1978, as the operations director of WNEW, Richard Neer faced a quandary. Free-form was in free-fall and, with the assistance of ever more reliable ratings from Arbitron, WNEW management was keeping close watch on its audience share. The station trailed WPLJ, its chief rival, in the ever-important twelve-plus share, as the radio industry constructed anew the entry age for teenagedom.

To help solidify its position, WNEW played to its strengths. In February 1979, a full-page advertisement in the *Voice* showed a studio wall of over ten thousand records, in order to contrast "Our Play List" and "Their Play List": a table-top rack of perhaps thirty LPs:

> It's the main source of music for the personalities who choose the daily sounds of WNEW-FM. . . . They play hits, too. But only when they want to. . . . Most other stations that play rock and roll limit their play list to a few best sellers, a few pick hits of the future and a few golden oldies. Which isn't bad if you don't mind the repetition, repetition, repetition, repetition, repetition.

The legacy of WNEW as a free-form station, and one with an expanding playlist courtesy of Griffin and Scelsa, remained intact, but the "your-show-reflected-you" legacy was subject to revision. In advance of the April-May Arbitron rating period, management provided deejays with new guidelines for playlists, instituted artist-of-the-day specials, and warned a handful of jocks about the implications of their episodic work ethics.[12]

If Muni understood the monetary side of the enterprise, he also maintained a robust skepticism over the merits of Arbitron. "They don't have contact with our audience. They claim the young adult is too busy to fill out a diary, or that the million students in our listening area can't be reached. But advertisers often only accept ARB results," Muni lamented, and then made clear his chosen side of the bed. "We based WNEW-FM on being an alternative, that's why listeners came to us. But there's nothing to fight these days, nothing to mobilize around." As it had for years, the research-driven format of WPLJ cut into the WNEW audience from the right. WPIX, with its new format, prepared to do the same from the left.[13]

"Mr. Berry? Hi, it's Joe Piasek at WPIX-FM in New York." Shortly after his 1979 stint in prison for tax evasion, Chuck Berry played in New York City. To promote the show, WPIX gave away tickets to the first 100 fans who brought IRS 1040 forms to the station (from the archives of Joe "from Chicago" Piasek).

At WPIX, Piasek took the helm of a wayward vessel. In 1975, 1976, and 1977, WPIX changed formats from adult top 40 to disco, back to adult top 40, and to top 40/rock, respectively. In spring 1978, Piasek wanted something fresh, disconcerting, even, and initiated the Live at CBGB's series. For the July kick-off, Jane Hamburger served as the on-air host for a concert by The Dead Boys and, on subsequent Fridays, performances by Richard Hell and Elvis Costello.

In September, Hamburger accepted an invitation to stack the turntables at Hurrah on Tuesday nights with the danceable grooves of punk and new wave. In November, Piasek became the acting program director and, on February 1, 1979, instituted a format change dubbed, alternately, "25 years of rock'n'roll," "from Elvis to Elvis," "New York's Rocknroll," and "The Next 25 Years of Rock'n'Roll." In his youth, Piasek savored the station wars between WPOP-AM and WDRC-AM in Hartford, Connecticut, and now had the chance to captain his own insurgency. With a well-stocked garrison at 'PIX, he prepared to engage WNEW and WPLJ.[14]

THE ART (AND MECHANICS) OF COMPOSING

WNEW's effort to establish and sustain its identity through the 1970s offered an early, inclusive version of the rack, which allowed the deejays room for dissent with near impunity and, in turn, to take pride in their transgressions. At the more paternal WPLJ, with liner cards for each album and a tight and closely monitored playlist, the program director offered little indulgence to deviant behavior.

Upon his 1977 promotion to music director at WNEW, Neer inherited the "rack": a rolling wooden bin that contained close to 250 albums. The rack contained five types of albums: new, progressive, folk, jazz, or instrumental. If a new album survived the weekly paring of the rack, Neer added a genre label to his notes about favorite tracks and some biographical information about the artist. Deejays, though, were under no obligation to make use of the liner cards—or "liners," in deejay parlance. Every six weeks, Neer penned a memo with details of the new albums added, the albums designated to the station library, and the albums designated to the landfill. Removal from the rack had a major impact on a disc's rate of exposure and, Neer noted, "Holy hell would be raised if [I] removed a record that a friendly promoter was hyping to Muni or Steele."[15]

At WPLJ, holy hell was reserved for deejays who dared violate the dictates of their version of the rack. In 1975, at WPLJ, Miller found relief from the breed of "radio-personality-creating-my-art-and-you'll-appreciate-the-musical-education-I'm-meting-out-to-you," and a structure designed to confirm, rather than challenge, their listeners' sensibilities. For program director Larry Berger, the task was clear: draw upon the progressive ethos of WNEW, mix in a selection of the top-of-the-pops tracks in rotation on WXLO, and forge a market share made of defectors from both camps. Tracks by members of the rock canon, including The Beatles, Bruce Springsteen, and The Kinks, appeared alongside the latest offerings of The Bee Gees, John Denver, and KC and the Sunshine Band—that is, until the consultants convinced Berger that "New York's Best Rock" needed less "dance music" (read: black music). Berger proceeded to pare the station's music library of black artists such as Eddie Kendricks and Earth, Wind & Fire, as well as too-soft rockers such as Joni Mitchell and James Taylor. Deejays' on-the-mic activities were expected to promote a sense of companionship, rather than pedagogical ends, and album liners prompted station-sanctioned deejay chatter. Deejays at WNEW and elsewhere took pride in their knowledge of their favorite bands, and pitied deejays whose raps merely reproduced the directives of program directors.[16]

At WPIX, deejays determined the mix of tempo and hardness, within color-coded categories designed to balance selections from Elvis to Elvis. Orange, to begin, included new releases bound to break big ("Pix to Click"). Tan included soul and Motown hits, and green comprised classic rock'n'roll, regardless of sales (e.g., New York Dolls). Blue indicated a British invasion oldie, and red represented "the PIX past": hits from the 1950s. Once discs were no longer considered new releases (yellow), the LPs representing rock's future history—for example, Costello's *Armed Forces* and Joe Jackson's *I'm the Man*—were affixed with white stickers. Taking cues from the old AM format, WPIX deejays worked from a dynamic list of the station's top 40 contemporary tracks, which they kept in heavy rotation until even they were tired of hearing them. Piasek's hope? The structure would inspire new forms of creativity on behalf of the deejays.[17]

The free-form mode was preserved on Sunday nights, on the "Radio/Radio" show, hosted by newsman John Ogle, with regular appearances by deejay Dan Neer, Richard's younger brother, and a host of who's who from the Bowery and beyond. For Piasek, "Radio/Radio" offered a "free-form four-hour audience participation and interview rock show covering everything from JFK's assassination to the latest thoughts of Lou Reed." The moniker represented an alternative to "*machine* radio," and included discussions of topical news, concert announcements for The Bottom Line, CBGB, and Hurrah, and the audio pictures painted by their guests.

Ogle and Neer shared interview duties and, when the guests included key musicians, served as engineers, while the musicians created playlists on the fly. Midweek at the Palm, Ogle reviewed the musical interests of his guests and, by Sunday evening's start time, would pull the LPs from the library or pick up new titles at Village vinyl shops. As Ogle reported to Will Keller, "Word got out among the musicians that you could play anything you wanted to. Todd Rundgren was about five minutes into [Ravel's] *Bolero*, before he realized I was going to let him play it all the way through. He said, 'You're going to let me do this?' And I said, 'This is your show, dude.'" The guests included David Byrne, Debbie Harry and Chris Stein, Lester Bangs, The Cramps, Nick Lowe, Iggy Pop, The New York Dolls and, on more than one occasion, Lou Reed, the godfather of punk, according to *Punk* magazine.[18]

ROCK 'N' ROLL HEART

For the first issue of *Punk*, Holmstrom and McNeil secured their interview with Reed as a matter of happenstance. In fall 1975, while waiting for The Ramones to take the stage at CBGB, Holmstrom and McNeil accosted Reed, demanded an interview, and Reed obliged. Afterward, McNeil was wary of celebrating a figure so dark, so condescending, as punk: "Lou always seemed like he wanted to go darker than sex, murder, mutilation, further. And you always got the feeling that you were definitely an idiot around him. I didn't want to sit at his feet that night. I didn't like him. He didn't seem like a nice guy. I mean, I wouldn't want to hang out with him." Holmstrom insisted and persisted, and his caricature of Reed dominated the tabloid's debut cover. In the subsequent issue, though, as noted above, the contemporary, "self-parody" of Reed (see *Lou Reed Live*) was skewered as a caricature of the early, virtuous Reed (*Transformer* and before), in a precocious example of the "kill-yr-idols" ethos of punk and post-punk.[19]

Punk, though, was late to the sparring exercises with Lou Reed. In the early 1970s, Lester Bangs served as a self-appointed hagiographer, harasser, and all-around hater of Reed. As Reed biographer Viktor Bockris notes, Bangs "set himself up as the conscience of Lou Reed and the Velvet Underground . . . writing obsessively about their influence and keeping tabs on the activities of Cale, Nico, and Reed." In 1975, though, when the two squared off anew, Bangs concluded, "Reed is a completely depraved pervert and pathetic death dwarf and everything else you want to think he is." During the 1970s, John Rockwell at the *Times* and Christgau at the *Voice* offered a more tempered variety of accolades and exasperation: for Rockwell, "His credentials are unshakeable"; for Christgau, Reed's self-consciousness proved "self-serving," and little more.[20]

Reed's most memorable counterpunches appear on *Live: Take No Prisoners* (November 1978), recorded during a March residency at the Bottom Line. His between-verse musings skewer Rockwell's Harvard education, Christgau's inclinations in the sack, and, in order to distance himself from the art-punk camp, the hippie poetics of Patti Smith's *Radio Ethiopia*. The mode of address is so excessive, though, it's difficult to gauge the level of artifice in his anger. It's good for Reed's ego, though, to play to the crowd, who delight in Reed's self-distancing from Smith, and the populist affirmation of Reed's idea of "Radio Brooklyn."

Under Piasek's lead, 'PIX proved a sufficient proxy for Reed's fantasy of Radio Brooklyn, and he dropped by the station a number of times to mix it up with news manager John Ogle. On Sunday, January 28, 1979, Reed hosted "Radio/Radio," and his musical selections evoked his life circa 1964, as a tunesmith for Pickwick Records and lead singer for The Primitives for the one-off, reverb-heavy "The Ostrich." Honey Cone's "Want Ads" opened the show, and segued into Crazy Elephant's "Gimme Gimme Good Lovin'" and The Turbans' "Sister Sookie." Reed enjoyed himself at WPIX, affectionately egging on callers on topics such as rock'n'roll, yesterday and today, and chiding them for their coarse language. Dan Neer offered a brief interlude with his interview of Charles Muster, playwright of *Rainbows*, a revolutionary theater piece staged around the corner from CBGB—which, you might have guessed, entailed the requisite opportunity for audience participation.

Other reverb-laden tracks included The Robins' "Smokey Joe's Café," Martha and the Vandellas' "Nowhere to Run," Dion and the Belmonts' "I Wonder Why" and "I've Had It," and "Oh My Soul," by Reed's dear friend Garland Jeffreys, who he invites, over the air, to come up to the studio.

REED: I really appreciate all the calls, all these people coming in and the thing is: yes, we would probably love to be playing at the Bottom Line again, because I like playing there for everybody. March or April, probably, for those who are interested, and—Oh, what were we listening to—do you have the list?

OGLE: We had just come from the interview . . . so we're all set.

REED: [Deadpans] Drugs do destroy some of the brain cells. There's no question about it. I thought it was Thursday.

After a quick break to note the time and station identification, Ogle noted that Sylvia Morales, Reed's eventual wife, and another friend were also in the studio. Next, Reed riffed on the history of Western concert music, invoking French composer Erik Satie, an avant-garde forebear of John Cage and Velvet Underground, as musical inspiration for closet cross-dressers.

REED: Here we are at WQXR, I would like to play some Erik Satie for you.

OGLE: [Laughs.]

REED: Close your closets. Take out your dress. Put it on. Really, nobody's looking. It's okay. Your wife doesn't care anymore. . . . [to Ogle] I noticed you have no commercials, does that mean you're not doing well?

OGLE: [To Neer] Do we have commercials or have we just been ignoring them?

REED: Is this like [W]BAI? The thing with BAI is that they're heavily into Puerto Rican lesbian liberation. You know, there's a limited audience for Puerto Rican lesbian liberation.

The ever-confrontational Reed, of course, invoked "Puerto Rican lesbian liberation" as a market-share problem, not a moral problem, for the listener-supported WBAI. He segued, then, to the matter of disco—"If Rod Stewart can do it, I can, too, right kids?"—and, as Ogle put "Disco Mystic" on the air, Reed continued his rant against the racket of transcendental meditation and, shortly after—to the sycophantic laughter of his inner circle—offered unflattering remarks about immigrant cab drivers. As Ogle cued up The El Dorado's "At My Front Door," a fevered doo-wop track from 1955, Reed's free-form ramble turned personal: "I went to school to stay out of the Army—yeah, [I'm] one of those. I didn't say I'm proud of it, but I'm not unproud of it: I was finding myself. And I didn't want to find myself in the Army [laughs]."

With Hank Ballard and the Midnighters' "Your Sexy Ways" swinging in the background, Reed's bluster reprised the depravity of Rolling Stone magazine, and reflected upon the sensuality of Ballard and the black music aesthetic: "It's about sex. They were always afraid of rock'n'roll because it's about sex. It's very, very complementary to sex. It's very in favor of sex. I don't think things going on today are so pro-sex"—disco excepted, of course.

Upon the surprise appearance of John Cale, Reed's former bandmate in Velvet Underground, Reed shouted, "Cale! . . . In New York, Welsh city of the heart!" Following Reed's cues, Ogle segued from Al Green's "I Feel Good" to Nico's pitch-challenged "It Was a Pleasure Then," and from Bobby Short's "Miss Otis Regrets" to David Bowie's "The Width of a Circle," the opening track of The Man Who Sold the World (1970). Reed and Cale exchanged thoughts on youth corruption ahead of three tracks from John Cale's oeuvre, including a roaring live version of "Jack the Ripper in the Moulin Rouge." Ogle cued up the closing announcement for "Radio/Radio," as Reed, Cale, and their entourage disappeared into the streets of Manhattan.

For "Radio/Radio," Reed channeled his love for early rock'n'roll and, as he had on Live: No Prisoners, his inner Lenny Bruce. The vision for rock'n'roll he imagined in the Cale-less Velvet Underground—"Here She Comes," "Sweet Jane," to begin—was thriving in the capable hands of the CBGB doyen and The Clash. On his visits to CBGB, Reed offered paternal advice to his musical progeny and, within weeks of his "Radio/Radio" appearance, accompanied Byrne for Nico's performance at CBGB. In spite of Reed's influence through his glam rock days on the high-androgyny of disco aesthetics, he never secured a disco hit.

HOT IN THE CITY

If Reed and Christgau were often at odds circa 1979, they did share an affection for the virtues of 'PIX. Christgau advised Voice readers that April to take note of the new format at WPIX, and to do so quickly.

While it lasts—and maybe it will—I'd recommend tuning to WPIX-FM (102 on your dial), which is playing a whole lot of real rock and roll. I've even heard Jane Hamburger (my fave) play black rock and roll, albeit from the '60s . . . and a weekend jock dubbed Alfredo [Santos] played for an hour and a half one dreary afternoon without [my] hitting my tuneout button once.

At WNEW, Neer gauged the growing interest in Griffin's airtime, reshuffled the schedule, and Christgau—among others—took notice. "WNEW is also sounding a lot better these days, with Meg Griffin moving up in the airtime hierarchy and Vin Scelsa remaining Vin Scelsa. It's a disco counter-reaction, I think, and I hope it doesn't merely reflect a dearth of blockbuster AOR product." Christgau was a pop stalwart, and his concerns about "product" were earnest. He wanted the inclusion of The Ramones and The Clash on radio playlists to represent a genuine triumph in the industry, rather than merely a backlash against disco, which often harbored traces of anti-gay and anti-black sentiments.[21]

Christgau's suspicions were well-founded. With the growing clout of Griffin and Scelsa, WNEW's free-form ethic became elastic enough to include punk and new wave. For their listeners, though, disco remained largely taboo. In spring 1979, WNEW's Dave Herman became enamored with Donna Summer's "Hot Stuff," and added it to his playlists. An onslaught of anti-disco letters and phone calls quickly followed. Bewildered by the hysteria, Herman asked the *New York Times*, "Are people threatened that rock'n'roll is dying, or what?" Perhaps listeners were fine with one disco tune on their free-form station, but two was simply too much. According to Merly, who joined WNEW in September 1978, Muni himself had a touch of disco fever. Rod Stewart's "Do Ya Think I'm Sexy?," which topped the *Billboard* Hot 100 in early 1979, made it into heavy rotation on Muni's show. "Scott had a mind of his own, and a sensibility and a little world of his own, and he really liked Rod Stewart," Merly said. "And if he liked an artist he was going to play that stuff, regardless."[22]

Likewise, at KSAN, near San Francisco, deejay Richard Gossett offered a steady rotation of Costello, Talking Heads, and The Jam during his six-to-ten p.m. shift. Gossett also had a soft spot for the *Grease* soundtrack, and often segued from "You're the One That I Want," by John Travolta and Olivia Newton-John, into The Ramones' "Rockaway Beach."[23]

In May, Hurrah's Monday-Tuesday punch of Griffin and Hamburger continued apace. Griffin's matrimonial alliance with Piasek, as well as her affinity for The Clash, among others, hastened her spring departure from WNEW to become music direc-

At WPIX, Ms. Griffin selects tracks from a Deaf School LP for the mix (from the archives of Joe "from Chicago" Piasek).

tor at WPIX. Christgau again took notice, likening WPIX to "WMCA or WINS in the glory days of top 40, 1964 through 1966, with a spirit and enthusiasm like that of WOR-FM when 'progressive radio' was a daring idea." He highlighted Griffin's tastes in particular, and her penchant for playing Dave Clark 5 and The Supremes alongside Television and The Velvet Underground. Griffin also had The Clash in steady rotation, and "Bleecker Bob" himself not only ensured that these titles were available to New Yorkers, he made regular trips to the UK and kept his ear to the street. As Pennie Smith recalled,

> The groundswell came from the street, and there was quite a lot of interplay between London and New York at the time. . . . The Clash were very knowledgeable about who was who in New York. So [U.S.] radio stations may have been quicker than average to take it up, but the groundswell came from the street. . . . It all went through Bleecker Bob, he had a load of stuff. They knew him even in England. He was the bloke.

Serendipity rarely simply happened. It needed nurturing from doting figures in retail, in print, and on the radio.[24]

I'LL BE YOUR MIRROR

For The Clash, the first few months of 1979 included a short U.S. tour, intermittent UK gigs, and their return to the recording studio. The Pearl Harbour tour—or, under Epic's designation, the Give 'Em Enough Rope tour—commenced in Vancouver on January 31 and, over the course of three weeks, included performances in Berkeley, Los Angeles, and New York. The staff at Epic, with a close eye on the modest sales of *Rope*, initially balked at the idea of a U.S. tour. Luckily, for American punk fans, Clash allies held sway, and the tour included sold-out shows in theaters across the country.

By New Year's 1979, Caroline Coon had taken over the managerial duties of The Clash—if not the accompanying title. In fall 1978, The Clash reached the end of their rope with Rhodes and, following his sacking, Coon became the "not-the-Manager of The Clash." According to Coon, sexism remained the norm in the music industry in the UK, and The Clash's decision not to grant her the title of manager stemmed in part from Strummer's effort to maintain a (macho) punk façade. Unfazed, Coon inquired with Epic regarding The Clash's first tour of America, and received a definitive reply: not now. "They told us not to come. They said the album wasn't getting any airplay," Coon said. "We told them we didn't care, we were coming anyway. They told us they had The Fabulous Poodles and Toto on the road, and that they wouldn't, therefore, be able to look after us properly."[25]

The nature of Epic's near indifference was partly personal, but mostly business. The general manager of Epic (equivalent to president), departed in April 1978, and their VP of marketing followed shortly after. Don Dempsey of the marketing division took the helm and patiently instituted changes in personnel and priorities, with key changes continuing through February. Dan Beck joined Epic as U.S. product manager in January, and it was another month before Dempsey installed Ron McCarrell as the VP of marketing. (Beck reported to McCarrell, and their clients included The Clash.) Coincidentally, the record industry suffered a slump through the first half of 1979, which was attributed in part to the impact of the oil crisis on consumer confidence.[26]

Wayne Forte, a booking agent with William Morris, suffered no crisis in confidence regarding his vision for introducing The Clash to their fans in North America. "I thought the Pistols, The Clash, and The Jam were like The Beatles,

The Stones, and The Who," Forte told me. "The Clash were the bad boys, these dirty grimy guys, but the kids still loved 'em." Forte gauged the level of American love by reading the *Voice*, listening to The Clash on WLIR and WNEW, and placing the occasional phone call to Bob Plotnick, owner of Bleecker Bob's. Shortly after the UK release of *The Clash*, Forte called the shop and said, "Clash: what do you know?" Plotnick replied, "I've sold one thousand imports." In Forte's estimation, one thousand domestic LPs sold in New York would likely produce a concert-going audience of three hundred. For one thousand, premium-priced import LPs, he figured, "Everyone who bought it will show up and bring a friend."[27]

In late 1978, Forte secured an agreement with Coon to organize the dates and venues for the tour. Forte's plan? "Fuck the clubs, we're going straight into the theaters. Duluth and Omaha? They don't care about The Clash. I knew we weren't going to own the country. I went where the movement was the greatest: Boston, New York, and San Francisco." Forte contacted New York concert promoter Ron Delsener to request the Palladium, which had capacity for over three thousand fans. Delsener replied, "You're out of your frickin' mind." Forte also contacted Brian Murphy of Avalon Productions to book the Santa Monica Auditorium (three thousand seats). He replied, "Who? Where?" Forte assured Delsener and Murphy, and the promoters in Cleveland and Washington, DC, "It's going to be amazing." Forte's enthusiasm for the band, though, was not shared openly by key figures at Epic, and he knew it. When he pitched his plan to Coon, he told her, "If we pull this off, we'll make the record company pay attention."

After *Rope*'s release in November 1978, Epic's attention appeared to be elsewhere. For new releases and live appearances, the *Voice* served as a key domain for exposure in New York for old guard and new wavers alike. In anticipation of Thin Lizzy's show at the Palladium in 1978, for example, Warner Bros. secured a full-page ad for the band's latest LP, *Live and Dangerous*. Other issues included full-page ads for Devo's *Are We Not Men? We Are Devo* and, on the coveted back cover, Elvis Costello's *Armed Forces*, in advance of the Armed Funk tour, with Carl Perkins. Smaller ads, too, ran for new albums and upcoming appearances. Even the representatives for Crazy Cavan 'n' the Rhythm Rockers, for a three-night residency at Max's, saw fit to run a wallet-sized ad in the *Voice*. In the three months between *Rope*'s release and The Clash's first gig at the Palladium, the only Clash-related ad copy in the *Voice* included the two Palladium concert listings: in the January 29 issue, it announced the February 17 show and the "Give

The night after their American debut in Berkeley, California, in February 1979,
The Clash played a benefit in San Francisco for a youth organization promoting
affordable rock shows. By bypassing local promoter and oligopolist Bill Graham,
The Clash affirmed their commitment to kids willing to do it themselves.

'Em Enough Rope Tour." In the February 19 issue (available February 14), it announced that the show was sold out.[28]

If advertisements for The Clash in the *Voice* or *Rolling Stone* proved prohibitive, Epic did purchase single ads at the time in *Trouser Press* and *Billboard*. In 1978, Epic ran multiple ads for Cheap Trick LPs in the monthly *Trouser Press*. To kick off 1979, Epic bought a Clash ad on the inside cover in the January issue. In punky collage style, a rendition of *Rope*'s cover appeared above the brazen tagline: "THE AMERICAN DEBUT OF THE ONLY ENGLISH GROUP THAT MATTERS." Epic also ran an ad in *Billboard* with the same tagline—albeit too late to promote the tour. The Clash were regarded in the ad insert celebrating Epic's twenty-fifth anniversary, in the February 17 issue of *Billboard*, as one of CBS's key acts currently touring the United States. A member of Epic/Sony's international division noted how "Jeff Beck, Ted Nugent, Cheap Trick and Boston are all popular among high school and university students. We want to make Dan Fogelberg, Clash [*sic*] and Meat Loaf just as popular."[29]

Despite rave reviews in the UK and American press, and the tempered support from CBS, Epic staff appeared blasé about the only English client that mattered. Shortly after his arrival, Beck walked down the hall to album promotion and, regarding *Rope*, asked, "What do you think? What are our chances?" Allies were few, consensus ruled the roost, and the response was not encouraging. If a key figure in album promotion, for example, did not regard The Clash favorably, an ad or two might be purchased to honor CBS's interest in The Clash, but little more. Epic, Beck told me, supported the idea of The Clash touring—if not the timing of Coon's proposal. After Coon put up close to $6,000 of her own money to secure the dates, she convinced Epic to underwrite the nine-date tour for the modest sum of $30,000. The Clash's debut in the states, on February 7 at the Berkeley Community Theater, included a photo opportunity with Epic representatives flown in from across the country. As the photographer prepared for the shot, The Clash took the opportunity to protest Epic's neglect by staging a walkout. The gesture, though, hardly dampened Beck's enthusiasm—in fact, it secured it. "The show I had just seen totally nailed me," he later noted. "I was in! I loved this band!"[30]

Once Clash allies within Epic bore witness to The Clash onstage, they had more freedom for dissent. Still, they needed "product to service"—which was not forthcoming on their terms, or the terms of American radio, prior to *London*

Calling. Epic deemed *Rope*, for instance, to be a rock album in a niche market. "Servicing the album" entailed delivering the LP to select program directors and deejays. If a consensus developed around a particular track, it might be released as a single. "We admit we aren't likely to get a hit single this time around," said Bruce Harris, director of artists and repertoire at Epic, just as *Rope* entered the *Billboard* Top 200 LPs. "But *Give 'Em Enough Rope* has sold 40,000 copies and that's better than sixty percent of most new acts."[31]

Voice music critics found no reason to hedge their bets. *Rope* topped the "Pazz & Jop Product Report," for January 8, 1979. The following week, *Rope* held the number four slot in the best album list of the annual Pazz & Jop Critics Poll. In advance of The Clash's arrival in New York City, Christgau contacted Susan Blond, Epic's VP of media relations. "I called her up and I said, 'I want thirty tickets. I want everybody at the *Voice* to go see this band. . . . Look, you're trying to create a press blitz for these people, let's create a press blitz. You know damn well they're all going to be converted,' and she did it for me."[32]

On February 17, the brilliant performance of The Clash confirmed the devotion of early fanatics and secured the conversion of a few more, including Christgau's colleagues at the *Voice.* "I remember in particular [jazz critic Stanley] Crouch's response, which was very positive, to my pleasure and surprise. He just felt the power of it and went with it, instead of complaining that it didn't swing. He understood that it was significant," Christgau said. "Strummer was a fabulous performer, and that was a good night." Even their rivals conceded their brilliance: typically diffident Johnny Ramone professed, "At that Palladium show . . . I thought, 'Oh shit, these guys are as good as us.'"[33]

It was significant, too, that The Clash played The Palladium rather than a considerably smaller nightclub. Other British bands making their New York debuts in 1979 included Joe Jackson and The Police, and they, too, were signed to a major label and had recently released albums in the United States. Prior to their New York debuts, though, neither Jackson nor The Police held the allure of The Clash, and the ardor of local scribes and deejays appeared coy in comparison. For their debuts in New York, Jackson and The Police embraced the "corporate option": a WNEW live broadcast from the Bottom Line, with its maximum capacity of four hundred seats, on separate dates that April.[34]

Again, for the *Voice*, Christgau penned a glowing review of The Clash's Boston and New York performances, and profiled his fellow line-goers as sober looking, high-IQ fans, "a crowd that liked to read about music." (To his reported astonishment, Christgau had one fan ask for his autograph.) Laudatory concert reviews appeared, too, in *New York Rocker*, the *New York Times*, *Rolling Stone*, and *Time* magazine. At *Trouser Press*, Robbins was not amused by the national coverage and, in a lengthy feature that June on The Clash, slagged the mainstream press for its initial cowardice: "Where were they when only [*Trouser Press*] and the *Village Voice*'s Robert Christgau had the courage to run rave stories in the US?" The internecine wars of rock scribes, though, hardly mattered to the fan base that began at Max's and CBGB circa 1974. In the next few years, its members had attended gigs at the Palladium for hometown heroes Patti Smith, Blondie, and The Ramones, tuned into shows by Griffin, Merly, and Hamburger, and stocked their record shelves with a host of ground-breaking LPs by three-minute heroes from the U.S. and the UK. Forte's hunch was spot-on and, with the summer release of Epic's Americanized version of *The Clash*, tri-state punk-o-philes had another reason to pogo for joy.[35]

With the nine dates of the Pearl Harbour tour, with Bo Diddley supporting, The Clash confirmed its adoration for America. Fans from San Francisco to New York mirrored their adoration and, at the Agora Theater in Cleveland, in a crush at the front of the stage, nearly got themselves killed as a result. The Clash returned home brimming with confidence, ready to assemble the opus that, Jones later noted, might well have been named *New York Calling*.[36]

6.
London Calls, New York Answers

Following their triumphant, inaugural U.S. tour, The Clash focused anew on their third album. They ignored the rumors of spring 1979 that they might be dropped from CBS, and enlisted Guy Stevens—another hero from the manifesto T-shirt—to work on *London Calling*. "There was a real intensity of effort," Strummer said. "That's when we really showed our mettle." As noted above, Stevens's reputation for heterodoxy was fueled in no small part by his affinity for tequila and black popular music. Engineer Bill Price, who also coproduced *Never Mind the Bollocks*, explained Stevens' method, which involved swinging ladders, toppling chairs, and a wine marinade of the piano keys: "The idea was that the highly excited atmosphere would produce highly excitable music." On the west side of the Atlantic, WPIX embraced the virtues of the live simulcast, featuring bands from The Buzzcocks to The Cramps, and thereby expanded the tri-state fan base for punk and new wave. Upon The Clash's return to New York, for two dates in September, that excitability continued for the Palladium goers especially, and for those tuning in, on September 21, to the live simulcast on WNEW.[1]

AN ALBUM OF THEIR OWN

In spring 1979, the last gang in town faced the prospects of renewing a radically democratic method for assembling the next album. For the moment, no father figure loomed: Rhodes was gone, Coon wisely kept her distance and, initially, the figures at CBS scarcely knew where to find them. In the confines of a new studio, with the help of two roadies and little more, The Clash now had the opportunity to do it all themselves.[2]

At Vanilla Studios in Victoria, upstairs from an after-market auto painter, The Clash wrote, rehearsed, and recorded, six to seven days a week, for two months solid. Strummer and Headon both resided nearby, and Baker's responsibility included motorcar delivery of Simonon and Jones, and the latter never took a day off. "Each night before we left," The Baker recalled, "I would do a rough mix of the day's work and run off several cassettes for the band to take home." (A selection of these rough mixes were released in 2004 as "the Vanilla tapes.") In The Baker's estimation, two-thirds of the eventual album, with vocals and limited overdubs, was already complete when the band joined forces in Wessex with Stevens and Price.[3]

At an early Wessex rehearsal, as The Clash ran through "Brand New Cadillac," Price rolled the tape. At the cadence, Stevens shouted, "That's it! It's a take!" Headon pointed out an error in the band's tempo, and Stevens retorted, "All rock'n'roll speeds up!" "From then on," Headon recalled, "the atmosphere was just electric." For Simonon, Stevens's mania proved calming. "Guy Stevens was really great. He made me feel really at ease, and if I played wrong notes he didn't care," Simonon said. For Clash consigliore Kosmo Vinyl, the difference between Stevens and Pearlman loomed largest for Simonon: "Paul prefers a bloke that throws chairs and swings ladders at you, as opposed to an American guy who's like, 'Can you do it again? Can you do it again? Can you do it again?'"[4]

As a rule, each track began with a collective run-through by The Clash, and select performances provided the basic tracks for the drums and rhythm guitar. Next came Simonon's bass lines, Jones's guitar overdubs, and, in various sequences, tracks for brass, piano, acoustic guitar, assorted percussion, and vocals were blended into the mix. On select tracks, fine contributions from organist Mickey Gallagher, of Ian Dury and the Blockheads, and, the horn section from Graham Parker's band were added in, too. Passages of a seagull's cry and, according to Price, the muffled sounds of a copulating couple were also incorporated on the double album. The repeated tearing of Velcro enriches the opening passage of "Guns of Brixton."

If the sessions tested the band's mettle, the role Stevens played in this chapter of the Clash saga has been largely romanticized. Strummer and Jones, especially, painted Pollyanna portraits of life with Stevens at Wessex. For Jones, "His presence in the studio definitely makes all the difference. It's like all the mess going into him, like Dorian Gray's portrait, or whatever. All the messy sound goes and it becomes him, and what's left on the tape is . . . clarity" [ellipsis in orig-inal]. Others offer less rosy recollections of St. Stevens's contribution, especially once the novelty passed of having a besotted, if lovable, madman at the controls. "When it was time to do endless vocal and guitar overdubs," The Baker told me, "Guy wanted no part of that tedious process." Stevens turned up at the studio with decreasing frequency as the inspiration of the initial run-throughs turned to the perspiration of take-after-take for track-by-track overdubs.[5]

In the beginning, roadie Johnny Green's duties included ensuring that Stevens appeared as scheduled. Toward the middle of things, Baker recalled, Green "had his MO changed to trying to make sure Guy was diverted from the studio." If he did make it to Wessex, Stevens needed to be managed, or manhan-dled, with or without Baker's sympathy:

> [Stevens] became just a nuisance to me personally. There were enough liggers and hangers-on visiting the studio each day doing nothing, without another one getting in the way. His constant begging for more alcohol became evermore insistent and I didn't have time for the nonsense. One day it reached a fever-pitch and he started physically mauling me to go get him booze. That was it! I kicked him in the stomach and he fell across the room and slumped into a heap on the floor. He never harangued me again.

Stevens, alas, did not do much of anything ever again. *London Calling* was his swan song: in an eerie echo of the fate of Keith Moon, Stevens overdosed in August 1981 on drugs prescribed to aid his alcohol addiction. The Clash left Price on his own to return to the United States on September 6, content for now to reveal the greatest secret in rock'n'roll on the Take the Fifth tour, song by song.[6]

After a rollicking good time on September 8 at the Monterey Stomp Festival, The Clash kicked off the tour on September 12 in St. Paul, Minnesota. From the stage, Strummer offered his sympathy for American radio listeners: "I come over here and I switch on the radio and all I hear is The Eagles and Steely Dan." "Life in the Fast Lane" and "Peg" were hardly the only slushy sounds in heavy rotation in the summer of loathing of 1979.

RADIO SALVATION

From New York to San Francisco, disco fever still ran hot in 1979. For the spring equinox, The Bee Gees' "Tragedy" displaced Gloria Gaynor's "I Will Survive"—a single not content to go quietly into that cocaine-addled night and, two weeks later, resumed its spot at the top of the pops. Blondie's "Heart of Glass" spent a week at number one that April, and Peaches and Herb's downtempo "Reunited" settled atop the charts through May. In June, Donna Summer's "Hot Stuff" and The Bee Gees' "Love You Inside Out" wrestled for the zenith position. For two weeks, Anita Ward's "Ring My Bell" held off Donna Summer's next sortie at 45rpm, and "Bad Girls" straddled the apex through the dog days of July and August. Chic's "Good Times" offered the last disco hit of the summer, and The Knack rode in comfortably on the new wave with "My Sharona" in the number one position, from August, to the autumn equinox, and after.[7]

For the growing audience of WPIX, the sounds of spring and summer were markedly less soporific. On separate Sundays in May, Hilly Kristal and Lou Reed appeared on "Radio/Radio," selecting discs and speaking candidly about the musical powers that be. John Cale cued up discs the following Sunday, in order to promote a mid-June residency at CBGB. Two months later, David Byrne of Talking Heads stopped by.

On August 12, "Radio/Radio" opened with Elvis Costello's "Radio Radio" and Ogle then segued to Talking Heads' "Life During Wartime," The Normal's "TVOD," and Public Image Ltd.'s "Death Disco." Ogle, Dan Neer, and Byrne followed with introductions and Byrne, in his disarmingly specific emotional register, spoke about how the band selected their singles.

> **BYRNE:** Well the way we did it on the last record, and it looks like the way we're going to try to do it on this one, is just to release the album and see which record is the most popular, which song that some radio stations play.
>
> **NEER:** Now obviously when you record a record, you have personal favorites that you'd like to see as a single. Does that often times match or they never match?
>
> **BYRNE:** Yeah, they never match [laughs].

Rather than "Psycho Killer" or "Uh-Oh, Love Comes to Town," Byrne indicated, "Mine would have been 'No Compassion.' I thought that one's the best." "No Compassion" followed, along with tracks by The Jackson Five and The Mahotella Queens. After losing an opportunity to offer words of kindness to his band-mates—Neer: "There was a reviewer that said . . . the Talking Heads rhythm section is possibly the tightest in the world"; Byrne: [chuckles]—Byrne explained the origins of the title *Fear of Music*, which had just been released the week before.

> **Byrne:** A while ago I was reading a book called *Music and the Brain*. It was a medical book about trying to discover if there were musical regions in the brain . . . [and fear of music] hap-pened to be one of the musical diseases. . . . And the people that had this disease, if they were walking down the street and they heard music coming out of a bar, they would have to quickly walk the other way: so of course most of them have to live in the country. . . . I thought it was a great contradiction to call a record *Fear of Music*.

Later in the show, Byrne answered calls from listeners, including a woman who asked, first, about working with Robert Fripp—Byrne: "he likes to [record] by himself without anybody watching"—and, quite presciently, "Have you thought about using tape loops the way he does?" (Tape loops featured prominently in the recording of *Remain in Light*.) To wrap up the summer, WPIX aired a live broadcast of The Buzzcocks' show from Club 57. (The opening acts were The The and Gang of Four.)[8]

Piasek, too, continued to tinker with the limits of radio, filling the schedule with a rich mix of novel programming. "Alive at 11" aired on Saturday nights, mostly, and supplanted the "Live at CBGB" program, with on-air broadcasts from Hurrah, Club 57, Trax and, of course, CBGB. "Alive at 11" followed the "PIX Penthouse Party," which featured virtually nonstop dance music of a rock'n'roll variety. As Griffin noted that fall, "The music we play is contemporary rock'n'roll, not contemporary rock. . . . Our assumption is that if you listen to the new stuff, it is reminiscent also of the old stuff. And it is all still rock'n'roll." Weekend pro-gramming tilted heavily toward the new and even fairly obscure. The "No Major Record Show" kicked off Saturdays at eleven a.m. and featured bands who, when it came to vinyl, were pressing it themselves. On Sundays, just ahead of "Radio/ Radio," "The New Rock'n'Roll Show" also featured bands otherwise neglected in the New York market. The Clash were among the favorites of many of the deejays at WPIX—none more so than Jane Hamburger, according to Griffin: "No one else in New York did more to promote The Clash." The playlist from August 10, 1979, the "hot list" (under "H") included Charlie Daniels, ELO, and Lena Lovich ("Lucky Number" and "Say When"), and the new tracks to break (under "N") included "Police and Thieves," from *The Clash* (U.S. version—August 1979), The

WPIX

PLAYLIST AUG 10 1979

H

THE KNACK	MY SHARONA, HEARTBEAT, LITTLE GIRLS
SUPERTRAMP	CHILD OF VISION
B 52S	ROCK LOBSTER, 52 GIRLS
M	POP MUZIK
CHARLIE DANIELS	DEVIL WENT TO GEORGIA, BLUE SKY - RE ADD
CARS	LETS GO, DANGEROUS TYPE, GOT ALOT ON MY HEAD
JOE JACKSON	SI SHE REALLY ...?- RE ADD
E L O	DONT BRING ME DOWN
ROBT PALMER	BAD CASE
SNIFF N THE TEARS	DRIVERS SEAT
NICK LOWE	CRACKIN UP, CRUEL, LOVE SO FINE, BIG KICK
RACHEL SWEET	WHO DOES LISA LIKE
WINGS	SPIN IT ON
JOHN STEWART	GOLD - RE ADD
SOUTHSIDE JOHNNY	I REMEMBER LAST NIGHT
LENA LOVITCH	LUCKY #, SAY WHEN
NEIL YOUNG	MY MY, HEY HEY
KINKS	GALLON OF GAS NATIONAL HEALTH, CATCH ME...
LAUGHING DOGS	JOHNNY CONTENDER
BLUE OYSTER	IN THEE, YOURE NOT..
PAT TRAVERS	BOOM BOOM
CHEAP TRICK	AINT THAT A SHAME- RE ADD
TIM CURRY	I DO THE ROCK
BOB DYLAN	SLO TRAIN, SERVE SOMEBODY - ADDS
RECORDS	STARRY EYES, TEENARARM
CHUCK BERRY	THRILL, IF I WERE - ADD
RUMOUR	EMOTIONAL TRAFFIC
CHICAGO	ALOHA MAMA, MAMA TAKE - ADDS
THOROGOOD	NADINE, NIGHT TIME - ADDS
IAM GOMM	HOLD ON
POLICE (PROPAGANDA LP)	NEXT TO YOU LIVE

N

JOHANSEN	MELODY
STIV BATORS	ITS COLD OUTSIDE
THE CLASH	POLICE AND THIEVES
J J CALE	I'LL...ANYTIME
DAVE EDMUNDS	QUEEN OF HEARTS
RY COODER	LITTLE SISTER
GARLAND JEFFREYS (SAMPLER A&M)	MATADOR
CAROLINE MASS	QUOTE GOODBYE QUOTE
TALKING HEADS	LIFE DURING WARTIME - ADD
RANDY NEWMAN	MONEY- ADD
PROPAGANDA-JOE JACKSON	DONT ASK ME, COME ON(LIVE),LANDLORD-POLICE -ADDS
GARY NUMAN & TUBEWAY ARMY	ALIENS - ADD
SHIRTS	CANT CRY ANYMORE-ADD
ELLEN FOLEY	WHATS A MATTER BABY - ADD
TOM VERLAINE	RED LEAVES- ADD
EDDIE MONEY	GET A MOVE ON- ADD

General Playlist, WPIX, August 10, 1979 (from the archives of Joe "from Chicago" Piasek).

Shirts' "Can't Cry Anymore," and Talking Heads' "Life During Wartime." Merly shared the excitement at WNEW, as did their writerly comrades downtown. Their efforts had minimal impact on the top 40, but upon The Clash's return to Manhattan, the following LPs were among *Billboard's* Top 200: The Cars' *Candy-O* (#9), *The Cars* (#21), Nick Lowe's *Labour of Lust* (#31), Talking Heads' *Fear of Music* (#33), B-52's (#70), Joe Jackson's *Look Sharp* (#73), Blondie's *Parallel Lines* (#75), *The Clash* (Epic) (#132), Gary Numan and Tubeway Army's *Replicas* (#149), Patti Smith's *Wave* (#161), Peter Tosh's *Mystic Man* (#164), and Graham Parker's *Squeezing Out Sparks* (#198).[9]

THIS IS RADIO CLASH

On their September return to New York, for a two-night stint at the Palladium, The Clash were welcomed by the *Voice* as "the most intense rock and roll band in the world." Again, advance notice of the show through advertisements was scant: the Palladium bill in the *Voice* on September 3 and 17 included mention of the shows, as well as upcoming dates for Joe Jackson's return to New York. Christgau, meanwhile, continued to drum away at the nonbelievers. In the September 3 "Consumer Guide," on the recently released U.S. version of *The Clash*, he noted,

> Cut for cut, this may be the greatest rock and roll album (plus bonus single) ever manufactured in the U.S. . . . Yet the package somehow feels misbegotten. The U.K. version of The Clash is the greatest rock and roll album ever manufactured anywhere in some small part because its innocence is of a piece—it never stops snarling, it's always threatening to blow up in your face. . . . Nevertheless, a great introduction and a hell of a bargain. [Grade] A.

The following week, *The Clash* (U.S.) ranked number four in the "Pazz & Jop Product Report." Lastly, in the issue of the *Voice* on newsstands September 19, the Palladium show was included among "Voice Choices," and Christgau assured readers, "There are still tickets left as I write, Sam & Dave will open, and this is the greatest band in the world right now."[10]

Piasek reported that WNEW and WPIX often jostled to secure the live broadcast for new wave bands. Harvey Leeds of Epic indicated that, in the case of The Clash, the choice of stations was never in doubt. "There was no competition. PIX was a new station, and NEW had the history," he told me. "You would always have gone with NEW, which was the legendary station." (Piasek's consolation package? That same weekend, Andy Warhol made a cameo appearance on "Radio/Radio." Walter Stedding accompanied him and played violin, and Reed dropped by, too. "I told [Reed] to come down to the Mudd Club with us later because they were having a Dead Rock Stars Night," Warhol noted. "He said he would go as himself, but I told him he looks too good for that now.")[11]

Epic contacted Muni at WNEW and, Leeds noted, "We pitched it the way we'd pitch a record." Beck reported that a flood of line ads—that is, four-by-five-inch ads—were typically placed in the alternative weeklies, including the *Voice*, in advance of a concert. If considerable enthusiasm about a given band was generated by deejays and journalists, for instance, then the U.S. product manager had a different task: step out of the way. "It was just as important to know when to stay out of the marketing process as to get in and push it," Beck noted. "Audiences have always been able to smell the hype, and with all the energy coming from the street on The Clash, our role was to reinforce it, punctuate it, but never get ahead of it."[12]

LOADING THE GUNS OF BRIXTON

Reports from the first night's performance indicated that neither of the opening acts, The Undertones, from Ireland, and Stax legends Sam & Dave, were in top form, and even The Clash—after an electric opening—were unable to sustain their usual level of ferocity. For the second night, though, The Undertones and Sam & Dave performed valiantly. Barry Myers, a.k.a. DJ Scratchy, toured with The Clash on their first three trips to the U.S., and between sets he stitched together a lively mix of roots reggae, rockabilly, and 1960s soul. "Part of the reason I worked with The Clash was because I was a deejay who didn't think that music had begun in 1976," he told me. At the Palladium, Scratchy set up his turntables downstage left, with Headon's drum kit to his right, and a stack of bass monitors to his left.[13]

Scratchy had free reign with his musical selections, excluding the last song of the pre-Clash interlude. On previous tours, Scratchy noted, The Clash bounded onstage to The Coasters' "Cell Block no. 9" or Sam Cooke's "Chain Gang." On this night, it was Frank Sinatra's "High Hopes." As Sinatra's voice reprised the tale of the ram and the dam, Simonon's bass thumped to life. Jones strummed a chord that dissolved into feedback and then launched into the opening bars of "Safe European Home"—which was followed, without pause, by "I'm So Bored with the USA" and "Complete Control." Strummer stood front-center stage and—between their leaping about, the flying windmill chords, and the occasional scissors-kick—Jones stood to Strummer's right, Simonon to Strummer's left.

Strummer engaged the audience throughout the set, poking fun at American rock figures, drawing the audience into the song narratives, and proffering a didactic history lesson. Following "Complete Control," Headon tapped intermittently at his snare drum, while Strummer offered the evening's first in a series of earnestly charming improvisations. "Meanwhile, I think we is all on the radio now. Has everyone got good eyesight? You people up there, you see that alright?" pointing to a copy of the morning edition of the *New York Post*, whose headline announced, in *Mars Attacks!*–sized typeface, "THE BEATLES ARE BACK." (The subhead read "Fab Four to be reunited for big UN concert in New York"— which, of course, never materialized.)[14] Strummer held forth on the fate of Beatlemania, then Headon set a brisk tempo on his high hat, as Simonon tapped out the haunting *ba-da, ba-da-ba-da* that opens "London Calling." Strummer's voice, already strained, faltered on the opening verse. He mounted a valiant recovery and, at the coda, Strummer offered the audience a clear rendition of the final lyric lost in the fade-out of the album version: above all, London's drowning made Strummer feel like "singin' the blues."

Strummer, again, turned his attention to the audience. "Okay? Ah. If you don't mind, if you don't mind I'd like you all to—you can all pack your bags, you lot and all, and we're all going to Hammersmith on a Freddie Laker," referring to Laker Airways, which flew between Heathrow and JFK airports. "The flight to Hammersmith is leaving," said Strummer, pausing and, in a West Indies' accent, shouted, "No, mahn, no!" The respite served Strummer well, and he returned to form, snapping off sharply the last syllables of "Jah-may-kah!" in the opening stanza of "White Man in Hammersmith Palais."

Jones's proclivity for guitar effects was on full display and, courtesy of his MXR 100 phaser, nearly every song was awash in echo and reverb. Throughout the set, Headon ably demonstrated why Pearlman dubbed him "the human drum machine," and between songs, as Strummer engaged the audience, Headon could scarcely control his nervous taps or kicks. Simonon, meanwhile, kept pace ably and, on "The Guns of Brixton," tendered a full-throated, roots-reggae chant at the microphone.[15]

In addition to "London Calling" and "Brixton," the band played three tracks from the upcoming album: "Koka Kola," "Clampdown," and "Wrong 'Em Boyo." Strummer introduced "Kola" with a quip about "a word from our sponsors" and an earnestly clumsy reference to the live broadcast: "this is Radio W.S.H.I.T.!" He proceeded to miss a handful of lyrics in the third stanza, but Headon, Simonon, and Jones pressed on, with Headon beating out a thunderous segue between "Kola" and a rousing "I Fought the Law."

In a successive interlude, Strummer teased the audience about Ted Nugent— "Don't worry, Ted will be on in a minute!"—and melodically mocked roadie Johnny Green's dilatory effort to repair Strummer's homespun wrist guard. To protect his forearm during strumming frenzies, Strummer employed wraps of electrical tape above his wrist, and tonight they failed to hold. Green was summarily drafted to fix the "Strummer guard," and Strummer improvised a sardonic lament for the amusement of the audience: "Here comes Johnny Green with a gaffer tape / and he's a little too late / you're always too late, Johnny!"

Gallagher took his place at his organ midway through "Clash City Rockers" and kept pace as the group tightened up with rollicking renditions of "Stay Free" and "Clampdown." Following "Police and Thieves," Strummer gently chided the audience. "I hope you all know about Junior Murvin. I'll tell ya: shh shh. You should hear Junior Murvin doing that tune. Junior Murvin can sing in a voice as high as that roof. He sings it like, kinda: 'aah-ooo-aaaaahhhh!'" ending with a falsetto crescendo. The band charged through the first few minutes of "Capital Radio," and held steady during the Gallagher-led vamp. Capital Radio was established as the second commercial radio station in England, in 1973, and appeared on the manifesto T-shirt's list of hates. Strummer may well have been directing his sortie at WPLJ and other progressive radio stations that offered scant support for punk and new wave, as he iterated the guiding principles of "Capital Radio": "Since I am the DJ on this here Capital Radio,

Mick, with his pal Gibson. Palladium Theater, March 1980 (© Joe Streno, go2jo.com).

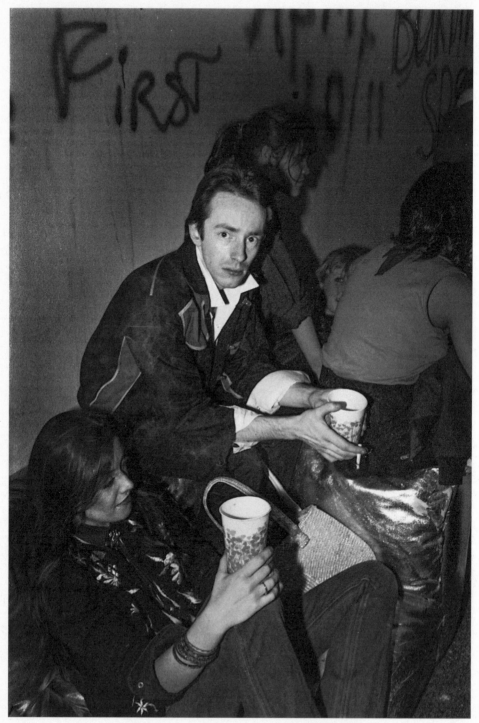

Topper, backstage at Bond, spring 1981, with cigarette,
drink, and birds (© Joe Streno, go2jo.com).

I would like to tell you a few of our station rules. Number one: we allow no rock'n'roll! Number two: we allow no rock'n'roll. Number three: we allow no rock'n'roll!"

Undeterred by his failing voice, Strummer bounced his way through the last four songs of the set. "Tommy Gun" featured Headon at his hard-charging best, and "Wrong 'Em Boyo," with Gallagher high in the mix, and Jones having fun with a smattering of "oohs" and "aahs," provided a bit of comic relief. The Clash concluded the set with "Janie Jones" and "Garageland," and the furious pace set by Headon and Simonon primed an already enthusiastic audience to demand an encore.

"It was loud, it was percussive, but it was well-balanced, too," Piasek told me. "The Clash pushed things over the edge, and pulled things back. It was a tight group . . . More often than not, you saw a lot of the punk bands back then, and they were about as sloppy as sloppy could be. But The Clash were not sloppy." Piasek, too, noted that his fellow fans were not merely attending another concert. "These people were *of the show*, they *were* the show . . . it had that kind of feel. The fans were a community. They were participants in the show." Griffin counted herself among the participants. "I had been on the air a little while, and I had gotten to know my listeners, and I knew all the people who ran the clubs, and the people who ran the cool magazines: *Soho Weekly News*, *Trouser Press*, *Creem*," Griffin recalled. Many of them attended each of The Clash shows that year. "As you looked around the room you knew were going to know most of the people there," Griffin told me. "We were bound together by an appreciation for this rebellion." Still, Piasek rued, "There were a lot of drugs involved through these years. That was the tapestry behind all this music." With the drugs, of course, came casualties. At a holiday party at Bob Gruen's West Village studio, in 1996, Valentine met up with Childers for the first time in years. "Sadly, as we spoke, we realized that a lot of the people we knew from back then were dead," Valentine recalled. "At one point we even tried to count them, but then stopped . . . it was too morbid."[16]

For this show, by choice or necessity, The Clash gave themselves permission to work things out on stage, to reach beyond their grasp to perform songs from *London Calling*, including tunes which they had yet to master. By 1981, when The Clash returned to New York for their spring residency at Bond International Casino, this would no longer be the case.

THE SECRET IN THIS SECRET HISTORY

For the cover of *London Calling*, Strummer selected a photo from Smith's contact sheets, and Ray Lowry's design mimicked the layout of Elvis Presley's debut album. Gruen, a long-time friend of Smith, regarded the photo with affection: "I wish I had taken it. It's a great picture." For Griffin, who played a key role in the good-spirited rivalry of the punk scenes in London and New York, the photo registered personally. "It was cool," she said, "that that was a New York shot."

Simonon's recollection focused on the feedback offered by the New York audience. At the Palladium, the press occupied the orchestra pit, as a rule, and thereby served as a buffer between the band and the audience—which, at most Clash gigs, pressed up against the stage. "The Palladium had fixed seating, so the audience was frozen in place," Simonon said. "We weren't getting any response from them, no matter what we did. I'm generally good-natured, but I do bottle things up and then I'm like a light switch, off and on, and it can be quite scary, even for me, when I switch, because it's very sudden."[17]

A key question emerged in my review of the antecedent conditions of that historic night: did the biographers of The Clash have the right date? Given the available information, is it possible that Simonon's outburst—and Smith's brilliant photograph—took place on September 20? Smith indicated that her categorization of proof sheets and images was by tour and year only, as she was not called upon to identify particular images by date. (Most images provided the necessary clues to identify location.) The dating, in this case, was delegated to Strummer, who first saw the proof sheet in mid-October and then provided the date for the photo's caption in Smith's gorgeous and brilliant *The Clash: Before and After* (1980). When asked, Smith replied, "If Joe's dated it in my book, then Joe's right." Once that date emerged from the ranks of The Clash, no one bothered to cross-check it. Eyewitness accounts are helpful to get the conversation started, but as Smith told me, "All I know is that if the amount of people who've written they were there on that night were there, then all of America was there." In the intervening years, then, has the ubiquity of Smith's image led an inordinate number of Clash fans to believe they witnessed Simonon's sacrifice to the rock gods? It's possible, I suggest, that previous Clash chroniclers have unwittingly embraced the adage offered by Maxwell Scott in *The Man Who Shot Liberty Valance*: "This is the West, sir. When the legend becomes fact, print the legend."

That possibility deserves consideration, if simply to add another playful topic to the mix for the nutters and fanatics. The pertinent elements include, to begin, the non-musical segments from the WNEW broadcast, which were excluded from the *Guns of Brixton* bootleg. These tracks include Richard Neer's pre-concert commentary during the playing of Sinatra's "High Hopes," the interlude ahead of the encore and, after the encore, his conversation with Pam Merly. Second, Strummer's memory for iconic events in Clash history was not foolproof. For a March 1979 issue of *NME*, Strummer's diary included his report of the band walking out of a photo opportunity with Epic brass in Los Angeles. Their protest actually took place in Berkeley, after their American debut, two nights before.[18]

Third, while Simonon's rationale for his outburst has varied over time, he reprised most frequently the theme of insufficient audience response. Their response, of course, hinged on a number of factors, including the enthusiasm generated by the band, and the proximity of the audience to the stage. On September 20, Strummer himself was off-kilter, according to Ray Lowry. "Joe was having a bad day," he recalled. "I remember he got really uptight and hurled an ashtray across the dressing room for some reason." Critics sensed the angst, concluded that The Clash (and the opening acts) sounded flat on the first night, and rebounded triumphantly on the second night. In subsequent interviews, Simonon highlighted the problem of separating the real fans from the stage by an orchestra pit full of press, and affirmed the band's commitment to having fans up against the stage. During a two-night residency, such problems could be fixed. "If we had two nights somewhere, and there was a problem, we'd fix it," according to The Baker. "We would have gone in the second day and said, 'Now listen: we ain't havin' all these fuckin' press people up against the stage. We want the audience.' We wouldn't have done two shows and put up with it. There's no way."

The bootleg itself testifies to the band's prowess on September 21, and video clips from that night show fans pressed right up against the stage. The missing tracks from the *Guns of Brixton* bootleg indicate that neither Neer nor Merly sensed that anything was amiss, either. The audio recording of their eyewitness account is the most reliable source in general, and about the fans' enthusiasm and their proximity to the stage in particular. Prior to the encore, Neer regarded the event with sober senses, and registered for at-home listeners the impact of the band on the audience: "The people are just *totally enveloped* in the music. I would say the entire orchestra section here—which is a good part of the whole house—they're all on their feet. They're dancing, they're jumping up and down and they are just totally into it! It's almost a hypnotic influence that the band has over the audience." With Griffin's defection to 'PIX, Neer took the assignment, even though he was not a Clash devotee. At the conclusion of the encore, Merly joined Neer at the microphone and, while they looked out onto the recently abandoned stage, neither mentioned anything as extraordinary as Simonon going momentarily mental.

Two more bits of evidence counter the photo's dating as September 21. First, as you can see on the cover of this book, a squat bouncer crosses downstage right to upstage right, in pursuit of an unruly female fan. Jones, alertly, stepped in and whisked her off to safety. In turn, it seems, Jones scarcely had time to lean into Neer's microphone to curse "Bollocks, you cunt!"—which he did on September 21, and elicited an uncomfortable laugh from Neer. To the radio audience, Neer says, "All right, you heard 'em go by." On the night of the broadcast, Jones and at least one of his bandmates exited stage right casually, past the set-up of the on-air host, with a dollop of punk agitation—perhaps the vision of the irate bouncer, from the night before, was still on Jones's mind.[19]

One last feature of the two-night residency at the Palladium is germane. Given the stage set-up, it's likely that very few people in the audience would have witnessed Simonon's outburst. Even in theaters the size of the Palladium, Green and Baker took efforts to reproduce the stage constraints of a club, by use of the curtains downstage, the location of the amp stacks, and the position of the drum kit at center-to-downstage-center, in order to keep the gang in close proximity. Smith, alongside Baker, reported how Simonon was but a few feet away at the time of the outburst, and Baker indicated that Simonon gave the offending bass a couple more thwacks:

> I was in my customary position at stage-left, standing right next to Pennie Smith, ready to go onstage as the band departed. . . . I certainly didn't see it coming. Paul looked pissed-off during the show but that wasn't out-of-the-ordinary as his usual look was pissed-off. It all happened in seconds . . . He just smashed it, and swung it over his head . . . two, three, four times, and

then he just walked off. The bass was in little bits. He just left
it there.

Simonon's *pas de un* was over and done in fifteen seconds and, with the narrow-ing of the stage, back to front, and side to side, was likely witnessed only by the fans with seats near upstage right, and a few on the second and third levels. The shadow cast by the left curtain extends from well-behind Simonon's right foot and, in turn, obscures the view for concert-goers in the middle and right side of the theater. Serendipity, it seems, led Simonon to be back lit for this moment of sublime brutality. Clash fan Kevin O'Marra reported, "I saw the Palladium show on the 20th. THAT is the night Paul broke his bass. . . . You can hear them walking off the stage [on September 21] and the announcer makes no mention of Paul breaking anything. A lot of people probably didn't see him break it because he was heading off stage. Me in the upper level cheap seats saw all."[20]

Other fans have shared similar testimonies, as has Clash biographer Marcus Gray, albeit indirectly, in his exhaustive survey of all things related to *London Calling*: "Strangely, in spite of the spotlight, [Paul's outburst] seems to have passed unnoticed or at least unremarked by all the other writers, too, and no photographers other than Pennie Smith appear to have recorded it visually." The contradictory testimony attests to the power of Smith's iconic image, and the fal-libility of human memory. Given the stage set-up, the position of the curtain, and Simonon's proximity to the left stage wing, it is likely that only a couple hundred spectators had the proper sightlines and were looking in Simonon's direction for his fifteen seconds of Fender-smashing fame.[21]

Whether there was, indeed, a night that separated *Simonon terrible* and the WNEW broadcast, the two sold-out shows at the Palladium in September 1979 represented an historic shift from the domination of disco and dinosaur rock. A week later, Joe Jackson headlined at the Palladium and, a few weeks after that, so did The Police. By fall 1979, New York was awash in new wave from the UK.

GET THE BALANCE RIGHT

The iconic qualities of Simonon's coda at the Palladium, and its celebration on the *London Calling* cover, also represent The Clash's reflexive engagement with the contradiction of art, politics, and commerce. "When all's said and done about the songs and the lyrics," Strummer said, "I always think of Paul Simonon smashing that thing around. And that says it all: I'd like to think The Clash were revolutionaries, but we loved a bit of posing as well." The Clash struck intricate poses, onstage and off, but rarely—if ever—did those poses contradict Strummer's early proclamation about their politics: "We're anti-fascist, we're anti-violence, we're anti-racist and we're pro-creative. We're against ignorance." The Clash and their associates also maintained a commitment to having a laugh. Epic's Beck and McCarrell reported how, on behalf of The Clash, Kosmo Vinyl fought tooth-and-nail with tongue-in-cheek. "When we came up with the phrase, 'The Only Band That Matters,' [Rhodes and Vinyl] literally came in the office and protested it," Beck told me. "'That's horrible!' they'd say, and they'd be bursting with laughter." Their laughter arose from the gap between the fantasy of the authenticity police and the aims of The Clash, which Strummer articulated prior to their first passage across the Atlantic: "We've got loads of contradictions for you . . . we're trying to do something new; we're trying to be the greatest group in the world, and that also means the biggest. At the same time, we're trying to be radical—I mean, we never want to be really respectable—and maybe the two can't coexist, but we'll try."[22]

In the ensuing years, the staff at Epic came to understand and respect The Clash's reflexive engagement with these contradictions. As radio expanded its sonic palette, and The Clash continued to shift musical directions, the moment ripened for airwave domination. After the release of *London Calling*, McCarrell told Vinyl, "Look, if we do this right, we can sell millions of records here. Are you guys okay with that?" Vinyl smiled and replied, "Yes. Yes we are."[23]

London Calling was released in the UK in December 1979, and in the United States the following month. If *Rope* was, as *Creem's* Dave DiMartino surmised, "the carefully measured, laboriously drawn-out Pearlman affair," *London Calling* represented a burst of freedom from their estrangement. For the March issue of *Trouser Press*, Chris Salewicz penned an affirmative profile of more than three thousand words, hoping plainly that *London Calling* would become "the definitive '70s rock'n'roll record, an ironic antidote to Me Generation selfishness and self-defeatism." Between the bookends of the anthemic titular single, and the pop-radio-friendly "Train in Vain," the *Village Voice's* John Piccarella savored The Clash's facility with the three "r's": rockabilly, rhythm and blues, and reggae, especially. Four months after the U.S. release of *London Calling*, *Rolling Stone*

Backstage at the Palladium, Mick takes pause with the pause
that refreshes (© Joe Streno, go2jo.com).

obliged once again. In a lengthy review essay for the April 3 issue, Tom Carson described the album as "spacious and extravagant," relished the historical grandeur of "Spanish Bombs," and celebrated the stubborn spirit rising in the coda of "Death or Glory." For the *Soho Weekly*, Bangs offered tempered enthusiasm, professing that he missed "the edge, the snarl, the unremitting tension" of earlier LPs. Still, Bangs reckoned, "There's an ease and a rightness about them that's as gratifying as the Stones of *Beggars Banquet*, and probably a good deal more straight-on."[24]

All four sides of *Calling* resonate with ease and rightness. It's gritty where it should be, and gorgeous everywhere else. It's a reckoning with the world of rock'n'roll, a negation of the narrow codes of punk, and a tribute to what The Clash achieved in Vanilla Studios, with the help of The Baker and Johnny Green, Gallagher and the horn players—and, for a little while, minimal interference from anyone else. Jones bore responsibility for sequencing the album and did a brilliant job. If the antics of "rock'n'roll Mick" would grow tiresome, even loathsome, in the next few years, his understanding of how to sequence an album reflected his diligent study of exemplary rock LPs. He also understood the pop aesthetic of the fade-out at the cadence, which he and Price employed on thirteen of the nineteen tracks on *London Calling*.

In the paragraphs that follow, I imagine *London Calling* as a cinematic montage, and The Clash as a single, peripatetic protagonist, wandering the avenues and alleys of London and New York, picking up stories and sounds in *al fresco* cafés, in movies in Times Square, and behind barricades in Brixton. My aim here is not to claim *London Calling* as a concept album, but to take stock of the aesthetic impact of the rarest of things: a triumphant double album.[25]

Side one commences, of course, with the opening bars of "London Calling," which are straight-on indeed. Our protagonist stands by the river, wondering aloud, plaintively, about the fate of this great city—of all cities everywhere—should nuclear errors persist. The anthem commences with Strummer's downstrokes and, for the moment, Headon's kit remains deep in the mix. Simonon joins in with the haunting bass refrain, and now Headon's drums charge to the foreground, marching the band to the opening verse. The amber waves of grain are desiccated, and meltdown awaits. The upshot? There's no more Beatlemania in the form of The Jam—cheer up, kids! Strummer sustains a hot vocal urgency from beginning to end, while the warm vocals of Jones and Simonon offer a reassuring sense of calm—a contrast reprised to great effect for the next hour. At the coda, the ease of the fade-out is betrayed by the warning transmission of Morse code, tapped out by Jones on his guitar, over Strummer's receding confession.[26]

Around the corner, our protagonist encounters a lovers' quarrel. The woman sits behind the wheel of a shiny, well-chromed gas guzzler, and her ex-lover is awestruck. But is it the presence of the Cadillac, or the loss of his woman, that he finds most vexing? Here The Clash break the rules once again, and include on track two their homage to Vince Taylor, a late-1950s rock'n'roller and the subject of the imaginative bio-LP *Ziggy Stardust*. (After 1965, covers rarely appeared earlier than track four on canonical LPs.)

Side one closes with tales of temptation and addiction. The Baker's glorious whistling opens "Jimmy Jazz," and introduces the thick arm of the law to the narrative. The action begins at the outdoor seating of a café, and the police approach the owner, who turns coy trickster, within earshot of our protagonist. "Jimmy? Here? He was, but not now." Strummer's slurred lyrics, over musical accompaniment with R&B horns and a relaxed reggae tempo, provides a hint for American listeners, who may have relied upon monikers other than "jazz" for marijuana.[27] "Jazz's" moderate rhythmic complexity serves as a nice bridge to the uptempo desperation of "Hateful," in which our protagonist wanders into Brighton's Powis Square, and turns a keen eye on a junkie he once knew, now bereft of mates and his memory. The following morning, on London's East End, he raises the prospects of lager as the breakfast of champions and, if there's no work to be had on Maggie Thatcher's Farm, the rude boys are, set to rights, doomed to fail. In its vinyl form, it's a triumphant end to side one, with Jones and Strummer barging in on one another mid-stanza, in chorus and verse—a feature well-reprised on a handful of songs that remain, and on "Spanish Bombs" in particular.

On side two, our protagonist finds himself in midtown Manhattan and stops for coffee to catch up on his reading. He tarries in a bilingual daydream about anarchists' fantasies in "Spanish Bombs." Upon leaving the café, he crosses 42nd Street and spies pimps and hustlers working the beat beneath the Mayfair marquee, where the films of Montgomery Clift, the drinking-and-driving anti-hero of "The Right Profile," once played. Our protagonist hits the shops on Broadway, but neither discotheque albums nor alcohol provides little more than fleeting satisfaction ("Lost in the Supermarket"). Back in Brixton, he encounters a band of young men who solicit his counsel. "Don't believe!" he shouts. "Refuse the clampdown! They're not after your money. They'll take much more than that!" He moves along, chin low against the wind, and notices the fraying hem in his navy pants, and the scuff atop his chestnut boots. That night, somebody's been murdered, and now it's rebels galore, awash in firearms, dreaming of death and glory, with fingers on the triggers of the "Guns of Brixton."

For side three, in Greenwich Village, our protagonist decides he needs a larger audience, and takes to a ramshackle stage at Washington Square Park. To bolster his faith in nearly clean living, he offers a rousing cover of Clive Alphonso's "Wrong 'Em Boyo." On vinyl, Jones and Simonon offer backing vocals at seemingly random intervals, and evoke—in its absence—the repressive order of the *Rope* sessions. The joy and ease of the vocal accents, along with the riff-heavy refrain of the horn section, confirms their facility with the musical codes of reggae. The urgency becomes palpable, and the stage becomes a soap box. In the rousing "Death or Glory," the options appear to our aging protagonist as neither palatable nor possible, and our hero extends compassion to the tattooed-knuck-led punk trying to get his baffled kids to understand . . . what exactly? He wishes he knew.

In "Koka Kola," our protagonist returns to the street, checking out the billboards along Madison Avenue, wondering about the world of the ad man, and whether it's life or death that goes better with coke. In the grooves, Headon keeps a resolute tempo, Simonon turns in some lovely bass figures, and the whole thing speeds by in under two minutes. Around the inarticulate message of "Lover's Rock," our protagonist returns to the Odeon in Times Square for a double feature of *The Cincinnati Kid*, an über-cool card sharp played by Steve McQueen ("The Card Cheat"), and *The Four Horsemen of the Apocalypse*, starring Rita-Hayworth-favorite Glenn Ford ("Four Horsemen").

As the credits roll, he leaves inspired, cocky even, and returns to Washington Square Park. Back on the bandstand, he affirms his tenacity with the hard-charging "I'm Not Down," and wraps things up with the more conciliatory "Revolution Rock." His between-verse patter indicates his need to keep his sights modest, to take any gig he can get, and to play in whatever musical style the host demands. And that is nearly how the montage concludes—from nuclear melt-down to the exigencies of the market, from the band's last gesture as a punk rock group, to their steady hands as reggae stylists, and the territory covered over the first eighteen tracks is vast and deep, black and white, and open to possibility. Our protagonist knows, though, for a kid raised in Wilmcote House, there are few options more alluring than singing for a rock'n'roll band. So he packs up his guitar, heads north on 5th Avenue, veers left onto Broadway, through Times Square, and into the Brill Building, with a one-song tape in hand, praying his efforts won't end in vain.

In the analog era, rock'n'roll was effectively urban in character, and punk and post-punk were no different. *The Ramones* and *Never Mind the Bollocks* evoke New York and London in all their grime and clamor, and reflect a metropolitan aesthetic. The musicianship and aspirations of The Clash eclipsed those of their rival quartets and, with *London Calling*, produced the first cosmopolitan album of popular music. On *Calling*, The Clash demonstrated their facility with garage-punk ("London Calling"), art-punk ("Spanish Bombs," "Right Profile"), and pop-punk ("Lost in the Supermarket," "Train in Vain"), as well as rockabilly, reggae, and rhythm and blues. Their rejection in 1977 of Elvis, The Beatles, and the Stones, led them away from the blues, and deep into the expansive sonic palette of Black Britain. With *Calling*, and with *Sandinista!*, too, they remodeled The Who's maxim of "Maximum R&B" into The Clash's "Maximum Rock Steady"—which proved convincing to fans, critics, and musicians alike. When The Clash returned to the states, and stopped in Detroit in March 1980 to headline a benefit concert for Jackie Wilson, Bootsy Collins himself—veteran bassist for James Brown and George Clinton—reported listening to "Train in Vain" every day. On their 1981 return to New York City, black radio stations had the hip-hop track "Magnificent Seven" in heavy rotation.[28]

The retail price for *London Calling* was as righteous as its sound, for The Clash insisted that CBS sell *London Calling* for the price of a single album. In turn, musical and economic forces make it difficult for any fan to select *Rope* as their favorite Clash LP. Still, *Rope* was certainly The Clash's most important album in terms of their musical development. Simonon assumed a new diligence in his mastery of technique, and reaped special dividends with his vigorous time-keeping for "Last Gang in Town" and, eventually, on a dozen tracks of *London Calling*.[29] Likewise, the Pearlman effect bolstered Jones's capacities as a producer's apprentice. For the mixing of *Rope* at the Automatt, in San Francisco, Jones forsook his fondness for marijuana, and paid rapt attention to Pearlman's practicum in audio engineering. "He was hanging over Sandy's shoulder the whole time," Simonon recalled. In turn, Jones was able to step in, as needed, during the engineering and mixing of *London Calling*. Disdain for Pearlman's heavy-handed production technique only emerged later among American rock critics, and it shaped their assessment of The Clash's position in the rock canon. In *Rolling Stone*'s commemoration, in 1987, of the best one hundred albums of the past twenty years, their critics selected only *The Clash* (number twenty-three) and *London Calling* (number fourteen).[30]

7.
Clash in Hitsville / WPIX's Train in Vain

At the Palladium once again, on March 7, 1980, The Clash distanced themselves from the sonic tenets of punk and still delivered a torrent of energy—and the crowd reciprocated in kind. *New York Rocker* noted how The Clash "no longer raced against each other; their sound cohered and connected . . . they were now more of a regular rock'n'roll band (albeit a great one) than they'd ever been before." The politics of The Clash that galvanized fans and journalists alike were, at this point, more subtly manifest in their musical choices. The Clash's decision to select supporting acts such as Bo Diddley, Sam & Dave, Mikey Dread, and Lee Dorsey, as well as the performers featured during the Bond's residency—Grandmaster Flash, The Sugarhill Gang, and Lee Perry, to begin—challenged their audiences to recognize the tangled, racial roots of popular music. The reggae tunes on *London Calling*, including "Wrong 'Em Boyo," by Clive Alphonso, and "Revolution Rock," by Jackie Edwards and Danny Ray, constituted acts of egalitarian prescience. In the 1980s, skinhead factions embraced the sentiments of the National Front, and took perverse delight in the anti-Semitic, anti-immigrant, pro-hooligan songs of Skrewdriver, Skullhead, and RaHoWa—short for Racial Holy War.[1]

With The Clash in ascendance, WPIX entered its twilight. In a February issue of *New York* magazine, Frank Rose's feature on WPIX focused on Piasek and Griffin and noted how, by the summer of 1979, "These two had created the only hip radio station in New York." Hipness depended, according to Rose, upon the exclusion of "disco and the soulless corporate rock that had turned AOR [album-oriented radio] into a teenage wasteland." "London Calling," the single, was in heavy rotation, as were tracks by Tom Petty and Joan Armatrading. That same week, *London Calling* was singled out for distinction as the "album-PIX" by Griffin herself. In the photo accompanying the article, a smiling Piasek rests his chin gently atop the crown of Griffin's Dorothy Hamill wedge. Griffin's eyes sparkle just beneath her bangs.[2]

Ray Yorke, the new general manager at WPIX, had arrived in December from a disco station in Washington, DC. Arbitron figures from October and November indicated that WPIX's audience share of 1.2 trailed WNEW, at 2.7, and WPLJ, at 3.2, which allowed the latter to charge their advertisers more per minute of air time. To improve ratings and revenue, Yorke decided WPIX needed musical and sartorial discipline. AOR standards such as Queen and Pink Floyd joined XTC and The Specials on the station's top-twelve lists, and Yorke ordered Piasek to institute an office-attire dress code. Piasek replied, "That'll be fine, if it goes along with a raise for the entire staff." The allure of working for WPIX included the occasional promotional record for home use, as well as an unlimited supply of T-shirts. "Nobody's dirty. It doesn't smell," Piasek told me, laughing. "These are T-shirts of their culture, and we are representatives of the culture. He did not get it entirely."[3]

Another lesson missed by Yorke was the one Karmazin had offered, while at WNEW, to a disheartened Dave Herman, who was ruing another ratings loss to WPLJ. Karmazin steered Herman's attention to the financial ledgers and the steady growth in revenue. "These are the only numbers that count," he assured Herman. "The hell with Arbitron ratings." Vince Cremona, the managing director at WPIX, reported in December that losses over the previous two years were at an end. Cremona was unable to confirm the December figures, though. By the time they were tallied, he had been transferred to the company's station in Bridgeport, Connecticut. A reporter for the *Voice* expected the worst, fearing featured artists such as Chuck Berry, Lena Lovich, and The Clash could give way to ELO and Linda Ronstadt.[4]

By the first week of March, the "Elvis to Elvis" experiment was over. Piasek was pushed out of his position, and then out of the building, by Yorke. While collecting his interview tapes, deejay Dan Neer ran into Yorke and was fired, on the spot, for thievery. By week's end, the guards received photographs of Neer and fellow deejay Rick Allison marked "Do Not Admit": at the time, both men were still awaiting written notice of their dismissals. Neer told Will Keller, who is compiling an oral history of the Elvis-to-Elvis experiment at WPIX, "That was

Simonon to Headon: "Feck off! Play the tempo!" On occasion, Headon
would play songs at double time, simply to get a rise out of Simonon.
At the Palladium, March 1980 (© Joe Streno, go2jo.com).

my first experience with the reality of radio. Before that, it was like a dream . . . everyone who was there at that time understood that we were involved in something special."

Once again, local music journalists expressed solidarity with their allies on the airwaves. A reporter in the *Village Voice* lamented, "WPIX-FM's distinctive rock & roll format didn't disappear last week so much as fade away; it was like watching a friend turn into a zombie." By March 7, when The Clash returned to town, WPIX had been scrubbed free of Clash tunes, replaced by Paul Simon, James Taylor, and Yes. The top-twelve playlist originally slated for the first week of March included The Specials' "Message to You, Rudy," The Ramones' "Rock'n'roll Radio," and The Clash's "Train in Vain." Within four weeks, the album pick-of-the-week went from *London Calling* to Linda Ronstadt's *Mad Love*. Hamburger survived the purge, but quit by telegram days later in order to join her friends and The Clash at the Palladium. The shout-out offered by DJ Scratchy during the evening's prelude to The Clash—"We've lost PIX, now let's get something even better!"—offered Hamburger and her comrades a measure of fleeting solace.[5]

Griffin returned to WNEW a few months later, and began hosting the Prisoners of Rock'n'roll Show at the Bottom Line, which helped break The Bongos, The dB's, and The Smithereens. Richard Neer became the program director in 1981, knowing full well that the management of WNEW, one of the final holdouts of free-form in commercial radio, was serious about a boost in the ratings. To that end, Neer established a new rack, which held sixteen singles designated for heavy rotation. Deejays were instructed to play their choice of two of these songs every hour, move the played songs to the rear of the rack and, in turn, make certain nearly every track aired three times daily.[6]

Coincidentally, WNEW management hired a consultant to help the transition to a more disciplined structure. The consultant encouraged the staff to prepare for shows, to treat each minute on the microphone deliberately, and to stop treating improvisation as a sacrosanct form of artistic expression. Some deejays understood the exigency of the market; others, Griffin and Merly among them, did not. (Merly had joined WNEW shortly after Griffin's departure for WPIX.) "I was listening to Vinny Scelsa, and Vinny [pause] Vinny was my hero," Merly reminisced. One evening, "The studio door opened, Vinny's head pops in, and he looked at me and said, 'Hmm. I detect a kindred spirit.' I just smiled. That made me feel like a million bucks." To earn the kudos of the figure she considered the black sheep of the station, Merly figured she must be doing something righteous. Following Griffin's return to WNEW, she and Merly, along with Scelsa and Morrera, were now allies, employing their collective, optimistic will against the tight formats established at competing radio stations.

"To think that I was going to be able to stop this rolling radio machine, which was already on its way to 'Hitsville,'" Merly told me, and then paused, and left her sentence unfinished. As she spoke, Merly became agitated, thinking about the stakes of those days. "It felt so important to try to stop it," she said, "and yet it was out of control." Likewise, in my interview with Griffin, the timbre of her voice and the cadence of her speech resonated with an urgency largely absent from her Sirius XM shows, "Deep Tracks," "Classic Vinyl," and "The Loft," especially, for which she featured musicians more closely associated with roots music than riotous desire.

When Tom Donahue left San Francisco's KMPX in 1968, and his staff walked out in solidarity, Metromedia sided with the free-form advocates, by switching the format of nearby KSAN from classical music to free-form, and hiring Donahue and his honorable free-form bandits. Ten years later, Metromedia turned against the free-form veterans at KSAN, and began close monitoring of increasingly strict playlists. Richard Gossett defied the edict, allegedly played The Clash's "Complete Control," and was subsequently fired. (After a short stint at KQAK, Gossett left radio and, in 2008, he retired as the Senior Brewmeister of Anchor Brewing Company.) In November 1980, KSAN switched to a country music format.[7]

In the meantime, The Clash were gathering momentum along the route to "Hitsville USA." In December 1980, the band released *Sandinista!*, a triple album of dub, ska, and, according to Christgau, a few "discursive moments." Among these moments were enough gems to inspire Beck and Bob Feineigle, Epic's director of national album promotion, to use a Clash-inspired ploy to get The Clash more airplay. Beck and Feineigle wanted to send the disc to (black) urban radio, which, Beck told me, "would cost us $2,000, $3,000 to manufacture and mail, and we knew nobody would play it." Still, he figured, program directors in urban radio who received the disc might be impressed. "They would say, 'Hey, I can't play that, but that was pretty cool,' and word would get around, and it would just be one of those things floating in the air." Feineigle pitched the idea to T.C. Thompkins, director of regional promotion, and the gatekeeper for Epic releases sent to urban radio. Thompkins declined Feineigle's offer. "Bob came back to my office, and he was pissed," Beck recalled. In the quiet confines of Beck's office, Beck asked Feineigle, "Bob, do you hear that fly? That fly that's buzzing around here?" Feineigle said, "What fly?" and Beck slammed his open palm down upon his desk. "The one I just killed that left a spot on the paperwork," Beck replied. Feineigle checked the approval box himself, submitted it for processing, and Clash vinyl was sent off to urban radio.

When The Clash returned to New York City in May 1981, for a three-week residency at Bond International Casino in Times Square, a new New York demographic had become smitten with The Clash. "These guys were at the peak of their game, man," recalled Don Letts, documentarian, deejay and, with Mick Jones, an original member of Big Audio Dynamite. "They basically ran New York for the few weeks they were playing there. There was this amazing cultural exchange going on. I can't tell you what a buzz it was. WBLS, a totally black station, started playing 'The Magnificent Seven' on heavy rotation," Letts recalled. "That was the soundtrack of the city for the whole period that the Clash were there, and beyond."[8]

The promoters oversold the Bond shows by double and, on May 30, following the cancellation of the matinee show by the New York City Building Department, fans denied entrance rioted in the streets. To honor all the tickets sold, The Clash extended their residency to play seventeen shows in three weeks and, by all accounts, performed brilliantly. The *Trick or Treat* bootleg from the June 9 show reveals a band at the height of their prowess, clanging brilliantly from rock anthem to rock steady, with segues tightly bound by sustained reverb from Jones's guitar. In short supply, though, were Strummer's between-song improvisations and the opportunities for serendipity. MTV debuted that August and, in 1982, *Combat Rock* reached number twenty on the *Billboard* LP charts. Upon their return to New York City, The Clash opened for The Who at Shea Stadium.[9]

★ EXTRA ★

SOLD OUT!

THE CLASH
BOND'S INTERNATIONAL CASINO
TIMES SQUARE -- NEW YORK CITY
MAY 28 -- JUNE 3 1981

The Clash sell out, and then sell out again, for seventeen shows at Bond.

Afterword:
All That Is Solid Melts into Air

Long after those brilliant nights at the Palladium, rock and radio and the written word have shape-shifted again and again. The effervescence of analog radio, in which the joy of listening was a serendipitous, real-time affair, shared with friends in the car and elsewhere, has largely been lost. In its place we have the immediate gratification—often enjoyed in personal isolation—provided by hard drives, allegedly smart phones, and "the cloud." With the archive fever of the digital music age, radio transmissions can be stockpiled and subject to immediate retrieval. For the BBC, from 1999 to 2002, Strummer rotated discs from Big Youth, The Beach Boys, and Billie Holiday on his "London Calling" radio show, and episodes were made available for free, in perpetuity, on iTunes. All that glitters in the past, though, is not gold. As Edward Gibbon has written, "There exists in human nature a strong propensity to depreciate the advantages, and to magnify the evils, of the present times." I am certainly grateful for the instantaneity of iTunes and YouTube, and for access to Joe Strummer's last gig as a composer.[1]

Still, the differences between the analog and digital eras are stark, for musicians, deejays, and listeners alike, and merit due consideration. This consideration reviews how key players in the analog era maintained analogous positions in the digital era. Likewise, it explores the shared experience of free-form deejays and utopian artisans of an earlier era in their resistance against workplace rationalization—as well as the deployment of music in artisanal acts of refusal. The coda surveys the impact of digital recording and playback technologies upon how we listen, how we write, and how we read.

YESTERDAY AND TODAY

In just a few years, The Clash and the dozens of new wave and post-punk bands that emerged in their wake jumped from playing Palladium-sized theaters to the bills of some of the largest music festivals this side of the pond. Less than four years after *London Calling*, which yielded one hit single ("Train in Vain," #23 U.S.), The Clash headlined New Wave Day at the May 1983 US Festival, which attracted fans by the hundreds of thousands. Four months later, The Police shared the bill with The Thompson Twins, Oingo Boingo, Madness, and The Fixx at the Day on the Green, at the Oakland Coliseum, to an enthused audience nearly sixty thousand strong.[2]

Following the dismissals of Headon in 1982, and Jones in 1983, The Clash disbanded in 1985. Jones's subsequent projects included Big Audio Dynamite and, with former bandmate Tony James, Carbon/Silicon. Strummer found success years later with The Mescaleros and, in 2002, died unexpectedly of a congenital heart defect. One of Strummer's final gigs was a benefit for striking firefighters, at which Jones leapt onstage for the encore. With a nod to Strummer's adoration of America, a mourner graced his coffin with a Stetson hat. With a nod to his enduring sense of humor, another mourner affixed two stickers to his coffin lid: "Vinyl Rules" and "Question Authority: Ask Me Anything." In 2004, The Clash were inducted into the Rock and Roll Hall of Fame. Simonon returned to painting, and his work has been featured at the Thomas Williams Fine Art Gallery in London. After a drawn-out battle with heroin addiction, Headon started drumming once again, appearing onstage with Carbon/Silicon.[3]

With the advent of satellite radio, free-form fans could find their favorite music in heavy rotation, with their favorite deejays and musicians providing the playlists, under the command once again of Mel Karmazin. Veterans of WNEW, including Scelsa and Griffin, as well as David Johansen and Lou Reed (rest in peace), have hosted shows on Sirius XM's "The Loft." Dan Neer and Merly, as well as WLIR veterans Earle Bailey and Joe Bonadonna, shared the schedule with Tom Petty and Bob Dylan on "Deep Tracks." The commercial-free format of satellite radio, and its effort to construct narrow and deep audience segments, coincided closely with the vision of radio imagined by the FM renegades. With reference to her shows on WNEW and "The Loft," Griffin said, "I would prefer to have an audience that wasn't so gigantic, but one that is loyal, rather than try to please everybody and turn it into pabulum. Then people don't really have it on for loyalty, they have it on for wallpaper. I like people to really listen."[4]

Following his departure from WNEW, Karmazin took positions at Infinity, CBS, and Viacom, and became the most powerful executive in radio. In 2013, as the CEO of Sirius XM, Karmazin faced the difficulty of finding a loyal, listening audience willing to pay for commercial-free radio (and other products) in abundance. The present abundance in satellite radio may shrink considerably, though, if the satellite options for Sirius XM television are expanded in order to raise revenue.

Between the last trading days of 2006 and 2008, respectively, Sirius XM common stock lost 97 percent of its value (falling from $3.54 to $0.12). In December 2012, Standard & Poor's raised the corporate credit rating for Sirius XM from B to BB. The next December, Sirius XM common stock was valued once again at $3.49 per share, but concerns remained about the company's long-term debt problem ($3 billion)—and, as was the case with free-form radio, no silver-bullet solution for the financial health of Sirius XM Radio appears forthcoming.[5]

CAPITAL AND CULTURE

If the era of free-form radio represents a distinctive chapter in the history of popular music, the resistance of artisans to the automation of their craft has a rich and often tragic history. Merly, Griffin, and Piasek, to begin, occupied the last frontier of the analog music era and, when management sought to rationalize the labor process, they balked. In order to understand the principles informing the last stand of the free-form aficionados at WNEW and WPIX, it's necessary to review the culture and convictions of artisans of an earlier era.

In *The Making of the English Working Class*, E.P. Thompson offers a sympathetic reconsideration of the agency of working people in the forging of history. To that end, he seeks to rescue the "utopian artisan [from] the enormous condescension of posterity." The historical accounts of the victors set the terms of condescension: the aspirations of the triumphant are deemed normal, natural, and inevitable, while "the blind alleys, the lost causes, and the losers themselves are forgotten." These causes often took shape in different customs, including the custom of "rough music."[6]

Since the seventeenth century, rough music in England assumed various forms, and included an amalgam of the following elements: a "rude cacophony" of "satiric noise," characterized by "mockery or hostility," in a ritual "attenuated to a few scraps of doggerel." With stones in a tin kettle, or cleavers, tongs, and tambourines, the performers directed an ear-splitting clamor toward a philanderer, a cuckold, or even the King's ministers. The latter bore witness to the performance of fisherman John Hart, who in 1724 came accompanied by "two hundred others of equal infamy," and "made signs with his hands intimating that [the ministers] might kiss his Arse."[7]

For Thompson, Hart's invitation and its musical accompaniment were offered in defense of customs and moral codes under assault by the crown, captains of industry, or both. From bread riots to workplace sabotage, blacksmiths, ploughmen, and their sisters and wives, especially, resisted the efforts of kings and capital to tighten social and workplace control, through taxes and time-discipline.

The punk era revived this long-dormant musical tradition. The Clash and the Pistols issued clamorous edicts of mockery ("Garageland" and "God Save the Queen"), satire ("Tommy Gun" and "Holidays in the Sun"), and slightly tempered hostility ("Guns on the Roof" and "EMI"). The accompanying doggerel ranged, of course, from rabble-rousing to the Rabelaisian.

By pedantry or happenstance, the utopian spirit of punk lovingly channeled the first principle of the Situationist International: "Be reasonable, demand the impossible." The sound and the DIY spirit of The Clash and the Pistols inspired dozens of listeners to create their own bands, write about these bands, and get these bands on the radio. Let us remember the deejays at WNEW and WPIX (and elsewhere) as utopian artisans of the late twentieth century. For Merly and Griffin, especially, their resistance to the rack emerged as a matter of principle, not remuneration, and thereby honored the resistance of artisans of yore. For previous generations of craft workers, "Their communitarian ideals may have been fantasies. Their insurrectionary conspiracies may have been foolhardy. . . . [But] their aspirations were valid in terms of their own experience," Thompson surmises. "Our only criterion of judgement should not be whether or not a man's actions are justified in the light of subsequent evolution. After all, we are not at the end of social evolution ourselves."[8]

Utopian deejays imagined radio as a place for skilled labor and forging community, and "rough music" and smooth transitions. With artisanal pride, Merly emphatically reminded me, "Segues rule!" Her first weekend shifts at WNEW included the eight-to-midnight block, for which she assembled the "Saturday Night Jam Program." For those playlists, Merly told me, "I used to include a lot of really danceable stuff," including the latest tracks by Ian Dury, The Clash, the Two-Tone bands, and Peter Tosh. "I used to concentrate a lot on the segues, like it was a little dance mix happening in a club." The art of the segue fell from grace long ago on commercial radio. Today's deejays, Merly mused wistfully,

> They don't give a shit. They'll go from Black Sabbath into some crappy poppy tune, and they don't even care. And if they get away with that, does that mean the listening audience doesn't care about that? That just drives me crazy.
>
> That's the musicality of radio that attracted me in the first place: the idea of presenting the music in such a way, to take people on a trip, to put them through moods. The idea was not to jar people from one mood to another. That was the art of it. The art of radio: it's almost an oxymoron anymore.

Segue after segue, too, entailed making selections from thousands of records, often within a four-minute span, and ran counter to the dictates of artists-of-the-day and the rack.

The craft labor of the segue, though, was just one element in the pleasure of free-form radio, for deejays and listeners alike. As Susan Douglas explains in *Listening In*, her delightful history of American radio, the death of free-form entailed a loss of deejay creativity and, in turn, the listeners "miss learning about new music, the juxtaposition of genres, and the intimate, conspiratorial mode of address. Ideologically, many listeners miss an outpost on the airwaves that was avowedly left-wing and anti-commercial." Likewise, listeners miss the challenge of free-form radio, for it required a depth and duration of attention rarely nurtured in the digital age.[9]

In those analog days in Stockton, California, I listened to KQAK, a new wave station in San Francisco, but otherwise listened to music primarily on vinyl or cassette. The recordable cassette provided us with the opportunity to compose our own sonic collages, which circulated almost exclusively in the gift economy of adolescent passions—hoping to "create moods" of a specific sort, with a specific recipient in mind. In my experience, the labor embodied in the mix tape rarely converted well in terms of exchange value—but when it did, the pleasure of sharing that music (and some passion) embodied adolescence writ large. It also represented an aesthetic experience for which I have found few rivals, three decades hence. Likewise, the analog quality of that object mattered. As Rob Sheffield argues in *Love Is a Mix Tape*, love is a mix tape. It's not a mix compact disc. It's not a mix flash drive, nor a mix playlist in the cloud. It's a mix tape.

I still listen to a mix tape I made in 1985 for my own enjoyment from a selection of LPs, on which the gap between the final a cappella bars of The Specials' "You're Wondering Now" and the flamenco guitar line on The Selecter's "Celebrate the Bullet" is but a one-beat rest. On episodic listens, I take pride in my assembly of the sort of seamless, serendipitous, sonically perfect segue that was routine for free-form deejays.

With Extreme Prejudice / On a Terminator Mission

At WNEW, the beginning of the end varies, depending upon who tells the story. In *FM: The Rise and Fall of Rock Radio*, Richard Neer reports on the transition from free-form to a more conventional structure, at the last major-market free-form station in commercial radio. Following the demise of free-form mainstays such as KMET in Los Angeles, and KSAN, Neer knew the end was nigh. Some WNEW deejays—including Dennis Elsas, Pete Fornatale, and Muni—understood the imperative of profit. Still others, Neer noted, "saw their every program as inviolable art that was beyond the reproach of those barbarians who only saw radio as a business and wanted to make money."[10]

The logic of the bean counters seemed infallible: in order to maintain ratings, deejays needed to play the songs people wanted to hear, and to play them often. Audience share determined ratings, and ratings determined rate cards for advertisers: the greater the audience share, the higher the premium. High premiums meant higher profits, for the most part. As noted above, when Karmazin reviewed with Herman the ledgers at WNEW, he drew Herman's attention to the steady growth in revenue, to remind him that ratings represented but one figure in terms of the station's fiscal health. His advice to Herman, "the hell with Arbitron ratings," might have included the following rejoinder: "for the moment." In order to appease Metromedia and its shareholders, WNEW revenue needed to outpace the growth rate at WPLJ, for example. Eventually, the Arbitron ratings were not as easy to dismiss as the rabble-rousers.[11]

The songs people believed they wanted to hear, though, were not the primary unit of analysis in radio. Deejays played music and commercials, forged segues, and chatted with their listeners. Each hour of this composition was the key object of consideration. The sales staff bore responsibility for selling the personalities of the deejays, their compositions, and the station's ethos to the advertisers. Ad revenue derived from securing deals with the advertisers that did the most radio business, rather than maximum audience share. The profit burden was distributed among the managers, the deejays, and the sales staff alike. It was the job of the latter to ensure that advertisers found credible their story about the ratings and their listeners. Is it possible that the demise of free-form was a failure of imagination on behalf of the sales staff? If so, why was it so difficult for them to sell the artisanal craft of serendipity?[12]

As George Harrison concluded in 1970, All Things Must Pass. In the late 1960s and early 1970s, the free-form deejay served as the conscience of the counterculture. From Bob Fass's use of the WBAI signal in 1968 to promote a Yippie-organized happening at Grand Central Terminal, to the use of the KSAN signal in 1971 to coordinate an oil spill clean-up campaign on behalf of Bay Area wildlife, deejays prompted listeners to put boots on the ground in service of the common good. By the time The Clash took over Times Square, deejays still got listeners tuned in and turned on, but primarily in discotheques, through booty-shaking solidarity for the common cause of non-monogamous love.[13]

THIS IS RADIO CLASH . . . / STEALING INFORMATION

Following The Clash's September 1979 show at the Palladium, insubordination continued apace at WNEW, and management's patience waned with the righteous clamor for artisanal rights. After Steele's dismissal from WNEW in 1979, Scelsa took over the ten-to-two a.m. shift, and music director Thom Morrera staffed the mic from two to six. Before long, the two combined forces as The Butch and Brick Show: Bayonne Butch represented Scelsa's punk alter ego, and Brick—from "hashish brick"—served as Morrera's on-air moniker. They represented themselves as the resident radicals, spinning punk and new wave discs for insomniacs and late-night revelers. In August 1980, they staged a station takeover (with management's endorsement), complete with ransom demands, during which a sleep-deprived Morrera pulled a hunting knife on Mike Kakoyiannis, a sales manager who had the audacity to violate their fortress to update the commercial log.[14]

Kakoyiannis laughed last. In January 1982, in the role of general manager, Kakoyiannis sought deejay cooperation with some format changes, and Scelsa balked. He reprised his long-standing routine of walking out, expecting once again to be coaxed back into the fold. No coaxing commenced. Kakoyiannis went public with the news and, rather than cite Scelsa's obstinacy, Kakoyiannis denigrated his musical taste: "He likes free-form esoteric radio of the 1970s. He thought I was stepping on his poetic license." The coda of Scelsa's nine-year run at WNEW looked more like an agonizing death than heroic glory.[15]

By the time of Scelsa's dismissal, Merly was spinning discs at WYSP, in Philadelphia. Like Scelsa, her Strummer-esque indignation led to conflicts over song selection: "It was against my sensibilities, my music and radio sensibilities, to play Foreigner and Journey. They were *corporate* rock . . . okay? We hated corporate rock. I hated corporate rock. I loved all the little indie guys, I loved all the British stuff." Her sensibility was visceral and social and shared in part by Christgau, who once contrasted the thrill of The Clash to "the goo of Foreigner." Merly had left on her own accord, in October 1981. Griffin persevered, taking over Scelsa's slot in 1982, only to be fired in 1984—which, not-so-coincidentally, opened up a slot for the more compliant Carol Miller to return to WNEW.[16]

Changes in the spirit of rock'n'roll and its mode of transmission coincided roughly with changes in the "tapestry of that culture": the economy and availability of marijuana and cocaine. The "getting loose" ethos of the counterculture was characterized in part by its irregular rhythms and mellow affectations. In marijuana, its practitioners found an amicable ally for resisting the time-work discipline of straight culture, and for enjoying serendipitous trips on the radio. Between 1969 and 1973, the percentage of Americans who had tried marijuana tripled and, in the next four years, doubled again. In the early 1970s, cocaine remained the preserve of a selective, well-to-do few. By mid-decade, its use among young people was on the rise. Rock deejays, too, were threads in this tapestry, and often socialized with well-supplied musicians. By 1979, with Donna Summer (and disco backlash) on the rise, and cocaine use among young Americans at an all-time high, program directors across the country ensured that the spirit of the radio mirrored the rhythm and cadence of the drug *du jour*. They put the screws to their deejays for more hit records and less between-song chatter, in order to keep their audience properly adrenalized. As Andrew Kopkind noted, in 1979, "The '60s were a mind trip (marijuana, acid); Disco is a body trip (Quaaludes, cocaine)."[17]

THE NEW WAVE CRESTS

In 1982, just four short years after the post-mortem of punk and new wave in *New York Rocker*, New York City hosted the third annual New Music Seminar, which featured addresses by Clive Davis, president of Arista Records, and Malcolm McLaren. The tenor of the seminar was upbeat, buoyed by recent hits by The Human League, The Go-Go's, Soft Cell, and The Clash. The people responsible for the success of these bands were regarded by Davis, though, as atypical of the music industry. "Why are there no Spielbergs and Lucases in this field?" Davis asked. "And why is AOR closer to Lawrence Welk than PacMan?" Davis lauded KROQ, the Los Angeles station with an early stake in new wave, as an industry exemplar, and goaded his colleagues to take more risks, in part because the changes were clearly upon them. The new kids wanted a new sound, Davis surmised: "The floodgates will open. The tide can't be stemmed."

McLaren, in turn, waxed nostalgic about the virtuous, musical mayhem of 1977. He bemoaned the dearth of "sex, style, and subversion" of the new wave, noting that these forces collectively represented rock'n'roll at its most dangerous and most marketable. McLaren, too, offered a prescient, radically democratic vision of music in the cassette age. Compared to the LP, McLaren claimed, "A cassette is actually more attractive because the human hand can hold it or even shove it in a pocket. A cassette doesn't look like it's in control. You can wipe it out and use it again and again. You can't do that with a record and the industry fears that. . . . [The cassette] destroys the music selling ethic." Soon thereafter, the cassette was subsumed by the compact disc, and the future of the music industry was rendered less certain than ever before.[18]

The advent of digital music technology has, in fact, given rise to listening practices that may render commercial radio obsolete. The rise of mp3 technology, as well as iTunes and its rivals, secured the death of the album and the return of the single as the key unit of the marketplace. For younger deejays and station managers alike, the late 1990s now represent the halcyon days, when they could expect their listeners to tune in for a whole song (or longer) before switching stations. By 2012, the key unit of music was changing again, and musicians and managers changed their composition strategies to keep pace with the listening modes of Generation Me. According to Jay Brown, president of Jay Z–owned Roc Nation, each track designed for radio play must include the following features: "a hook in the intro, a hook in the pre-chorus, a hook in the chorus, and a hook in the bridge." Why? "People on average give a song seven seconds on the radio before they change the channel," Brown claimed, "and you got to hook them."[19]

Marxists of the Bernie Rhodes variety must be pleased as the modes of musical production, and the apps and devices of consumption, continue to be revolutionized. By 2013, the radio was merely one of many outlets for finding new music. Listeners were able to find, for free, whole albums on YouTube and song snippets on iTunes, whose top-sales lists closely mirrored *Billboard*'s Hot 100, which is derived from radio play and sales.[20] The art-commerce contradiction that informed deejay identity (and insubordination) in the analog era was, by this time, largely resolved: with all art understood as unapologetically commercial, bands were able to forego radio exposure for heavy rotation on television by composing the micro-soundtracks of commercials for Chevrolet, iTunes, and Old Navy. In addition, motor vehicles from Acura to Winnebago came newly equipped in the United States with Sirius XM Radio technology. At the end of their commutes, Americans could stay connected to Sirius, or tune into Spotify or Pandora at their desktops, and thereby bypass any connection to regional deejays on the FM dial. With more data transmitted daily through "the cloud," the designation of the airwaves as a public good may be rent asunder. If all that is solid eventually melts into air, we might imagine a not-too-distant day when the staff of National Public Radio, following the privatization of the airwaves, is asked to turn out the lights and lock the door.[21]

The prospect of the death of FM radio highlights the magical connections it once fostered in the domain of popular music. The magical romance mediated by the analog transmission of a regional deejay at two turntables and a microphone, constructing a community among punks, freaks, and geeks about the sublime power of The Clash, may never bloom again. Such redemption proved possible because it was relational: I needed The Clash to get through adolescence, but I needed Van Halen, too, if only to construct my sense of self in contrast to the opposition. The changes in the music industry noted above seem likely to prevent the emergence of another Clash or Van Halen, for these changes seem likely to prevent the emergence of another Jane Hamburger or Robert Christgau.

The DIY spirit of punk and new wave contradicted the power held then by a precious few players in the music industry. As cultural intermediaries, deejays and rock journalists played key roles as gatekeepers of new music through the 1970s and '80s, as they determined the rate of rotation of albums and singles, and showered praise or derision, respectively, as they deemed fit. Christgau, too, not only wrote some of his finest pieces about Strummer, Jones, and Co., he helped convert a dozen other *Voice* writers who would, in successive years, issue their own edicts on the virtues of The Clash.

Under these conditions, bands like Van Halen eventually occupied a dominant position in the world of rock and, through 1979, bands like The Clash occupied the margins. The duration of both bands' success focused the attention of (mostly male) American teenagers, and fostered among them a shared musical experience. Rarely were you permitted to choose both: you were either for or against, The Clash or Van Halen, and proudly so.[22]

The diligence of Clash fans employed at Epic also played key roles in shaping these conditions. Dan Beck and Susan Blond, especially, ensured that transmissions of The Clash were beaming from mountaintops into millions of American households. If the deejays, journalists, and record-shop owners helped ensure teeming audiences for each Clash show at the Palladium, Beck and his colleagues helped ensure a teeming audience at the Spanos Center in 1984, for The Clash's lone visit to Stockton, California. In appreciation for his marketing of *London Calling*, Beck received an English gold album from CBS. Of the two hundred comparable tokens of gratitude in his possession, on behalf of work for artists from Michael Jackson to Pearl Jam, Beck told me, "It is my most prized possession."

In the mp3 era, changes in the production, circulation, and consumption of popular music invited listeners to embrace the DIY spirit wholeheartedly: the roles of musician, critic, or both were available to all. These freedoms, though, had their own casualties, including the common musical experience and, for generations to come, the righteous nostalgia trip offered by popular music histories.

How We Read, Write, and Listen

On September 21, 1979, The Clash played at the Palladium, in New York City, and the concert was broadcast live on WNEW. An unidentified recording was eventually pressed onto two slabs of vinyl, designated *The Guns of Brixton* bootleg and, circa 2010, circulated widely on illegal file-sharing networks. Deejays at WNEW, WLIR, and WPIX, and writers at the *Voice*, *Trouser Press*, and *New York Rocker* decided that The Clash were the currency, that their audience had to deal with it, and filled the airwaves and their column inches accordingly.[23]

Stealing itself was made possible by these decisions, too, for it was constructed from their memories, and from the raw materials of their articles, profiles, and record reviews. The possibility of this book confirms that Coon's 1977 prediction on the cultural resonance of punk—"the force of punk rock will be felt in society at least until 1988"—proved immeasurably modest, and recently Clash fans have been rewarded by an embarrassment of historiographic riches. Since 2004, the market has borne five biographies of Joe Strummer, two documentary films, two coffee-table books, an oral history, superlative biographies, respectively, of the group and the *London Calling* LP, two CDs of live performances, vinyl reissues, a Clash singles box set, and *Sound System*—a twelve-disc box set, complete with stickers, fanzines, buttons, a new DVD, dog tags, and a poster. The books, especially, have allowed my generation to wax rhapsodically with greater accuracy about the righteousness of our youth. Perhaps U2, Madonna, and Radiohead, should they call it quits soon, will be subject to a comparable renaissance, thirty years hence.

The reasons are many, and the unrivaled brilliance of The Clash, and Strummer-alongside-Jones in particular, is paramount. As Nick Kent surmised, "If rock'n'roll immortality was based on physical energy alone, Strummer would be at the very top of the heap. His voice may have been a gnarly abomination, his guitar-playing just a blur of rhythmic chicken-scratching and he wasn't particularly good-looking [ahem!], but no one apart from James Brown and Jackie Wilson ever sweated more on stage in order to incite some form of rapture from their audience." The claim of rapture as a possibility, as a legitimate hope for a mere fan of rock'n'roll, recalls an era, a decisively analog era, in which art and commerce danced in productive tension, a time before every relation was reducible to a money relation, a time in which we could temporarily suspend our disbelief that we might ever be fooled again.

Likewise, few bands coming of age in the past ten years have been subject to the lengthy profiles and features that characterized the rock press in the 1970s, '80s, and early '90s. The ten-thousand-word profile has been cut in half and appears less frequently, in fewer magazines. The four-month lag between the release of *London Calling* and Tom Carson's thoughtful review in *Rolling Stone* clearly reflected the requisite six-week lead time, and the fact that he listened to it over and over, commensurate to the weight at that time of a glowing review in *Rolling Stone*. (In our youth, we pored over the album reviews, looking for just the right combination of adjectives and analogies—"lo-fi," "the Velvets"—as we prepared for our next trip to Tower Records.) In 2013, record reviews happened nearly instantaneously, typically within the confines of a few column inches.[24]

With its latest revamping, *Rolling Stone* was reduced to little more than a vehicle for advertisements ("just 65¢ an issue with a subscription") and included, at best, one feature close to five thousand words. The advent of the sixty-word album review represented the perfect literary analog for songs with hooks coming every seven seconds. *Rolling Stone*, though, continued to cover the latest tour information of "heritage acts" such as Bruce Springsteen and Aerosmith, and had yet to fully abandon the generation of readers who tune into "Deep Tracks" on Sirius XM. The moniker "Deep Tracks," of course, resonates primarily with consumers who once purchased their music in analog form, and recalls the joy of becoming acquainted with the songs on an album not subject even to light rotation on commercial radio. "Deep Tracks" is for listeners who possess the sense of patience and duration associated with a Protestant leisure ethic: they are not averse to working for their pleasure. They find fascination with albums and recognize neither the virtue nor necessity of the eight-hook-per-minute song format.

In turn, it is difficult to imagine, in the near future, a writer devoting the time to compile a five-hundred-and-twenty-four-page biography on a contemporary band or artist (see Marcus Gray's *The Clash: Return of the Last Gang in Town*), for neither the raw materials nor the audience for such a project will exist. With digital screens and digital audio players, we read differently—and we listen differently. In his biography of Joe Strummer, Salewicz takes the motto from a Clash badge as the first principle of Strummer's politics: "the future is yet unwritten,"

The future is unwritten, and rich with possibilities for honor, camaraderie, and joyful clamor (© Joe Streno, go2jo.com).

and thereby anything is possible. I suggest, with regrets, that the pasts of many great bands of the present era, will not be written at length, if at all.

Still, to conclude this narrative on a bitter note would betray the legacy of Rolland, Gramsci, and Strummer, especially. Let us instead maintain our willful optimism that the irrational exuberance of capitalism will continue, that another revolution of the modes of musical production and consumption will commence, and that future histories will include rock'n'roll bands that truly matter.

Notes

PRELUDE

1.   The Clash, *Guns of Brixton* bootleg recording, WNEW-FM broadcast, September 21, 1979. Many thanks to Dave Marin for providing the content from the on-air broadcast omitted from the *Guns* recording.

2.   Mary Harron, "Clash in NYC–Waiting for Ivan," *Melody Maker*, October 6, 1979, http://rocksbackpages.com/article.html?ArticleID=512, last accessed July 11, 2009; Pat Gilbert, *Passion Is a Fashion: The Real Story of The Clash* (London: Aurum Press Ltd., 2004), 245, 252.

3.   Dan Beck, U.S. product manager at Epic Records in 1979, reported that this motto was used in other materials, and he credits Gary Lucas as the author of this designation. The quip reads "the only English group that matters" in early advertisements. See The Clash advertisement, *Billboard*, March 10, 1979, 95. In 1977, while trying to overcome his addiction to heroin, Nick Kent faced a severe case of the shakes: "Tryptizol . . . this was the same drug that had killed Nick Drake. . . . I'd been given a potentially life-threatening drug by a registered physician without being advised beforehand on the quantity I was supposed to take. A year later, this same physician took on Keith Moon as one of his patients and prescribed him a drug called Heminevrin to combat the drummer's alcoholism. Again he failed to alert his patient to the dangers of taking too many and Moon died as a result." Kent, *Apathy for the Devil: A Seventies Memoir* (New York: Da Capo, 2010), 283. The use of Heminevrin for treatment of alcoholism was controversial at the time: see Tony Fletcher, *Dear Boy: The Life of Keith Moon* (London: Omnibus Press, 2005), 552.

4.   Gilbert, *Passion Is a Fashion*, 250–51; Pennie Smith, interview by telephone, June 13, 2012. All Smith quotes from this source unless indicated otherwise.

5.   Robert Christgau, *Grown Up All Wrong: 75 Great Rock and Pop Artists from Vaudeville to Techno* (Cambridge, MA: Harvard University Press, 2000), 220–21.

6.   Terri Judd, "One Hundred Timeless Rock'n'roll Moments, and the Photographers Who Turned Them into Icons," *The Independent*, January 24, 2002, http://www.independent.co.uk/arts-entertainment/music/news/one-hundred-timeless-rocknroll-moments-and-the-photographers-who-turned-them-into-icons-667442.html, last accessed February 13, 2010.

7.   The "you" slur is a rough paraphrase from a quote by Hamell on Trial, *Rant & Roll*, DVD (Righteous Babe, 2008).

8. Jack London, *The Road* (New York: Macmillan, 1907), 173; Thomas Pynchon, *V.* (Philadelphia: J.B. Lippincott Company, 1963), 145.

9. Gilbert, *Passion Is a Fashion*, 39; Bernard Gendron, *Between Montmartre and the Mudd Club: Popular Music and the Avant-Garde* (Chicago: University of Chicago Press, 2002), 237–38. Episodes of this secret history were mined in previous narratives of punk and post-punk. My favorites include Jon Savage's *England's Dreaming: Anarchy, Sex Pistols, Punk Rock, and Beyond* (New York: St. Martin's Press, 1992), Pat Gilbert's *Passion Is a Fashion*, and Simon Reynolds' *Rip It Up and Start Again: Postpunk 1978–1984* (New York: Penguin, 2006), which cover the key scenes on the east side of the Atlantic deftly and delightfully. Marcus Gray's *The Clash: Return of the Last Gang in Town* (London: Helter Skelter, 2004) and *Route 19 Revisited: The Clash and the Making of "London Calling"* (London: Soft Skull Press, 2010) set and exceed, respectively, standards for the proper level of detail for tales about The Clash. Clinton Heylin's *From the Velvets to the Voidoids: The Birth of American Punk Rock* (London: Helter Skelter Publishing, 2005), Gina Arnold's *Route 666: On the Road to Nirvana* (New York: St. Martin's Press, 1993) and Will Hermes's *Love Goes to Buildings on Fire: Five Years in New York That Changed Music Forever* (New York: Faber & Faber, 2012) cover stateside developments in punk, from Lou Reed's days at Syracuse to Nirvana's *Nevermind*. Ryan Moore's excellent *Sells Like Teen Spirit: Music, Youth Culture and Social Crisis* (New York: NYU Press, 2010) traces punk's roots to the post-Fordist and postmodern turns, and ably demonstrates how punk arose in response to the broken promises of the hippie counterculture. Gendron's *Between Montmartre and the Mudd Club* provides a rigorous account of the collision of artistic and populist discourses at key historical moments in Western art, including punk and new wave. Honorable mentions for beauty and obsession go to Stephen Colegrave and Chris Sullivan's *Punk: The Definitive Record of a Revolution* (New York: Da Capo, 2005), George Gimarc's *Punk Diary: The Ultimate Trainspotter's Guide to Underground Rock, 1970–1982* (New York: Backbeat Books, 2005), Heylin's *Babylon's Burning: From Punk to Grunge* (New York: Canongate, 2007), and Chris Knowles's *Clash City Showdown* (PageFree Publishing, 2003).

10. Gendron, *Between Montmartre and the Mudd Club*, 238; Robert Walser, *Running with the Devil: Power, Gender, and Madness in Heavy Metal Music* (Hanover, NH: University Press of New England, 1993), 44; Robert Christgau, "Avant-Punk: A Cult Explodes—and a Movement Is Born," *Village Voice*. October 24, 1977, 71; Heylin, *Babylon's Burning*, 336.

11. Of the key vocalists in punk, neither Johnny Rotten, Joe Strummer, Elvis Costello, Joey Ramone, nor Dave Vanian, of The Damned, saw fit to perform under his given name. As Keith Richards notes, The Rolling Stones *performed* getting thrown out of the Grand Hotel in the Bristol, following advance warning to the media, in order to have it properly documented. See Keith Richards, *Life* (New York: Little, Brown and Company, 2010), 168; Carola Dibbell, "Inside Was Us: Women and Punk," in Barbara O'Dair, ed., *Trouble Girls: The Rolling Stone Book of Women in Rock* (New York: Random House), 280. Gendron, for example, did not cite this piece, which may be the smartest bit of writing on gender and punk ever.

12. Heylin, *From the Velvets to the Voidoids*, xii–xiii, with corrections. From 1974 to 1976, the first wave included, in New York, Suicide (in 1970!), Television, Patti Smith, The Ramones, Blondie, The Dictators and, in Cleveland, The Mirrors, The Electric Eels, and

Rocket from the Tombs. The successive wave included The Heartbreakers, Richard Hell and the Voidoids, Pere Ubu, Talking Heads, and The Dead Boys. See Gendron, *Between Montmartre and the Mudd Club*, 273. For an extended meditation on the complexity of the concept of "new wave," see Theodore Cateforis, *Are We Not New Wave? Modern Pop at the Turn of the 1980s* (Ann Arbor: University of Michigan, 2011).

13. Susan Douglas, *Listening In: Radio and the American Imagination* (Minneapolis: University of Minnesota Press, 2004), 269; The appearance of Public Image Ltd. on *American Bandstand* on May 17, 1980, was a compelling exception to the rule. See: https://www.youtube.com/watch?v=hZLhqTzjpUM, last accessed May 26, 2014; Thomas Thompson, "The New Far-Out Beatles," *Life*, June 16, 1967, 100–106; Since free-form radio is associated with the FM dial almost exclusively, it's referred to herein without the FM designation. Unless noted otherwise, all station call letters refer to FM stations.

14. Max's Kansas City presents New York Rock Festival poster, Danny Fields Collection on the Ramones, Rock and Roll Hall of Fame and Museum Collection, ARC.0302, Box-Folder: OS1-2. See also Gary Valentine's recollection of this event, in his memoir, *New York Rocker: My Life in the Blank Generation, with Blondie, Iggy Pop, and Others, 1974–1981* (New York: Thunder's Mouth Press, 2006), 125–26.

15. WNEW-FM shared call letters with their AM affiliate, to which I never make reference. All references to WNEW in this document refer to the FM station.

CHAPTER 1

1. Gilbert, *Passion Is a Fashion*, 57.
2. Ibid., 59.
3. "It is undoubtedly [Paul's] combination of mischievous boychild and Paleolithic primate which has sent swoonblips quavering through feminine hearts as disparate as Patti Smith and Caroline Coon." Lester Bangs, "The Clash," in *Psychotic Reactions and Carburetor Dung*, edited by Greil Marcus (New York: Knopf, 1987), 235. In my interview with Susan Blond, who worked for CBS in the late 1970s, she affirmed that Paul was "the handsomest boy I'd ever seen in my life." Susan Blond, interview by telephone, June 23, 2009; John Robb, *Punk Rock: An Oral History* (Oakland: PM Press, 2012), 90.
4. Gray, *Return of the Last Gang in Town*, 46, 54.
5. Gilbert, *Passion Is a Fashion*, 81–82; David Black, "Critique of the Situationist Dialectic: Art, Class Consciousness and Reification." *The Hobgoblin* 4, 2001, http://www.thehobgoblin.co.uk/journal/h42002_DB_Situ.htm, last accessed March 25, 2014; Savage, *England's Dreaming*, 84–85.
6. Antonio Gramsci, *Selections from the Prison Notebooks* (New York: International Publishers, 1971), 474–75; Steve Connolly, a.k.a. Roadent, offered a similar assessment in an interview with Jon Savage: "The Clash were the first band to steal from the Pistols: they were the construction to the Sex Pistols' nihilism," in *England's Dreaming*, 239.
7. The Modern Lovers were a key intermediate force between the Velvets and American punk bands. The Boston band shared the bill on a 1972 New Year's Eve gig with the New York Dolls, Suicide, and Wayne County, at the Mercer Arts Center, where The Ramones and others often played prior to, dare I say, the institutionalization of punk rock at CBGB. The

original Modern Lovers' recordings, on 7" and LP, on Beserkley Records, benefited from the label's distribution by Playboy Records, which itself was distributed by CBS, and thereby crossed the pond in an easterly direction. See Tim Mitchell, *There's Something about Jonathan: Jonathan Richman and the Modern Lovers* (London: Peter Owen, 1999); Gilbert, *Passion Is a Fashion*, 65.

8. Sean O'Hagan, "'The Buzzcocks Were Very Mondrian and We Were Pollock,'" *The Observer*, March 30, 2008, 14, http://www.guardian.co.uk/music/2008/mar/30/popandrock.art, last accessed January 28, 2010.

9. Chris Salewicz, *Redemption Song: The Ballad of Joe Strummer* (New York: Faber and Faber, 2006), 140–41; Kent, *Apathy for the Devil*, 277.

10. Gilbert, *Passion Is a Fashion*, 73; Savage, *England's Dreaming*, 167–68; Heylin, *Babylon's Burning*, 97.

11. Gilbert, *Passion Is a Fashion*, 75.

12. Valentine, *New York Rocker*, 150.

13. Bryan Ray Turcotte and Christopher T. Miller, eds., *Fucked Up + Photocopied: Instant Art of the Punk Rock Movement* (Corte Madera, CA: Gingko Press, 1999), 206; CBGB Concert Listing, *Village Voice*, April 12, 1976.

14. Jon Dolan, "Lou Reed, Velvet Underground Leader and Rock Pioneer, Dead at 71," *Rolling Stone*. October 27, 2013, http://www.rollingstone.com/music/news/lou-reed-velvet-underground-leader-and-rock-pioneer-dead-at-71-20131027#ixzz2wyMTa3Y4, last accessed March 25, 2014; Ellen Willis, "Beginning to See the Light," in *Out of the Vinyl Deeps: Ellen Willis on Rock Music*, edited by Nona Willis Aronowitz (Minneapolis: University of Minnesota, 2011), 156.

15. Frantz informed me that Johnny Ramone regarded all the members of Talking Heads as "super-intellectuals," since they had been to art school. Chris Frantz, interview by telephone, February 27, 2014. All Frantz quotes from this source unless indicated otherwise. John Holmstrom and Bridget Hurd, eds. *Punk: The Best of Punk Magazine* (New York: HarperCollins, 2012), 58.

16. Norman Mailer, "The White Negro," *Dissent*, Fall 1957, http://www.dissentmagazine.org/online_articles/the-white-negro-fall-1957, last accessed March 26, 2014; Ralph Ellison and Albert Murray, *Trading Twelves: The Selected Letters of Ralph Ellison and Albert Murray* (New York: Vintage, 2001), 211; I have great admiration for Dick Hebdige's argument about punk, reggae, and the "present absence" of the latter in punk, and I hope my argument here charts territory more particular to American punk. See Hebdige's *Subculture: The Meaning of Style* (New York: Routledge, 1996 [1979]), 62–70.

17. For telling insights on racialization, the body, and rock'n'roll, see Ellen Willis's "Dylan's Anti-Surprise," 207, and "Beginning to See the Light," 156, in *Out of the Vinyl Deeps: Ellen Willis on Rock Music* (Minneapolis: University of Minnesota, 2011).

18. Paul Morley, *Words and Music: A History of Pop in the Shape of a City* (London: Bloomsbury, 2003), 135.

19. Everett True, *Hey Ho Let's Go: The Story of The Ramones* (New York: Omnibus, 2002), 22.

20. Ibid., 74.

21. Heylin, *From the Velvets to the Voidoids*, 186; Robert Christgau, "Voice Choices," *Village Voice*, April 19, 1976, 89; For Ed Stasium, the first Ramones gig he attended was at CBGB

in September 1976, and by that time things had changed. "The crowd was pogoing, jumping up and down.... I couldn't understand where everybody had come from. It was a whole new world. The entire crowd was dressed in T-shirts and jeans." True, *Hey Ho Let's Go*, 73.

22. John Rockwell, "The Artistic Success of Talking Heads," *New York Times*, September 11, 1977, http://query.nytimes.com/mem/archive/pdf?res=F10E11F9395516768FD DA80994D1405B878BF1D3, last accessed March 16, 2014; Press Conference, 1999, *Stop Making Sense*, Blu-ray/DVD (Palm Pictures, 2009).

23. The Tom Tom Club, led by Tina Weymouth and Chris Frantz, draw unabashedly on Black American musical aesthetics.

24. Smith missed that gig and, through February, was on bed rest at her place in the Village, recovering from her January 26 fall from the stage of the Curtis-Hixen Hall in Florida. Hermes, *Love Goes to Buildings on Fire*, 220–21; Harry's quote, *Love Goes*, 112; Dave Thompson, *Dancing Barefoot: The Patti Smith Story* (Chicago: Chicago Review Press, 2011), 164.

CHAPTER 2

1. Douglas, *Listening In*, 269; see also Richard Neer, *FM: The Rise and Fall of Rock Radio* (New York: Villard, 2001), 86. In March 1968, Donahue submitted his resignation at KMPX, citing conflicts with station management. A solidarity strike followed and, after eight weeks, Donahue and his coworkers took job offers from Metromedia to work at KSAN, which had just abandoned its classical music format for free-form rock. Donahue eventually became general manager of KSAN, which was the number one station for years among the 18–34 demographic. When Donahue died of a heart attack in 1975, his station cancelled commercials for twenty-four hours. See Marc Fisher, *Something in the Air: Radio, Rock, and the Revolution that Shaped a Generation* (New York: Random House, 2007), 178, 197; Douglas, *Listening In*, 270.

2. Nigel Williamson, *The Rough Guide to Led Zeppelin* (London: Rough Guides, 2007), 66. Led Zeppelin was successful in this refusal in the UK, but less so in the U.S.

3. True, *Hey Ho Let's Go*, 8. Murray the K secured a name-check on the *End of the Century* LP, in "Do You Remember Rock'n'Roll Radio?"; Tom Wolfe, *The Kandy-Kolored Tangerine-Flake Streamline Baby* (New York: Macmillan, 2009 [1965]), 41; See also: John A. Jackson, *Big Beat Heat: Alan Freed and the Early Years of Rock & Roll* (New York: Schirmer Books, 1991), 309. This scandal also prompted Tom Donahue to leave the East Coast in 1961 for San Francisco.

4. *Time* magazine was especially helpful in deploying the rhetoric of the middlebrow aesthetic: "With characteristic self-mockery, the Beatles are proclaiming that they have snuffed out their old selves to make room for the new Beatles incarnate. And there is some truth to it. Without having lost any of the genial anarchism with which they helped revolutionize the life style of young people in Britain, Europe, and the U.S., they have moved on to a higher artistic plateau." See *Time*, "The Messengers," September 22, 1967, 60–68; Neer, *FM*, 54; Warren Bareiss suggests that deejays at WBAI, in 1963, sketched the blueprint for free-form radio. See "Free Form Format," in Christopher H. Sterling, ed., *The Museum of Broadcast Communications Encyclopedia of Radio*, vol. 2 (New York: Fitzroy Dearborn, 2004), 627–28.

5. Neer, *FM*, 64.

6. Claude Hall, "Progressive Rock All the Way in WNEW-FM's Format Future," *Billboard*, December 9, 1967, 40.

7. Douglas, *Listening In*, 272; Dorothy Kalins Wise. "Beautiful Rosko," *New York*, July 1, 1968, 42, http://books.google.com/books?id=luECAAAAMBAJ&pg=PA42&dq=WNEW-FM&hl=en&sa=X&ei=AH8cT62TCePd0QGasoiYCw&ved=0CEUQ6AEwBA#v=onepage&q=WNEW-FM&f=false, last accessed January 22, 2012.

8. Yvonne Sewall-Ruskin, *High on Rebellion: Inside the Underground at Max's Kansas City* (New York: Thunder's Mouth Press, 1998), vii.

9. Richard Neer, interview by telephone, January 29, 2009. All Richard Neer quotes from this source unless indicated otherwise; Dave Marsh, *Bruce Springsteen: Two Hearts, the Definitive Biography* (New York: Routledge, 2004), 115; Eric Hollreiser, "Rock of Ages," *New York*, February 6, 1989, 29.

10. Earl Abrams, "Radio Robots Come to Life as Automated Formats Score Ratings Gains," *Broadcasting*, September 23, 1974, 33–41; Douglas, *Listening In*, 277–78; "FM Rockers Are Taming Their Free Formats," *Broadcasting*, November 25, 1974, 47–49.

11. Neer, *FM*, 193–94; Richard Neer, interview; Karmazin secured a sponsor for the event: see Neer, *FM*, 199. The Springsteen show was the second live broadcast on WNEW from The Bottom Line. The April 1975 performance of Melissa Manchester was the first. See, for example, Ira Robbins, "The New Wave Washes Out," *Trouser Press*. October 1977, 22, in which he proclaims "From here on in everything that arises will be an imitation"; listings in the March 26, 1979, issue of *New York*, in which CBGB is dismissed as the home of "punk nostalgia," 39.

12. Dave Marsh, *Bruce Springsteen on Tour, 1968–2005* (New York: Bloomsbury Press, 2006), 74–77.

13. Ibid.; Neer, *FM*, 201; Dave Herman, "At WPLJ, One Day at a Time," *Village Voice*, October 21, 1971. According to Herman, the annual operating budget of WPLJ, in 1971, was $832,000. To lose $2.5M on seven stations, then, meant up to a 43 percent loss on investment.

14. Southside Johnny's repertoire included many tunes penned by Springsteen himself.

15. Roman Kozak, "No 'Experts' Hired By N.Y. WNEW-FM," *Billboard*. June 25, 1977, 32. In this same article, Muni deflected the success toward George Duncan, then the president of MetroMedia, who Muni hoped still considered WNEW to be "his first-born child."

CHAPTER 3

1. Heylin, *From the Velvets to the Voidoids*, 172–73.

2. Richard Goldstein, "The Possibilities of Punk," *Village Voice*. October 10, 1977, 40.

3. Legs McNeil and Gillian McCain, *Please Kill Me: The Uncensored Oral History of Punk* (New York: Penguin, 1997), 201; True, *Hey Ho Let's Go*, 45.

4. Chas de Whalley, "Power Pop Part 1: Suddenly, Everything Is Power Pop!," *Sounds*, February 11, 1978, http://www.rocksbackpages.com/Library/Article/power-pop-part-1-suddenly-everything-is-power-pop/, last accessed July 11, 2009; Simon Frith, "Beyond the Dole Queue: The Politics of Punk," *Village Voice*, October 24, 1977, 78.

5. Salewicz, *Redemption Song*, 145; True, *Hey Ho Let's Go*, 64. 10,1975.

6. Gilbert, *Passion Is a Fashion*, 86.

7. Salewicz, *Redemption Song*, 73–74.

8. Alan Clayson, *Ringo Starr: Straight Man or Joker?* (London: Sanctuary Publishing, 1998), 144; Salewicz, *Redemption Song*, 154; see also Gilbert, *Passion Is a Fashion*, 93–94, and Terry Chimes, *The Strange Case of Dr Terry and Mr Chimes* (London: Crux Publishing, 2013); True, *Hey Ho Let's Go*, 67.

9. Gilbert, *Passion Is a Fashion*, 94–95.

10. Savage, *England's Dreaming*, 232.

11. Gilbert, *Passion Is a Fashion*, 146.

12. Ibid.; The chronological order of key UK punk releases in 1977 includes: The Damned's *Damned, Damned, Damned* (February 18); The Clash's *The Clash* (April 8); The Stranglers' *Rattus Norvegicus* (April 15); The Stranglers' *No More Heroes* (September 23); The Sex Pistols' *Never Mind the Bollocks, Here's the Sex Pistols* (October 28); and The Damned's *Music for Pleasure* (November 18).

13. Robert Christgau, interview by telephone, March 29, 2012. All Christgau quotes from this source unless indicated otherwise. Other prominent stateside readers of *NME* included Cleveland-based Peter Laughner, guitarist for Rocket from the Tombs and writer for *Creem*, and Miriam Linna, one-time drummer for The Cramps and Nervus Rex. See Heylin, *Babylon's Burning*, 27; Christgau, "'We Have to Deal with It': Punk England Report," *Village Voice*. January 9, 1978, http://www.robertchristgau.com/xg/rock/punk-78.php, last accessed June 12, 2009; CBS's Bruce Harris, in artists and repertoire, noted "Radio is just not interested in this record.... Listeners would have to pay attention much too much." Heylin, *Babylon's Burning*, 389.

14. "The 1977 Pazz & Jop Critics Poll," *Village Voice*. January 23, 1978, http://www.robertchristgau.com/xg/pnj/pjres77.php, last accessed August 19, 2012; Robert Christgau, "Pazz & Jop 1977: Dean's List," *Village Voice*, January 23, 1978, http://www.robertchristgau.com/xg/pnj/deans77.php, last accessed August 19, 2012; Christgau, "Avant-Punk," 68–69.

15. Pam Merly, interview by telephone, June 6, 2009. All Merly quotes from this source unless indicated otherwise.

16. Alan Watts (1915–1973) was a British philosopher, writer, and speaker, who was best-known as an interpreter and popularizer of Eastern philosophy for a Western audience.

17. WLIR advertisement, *Village Voice*, April 10, 1978, 57.

18. Angela Phillips, *Good Writing for Journalists* (Thousand Oaks, CA: Sage, 2007), 193; Ryan Moore and Michael Roberts, "Do-It-Yourself Mobilization: Punk and Social Movements," *Mobilization* 14, no. 3 (2009): 273–91.

19. True, *Hey Ho Let's Go*, 71; John Cooper Clarke, Mancunian punk poet, noted, "In an age when guys looked like Open University lecturers and even your uncle wore flares, The Ramones came in like a breath of fresh carbona, inspiring Mark Perry from south London to launch *Sniffin' Glue*." Colegrave and Sullivan, *Punk*, 153; Mark Perry, *Sniffin' Glue & Other Rock-n-Roll Habits: The Catalogue of Chaos, 1976–1977* (London: Sanctuary Publishing, 2000), 141; Savage, *England's Dreaming*, 202.

20. "Intro," *Trans-Oceanic Trouser Press* 1, no. 1 (March 1974): 1–2; "Classified Ads," 23; Ira Robbins, "The Clash," *Trouser Press*, September 1977, http://londonsburning.org/

art_trouser_press_09_97.html, last accessed February 27, 2010; Bob Gruen, interview by telephone, April 29, 2009. All Gruen quotes from this source unless indicated otherwise.

21. Savage, *England's Dreaming*, 445–48; McNeil and McCain, *Please Kill Me*, 334.

22. Valentine, *New York Rocker*, 79–80; Ann Powers, "Alan Betrock, 49, Pop Critic and Record Producer," *New York Times*. April 15, 2000, http://www.nytimes.com/2000/04/15/arts/ alan-betrock-49-pop-critic-and-record-producer.html, last accessed December 31, 2013.

23. McNeil and McCain, *Please Kill Me*, 203, 206.

24. *Strangled*, out of the UK, provided a visual representation of three chords and simple counsel: "Now go away and form a band": Everett, *Hey Ho*, 71; Joe Koch, "Marlon Brando: The Original Punk," *Punk*, January 1976, 1; Robert Romagoli, "Do It Yourself Sixties Protest Song," *Punk* 1 no. 1, January 1976, 14.

25. Valentine, *New York Rocker*, 114; Mary Harron and Michael Zilka, "Talking Heads," *Punk* 1 no. 2, March 1976, 1.

26. Valentine, *New York Rocker*, 115, 71; Richard Hell, "The Ramones Mean Business," *Hit Parader* (originally September 1976), collected in Hell, *Hot and Cold: essays poems lyrics notebooks pictures fiction* (New York: powerHouse Books), 2001; The Wyndbrandts were Harry's bandmates in The Stilettoes, and played in Wayne County's back-up band, Queen Elizabeth. Also, in the peer-on-peer spirit, Richard Hell penned a glowing piece on The Ramones in *Hit Parader* that closed with the following counsel: "If they have a good audience they want to give more and if it's bad they play with a vengeance, so either way, they deliver"; Roy Trakin, interview by telephone, June 8, 2012. All Trakin quotes from this source unless indicated otherwise. If Lenny Kaye had yet to secure fame for his own musical chops, he penned one of the earliest peer-on-peer salutes for Iggy and the Stooges, in a *Rolling Stone* review of *Raw Power* on May 10, 1975.

27. The Ramones played over two thousand concerts over twenty-three years: see Monte A. Melnick and Frank Meyer, *On the Road with The Ramones* (London: Sanctuary Publishing Limited), 282–301; Alan Betrock, "Ramones 7520," *New York Rocker*, May 1976, 24, 34.

28. "Match These Stars with Their Pets," *New York Rocker*, March 1976; Alan Betrock, "Albums and LP's," *New York Rocker*, May 1976, 26–27; Alan Betrock, "AB's, ABC's & Abba," *New York Rocker*, December 1976, 15.

29. Robb, *Punk Rock*, 184.

30. Heylin, *From the Velvets to the Voidoids*, 243.

31. Mike Ragogna, "From Ike & Tina Turner, John Lennon and Led Zeppelin to The Clash, The Sex Pistols and Green Day: A Conversation with Bob Gruen," *Huffington Post*. December 24, 2012, http://tinaturneronlineblog3.cdn.tina-turner.nl/blog/wp-content/ uploads/2012/12/from-ike--tina-turner-joh_b_2357442.html, last accessed February 2, 2014; Gilbert, *Passion Is a Fashion*, 41; Gray, *Return of the Last Gang in Town*, 41.

32. Perhaps sour grapes spoiled the impression of The Clash held by John Perry of The Only Ones: "By [the time of their arrival in New York] they were a good rock & roll band— [though] not as good as the Pistols in '76—but at the expense of everything they claimed to stand for." Heylin, *Babylon's Burning*, 500; Christgau, *Grown Up All Wrong*, 214.

CHAPTER 4

1. Susan Krieger, *Hip Capitalism* (Beverly Hills: Sage, 1979), chap. 13; Meg Griffin, interview by telephone, April 8, 2009. All Griffin quotes from this source unless indicated otherwise.

2. Hermes, *Love Goes to Buildings on Fire*, 250.

3. Robert Kuczik, "For WRNW, a Different Drummer," *New York Times*, February 5, 1978, WC3.

4. Steven M. Gillon, *The Pact: Bill Clinton, Newt Gingrich, and the Rivalry That Defined a Generation* (New York: Oxford, 2008), 27. Rodham, too, took the opportunity during her commencement speech at Wellesley, in 1969, to chastise a fellow addressee who denounced the SDS.

5. "WNCN, WQIV, F.C.C.," *New York Times*, November 9, 1974, http://www. nyradioarchive.com/images/radioscans/WQIVFM_Editorial_NYT19741109. jpg, last accessed March 14, 2014. "The Battle Is Joined over WNCN Format," *Broadcasting*, September 30, 1974, 40; George H. Nash, "Simply Superlative," *The National Review*, February 28, 2008, http://article.nationalreview.com/ print/?q=YmZkMTRmN2MyZjcwYWVhYWI4YjhkNjE5YTA5NmY3ODg, last accessed February 7, 2010; Michelle Tsai, "Why Did William F. Buckley Jr. Talk Like That?," *Slate*, February 28, 2008, http://www.slate.com/articles/news_and_politics/ explainer/2008/02/why_did_william_f_buckley_jr_talk_like_that.html, last accessed June 11, 2012.

6. Rob Frankel. "Aircheck: WQIV First Day." NY Radio Archive, http://www.nyradioarchive.com /audio/WQIV_19741107_RF_Pt1.mp3, last accessed on May 30, 2014; William F. Buckley Jr., "Buckley vs. Rich," *New York*, February 2, 1976, 2; Jim Cameron, e-mail correspondence, May 30, 2014. Cameron was an original member of the Quad Squad.

7. "Two Officials of WQIV-FM Quit over Policy Differences," *New York Times*. January 14, 1975; Mark Martin, "Thom O'hair, KSAN DJ in the '70s and Web Broadcaster," *San Francisco Chronicle*. January 11, 2001, http://www.sfgate.com/cgi-bin/article. cgi?f=/c/a/2001/01/11/MNL161297.DTL#ixzz1tcrfT6O7, last accessed May 1, 2012; "WNCN Comes Back as Classical Station," *New York Times*. August 26, 1975; Carol Miller, *Up All Night: My Life and Times in Rock Radio* (New York: Ecco, 2012), 130.

8. "WNCN Comes Bach as Classical Station," *New York Times*, August 26, 1975, http:// www.nyradioarchive.com/images/radioscans/WQIVFM_WNCN_NYT19750826.jpg, last accessed June 2, 2014.

9. Miller, *Up All Night*, 131.

10. Fred T. Abdella, "As Pitch in Opera Rises, So Does Debate," *New York Times*. August 13, 1989, http://www.nytimes.com/1989/08/13/nyregion/as-pitch-in-opera-rises-so-does-debate.html, last accessed February 1, 2014.

11. Will Keller. "WPIX: Radio Radio." Unpublished manuscript, courtesy of the author. See also: Dan Neer, "WPIX-FM Years (September 1977-April 1980)," http://www.danneer.com/1/ post/2014/02/wpix-fm-years-september-1977-april-1980.html, last accessed June 2, 2014.

12. Salewicz, *Redemption Song*, 173–74.

13. Bangs, *Psychotic Reactions*, 231.

14. Kent, *Apathy for the Devil*, 264.

15. Vivien Goldman, "The Clash etc: Harlesden's Burning," *Sounds*, March 19, 1977, http://www.rocksbackpages.com/article.html?ArticleID=8334, last accessed September 20, 2009; Nick Kent, "The Clash/Buzzcocks/Subway Sect/The Slits: Harlesden Coliseum, London," *New Musical Express*, March 19, 1977, http://www.rocksbackpages.com/article.html?ArticleID=12581&SearchText=nick+kent, last accessed September 20, 2009; The Pistols' sense of humor is now the subject of reconsideration: see Heylin, *Babylon's Burning*, 103–5.

16. Caroline Coon, 1988: *The New Wave Punk Rock Explosion* (New York: Hawthorn Books, 1978).

17. Barry Auguste, e-mail correspondence, April 15, 2014; Gilbert's *Passion Is a Fashion*, 153, has April 10 as Headon's debut. Gray's *Return of the Last Gang in Town*, 245, indicates it was April 27. The April 10 show, for which they were scheduled to open for John Cale, never happened. Barry Auguste, e-mail correspondence, May 31, 2014.

18. Gray, *Return of the Last Gang in Town*, 153.

19. Robert Kuczik, "For WRNW." Rather than taking a stand on principle, it seems Howard Stern embraced the side of management and, upon the departure of Griffin and Piasek, moved from morning deejay to program director.

20. WNEW-FM advertisement, *New York*, November 7, 1977, http://books.google.com/books?id=EegCAAAAMBAJ&pg=PA90&dq=vin+scelsa&hl=en&sa=X&ei=-JnwcT67ZGobo0QHztJXlAg&ved=0CDYQ6AEwAA#v=onepage&q=vin%20scelsa&f=false, last accessed January 22, 2012.

21. Harvey Leeds, interview by telephone, June 20, 2009. All Leeds quotes from this source unless indicated otherwise.

22. "*Billboard* Album Radio Action," *Billboard*, December 3, 1977, 6.

23. Divine played an outsized role in the New York new wave scene. Blondie's Gary Valentine (né Lachman) and photographer Lisa Jane Persky (then a couple) acted opposite Divine in a production of *Medea*, as his "ill-fated children": Valentine, *New York Rocker*, 122; In 1972, County was the house deejay at Max's Kansas City and lead singer for the proto-punk band Queen Elizabeth.

24. Gendron, *Between Montmartre and the Mudd Club*, 276.

25. Ibid.

26. Hurrah advertisement, *Village Voice*, October 2, 1978, 94; The responsibility of Vicious's overdose remains in question. See Ann Louise Bardach, "Another Break for Sid Vicious," *Soho Weekly News*, January 18, 1979, http://www.bardachreports.com/articles/oa_19790118.htm, last accessed February 7, 2010; a short clip, from the "Final 24" series on Biography.com, suggests that Sid's mother, Anne Ritchie, played a calculated role in his overdose. See http://www.biography.com/video.do?name=tvshows&bcpid=1753218632&bclid=1768641487&bctid=1726714821 last accessed February 27, 2010.

27. The b-side to "Bondage" was "I Am a Cliché" (Virgin). The promises of the marketplace were equally cheap. "That was the era of real hip capitalism too, and you just didn't buy it anymore," said Mary Harron, scribe for *Melody Maker* and *Punk*. "I resented everyone telling me what to believe. I disliked the hippie culture, I found it nauseating and prissy and sentimental, and smiley-faced." McNeil and McCain, *Please Kill Me*, 282.

28. Nick Johnstone, *The Clash Talking* (New York: Omnibus Press, 2006), 34.

29. Dave Simpson and Will Hodgkinson, "Punk, How Was It for You?," *The Guardian*, August 10, 2001, http://20thcpunkarchives.tripod.com/id22.htm, last accessed February 27, 2010.

30. C. Dubois. "A Free Form in New Jersey?" *The Upsala Gazette*, March 18, 1969, 4–7, http://blogfiles.wfmu.org/ME/upsalagazette03181969.pdf, last accessed June 5, 2012.

31. Roy Trakin, "Trakin It to the Streets," *Sonic Boomers*, date unknown, https://sonicboomers.com/boomerangst/trakin-it-streets-red-star, last accessed July 22, 2012.

32. Jan Hoffman. "Vin Scelsa's Radio Free Radio," *Village Voice*, February 19, 1979, 40; McNeil and McCall, *Please Kill Me*, 344. Kaye, here, refers to the question of freedom as a matter of taste, rather than law—and Hoffman indicates Scelsa played the track four times that Friday afternoon; The Ramones, *Pleasant Dreams* (Sire Records), July 1981.

33. Rhodes pressed his charges to think of music as praxis, in rudimentary form with London SS, and in less vulgar terms with The Clash. As Tony James recalled, "Bernie was very clever at tutoring us through this maze. . . . Bernie would give me reading lists: 'You should read Sartre, you should go and read about modern art, you should read about Jackson Pollock.'" Seagrave and Sullivan, *Punk*, 105.

CHAPTER 5

1. Joe Piasek, interview by telephone, April 30, 2009. All Piasek quotes are from this source unless indicated otherwise.

2. Johnny Green and Garry Barker. *A Riot of Our Own: Night and Day with The Clash* (New York: Faber & Faber, 1999), 35.

3. Heylin, *Babylon's Burning*, 390.

4. Michael Goldberg, "The Clash–Revolution Rock," *Downbeat*, December 1982, http://www.rocksbackpages.com/article.html?ArticleID=10420, last accessed February 27, 2010; Bob Gruen, *The Clash* (New York: Omnibus Press, 2002), 57; Gray, *Return of the Last Gang in Town*, 286.

5. Bob Gruen, interview. Gruen's *The Clash* is a fantastic collection of images and text.

6. See studio image at http://2.bp.blogspot.com/_BsggawC46VM/ReW4WuxgvvI/AAAAAAAAAHM/CiTVe9ywVRY/s1600-h/CBS+Studio+2.jpg, last accessed June 3, 2012. I am indebted to Gilbert (*Passion Is a Fashion*, 211) for making this connection.

7. Frances Lass, "Fizzy Drinks & Flat Clash," *Melody Maker*, November 4, 1978; Ian Penman, "The Clash: Black'n White Drop Outasite," *NME*. November 4, 1978, http://www.rocksbackpages.com/article.html?ArticleID=12962&SearchText=the+clash, last accessed February 27, 2010; Gray, *Return of the Last Gang in Town*, 292.

8. Lester Bangs, "Clash in the Crossfire," *Village Voice*, December 11, 1978, 67. By referring to Strummer's "'political' lyrics" in scare quotes, Bangs gently whips that barbed wire toward John Rockwell of the *New York Times*. Along with his fellow *Times* scribes, Rockwell focused often in his dispatches on punk and new wave on the "leftist-anarchistic views" of the musicians, and thereby missed what Bangs deemed the first principle of punk politics: do-it-yourself. Bangs suggests here the importance of Strummer's desire not for revolution but freedom *writ large*—and who could stand opposed to that?

9. Ibid.

10. Ira Robbins, "The Clash: *Give 'Em Enough Rope*," *Trouser Press*, January 1979, http://rocksbackpages.com/article.html?ArticleID=10046&SearchText=the+clash, last accessed February 27, 2010; Greil Marcus, "The Clash: *Give 'Em Enough Rope*," *Rolling Stone*, January 25, 1979, http://www.rollingstone.com/music/albumreviews/give-em-enough-rope-19790125, last accessed May 1, 2012.

11. Handsome Dick Manitoba, interview by telephone, April 28, 2009.

12. WNEW advertisement, *Village Voice*, February 19, 1979, 68.

13. Jan Hoffman. "The Happy Medium," *Village Voice*, August 20, 1979, 43.

14. Roman Kozak, "WPIX-FM Moves up in NY: Old & New Rock Fattens Ratings," *Billboard*, November 3, 1979, 26–28; Joe Piasek, e-mail correspondence, June 24, 2012. As John Gorman notes, Cleveland radio figure Carl Hirsch rallied the FM troops with the following edict: "We don't go to work. We go to war." See John Gorman, with Tom Feran, *The Buzzard: Inside the Glory Days of WMMS and Cleveland Rock Radio, A Memoir* (Cleveland: Gray & Co. Publishers, 2007), 54.

15. Neer, *FM*, 122.

16. Miller, *Up All Night*, 131, 132, 158.

17. Joe Piasek, e-mail correspondence, June 24, 2012.

18. Keller, *Radio, Radio*, unpublished manuscript.

19. Victor Bockris, *Transformer: The Lou Reed Story* (New York: Simon & Schuster, 1994), 287.

20. Ibid., 260, 283.

21. Robert Christgau, "Consumer Guide," *Village Voice*, April 30, 1979, http://www.robertchristgau.com/xg/cg/cgv4b-79.php, last accessed December 19, 2013; "I'm not a genre-ist!" Christgau said sharply, at the beginning of our interview.

22. John Rockwell, "The Pop Life," *New York Times*, June 1, 1979, C12.

23. Arnold, *Route 666*, 22.

24. Robert Christgau, "Consumer Guide," *Village Voice*, September 3, 1979, 72.

25. Allan Jones, "Banging on the White House Door," *Melody Maker*, February 24, 1979, 35.

26. Adam White, "Names & New Talent on Alexenburg Label," *Billboard*, September 30, 1978, 95; "New Black Record Co. Born in New York: T-Electric," *Jet*, August 30, 1979, 61; James Henke, "Music Business Bouncing Back?" *Rolling Stone*, October 18, 1979, 10.

27. Wayne Forte, interview by telephone, July 17, 2012. All Forte quotes from this source unless indicated otherwise.

28. Gray, *Return of the Last Gang in Town*, 303; Gilbert, *Passion Is a Fashion*, 373; Thin Lizzy advertisement, *Village Voice*, October 2, 1978, 108; Devo advertisement, *Village Voice*, October 2, 1978, 111; Elvis Costello advertisement, *Village Voice*, January 29, 1978, 112.

29. The Clash advertisement, *Billboard*, March 3, 1979, 95; "Epic Records' Worldwide Expansion," *Billboard*, February 17, 1979, E-20.

30. Dan Beck, interview by telephone, June 13, 2012. All Beck quotes from this source unless indicated otherwise. Gray, *Return of the Last Gang in Town*, 304; Gilbert, *Passion Is a Fashion*, 219, and Gray, *Return of the Last Gang in Town*, 305. Numerous Epic representatives claim the photo-op and walk-out happened in Berkeley, rather than Los Angeles. See Dan Beck, "The Clash Meet Their Record Company," *Music Biz Fizz*, http://www.musicbizzfizz.com/

post/420316544/the-clash-meet-their-record-company-3-1-10, last accessed July 19, 2012. Memories diverge over the role Epic played in securing radio and print exposure for The Clash on their debut tour. Beck and Forte believe that their interview with their colleague Howie Klein on KSAN, for example, likely came together through Klein's initiative. Coon believes Epic and Blond had a hand in the busy nonconcert hours on key days of that tour; Dan Beck, e-mail correspondence, July 24, 2012; Wayne Forte, e-mail correspondence, July 24, 2012; Caroline Coon, e-mail correspondence, July 21, 2012.

31. Mikal Gilmore, "Clash: Anger on the Left," *Rolling Stone*, March 8, 1979, 22; "Sixty percent of most," in those days, would keep you in the big leagues.

32. Christgau, "Pazz & Jop Product Report," *Village Voice*, January 8, 1979, 53; Christgau, "Triumph of the New Wave: Results of the Fifth (or Sixth) Annual Pazz & Jop Critics' Poll," *Village Voice*, January 22, 1979.

33. Melnick and Meyer, *On the Road*, 80.

34. For a night's work in the Village, Christgau often started at the Bottom Line, with "something more corporate," and concluded at CBGB, with a conversation with Kristal. By the time of The Clash's New York debut, *Rope* had just entered the *Billboard* charts, topping out at one hundred twenty-six. In 1978, The Police released *Outlandos d'Amour* in November, along with three singles, and the album eventually reached twenty-three on the *Billboard* pop album chart. They performed at the Bottom Line on April 3 and 4, and four nights later at CBGB. Joe Jackson's *Look Sharp* LP was released in January 1979 in the UK, and April 1979 in the United States, and reached number twenty on *Billboard*. "Is She Really Going Out with Him?" peaked at number twenty-one, on the *Billboard* single charts. XTC, on Virgin Records, made their 1979 debut in New York at CBGB; Kent, on Sting: "the anti-Lydon of the late seventies. One was ugly and—relatively—shiftless, the other was an industrious pretty boy bent on self-improvement and self-empowerment," *Apathy for the Devil*, 325.

35. Christgau, *Grown Up All Wrong*, 212.

36. Lammo, "Classic Album of the Day—The Clash: London Calling," BBC Radio 6 Music, http://www.bbc.co.uk/programmes/b01g8bxy, last accessed April 18, 2012.

CHAPTER 6

1. *The Last Testament*, dir. Don Letts, DVD (101 Distribution, 2009); Gilbert, *Passion Is a Fashion*, 238.

2. Suspicions abound about "Bernie sightings" during his alleged separation from the band.

3. Barry Auguste, e-mail correspondence, January 14, 2014.

4. Gilbert, *Passion Is a Fashion*, 237; Letts, *The Last Testament*, 2009.

5. Gray, *Route 19 Revisited*, 174.

6. Barry Auguste, e-mail correspondence, January 14, 2014. A "ligger" attends parties and events with the sole intention of obtaining free food and drink.

7. Billy Parrott, "Number One Hits for the Year: 1979," *New York Public Library*, http://www.nypl.org/blog/2013/09/11/hits-of-1979, last accessed April 9, 2014.

8. WPIX "Radio/Radio", with John Ogle, Dan Neer, and David Byrne (The James Brawley Collection, Rock'n'roll Hall of Fame Archive), August 12, 1979; The tape loops, too, were

a flashpoint for tension between Byrne and his bandmates. Cateforis, *Are We Not New Wave?*, 211.

9. Kozak, "Old and New," 6; "Top LPs & Tape," *Billboard*. September 22, 1979, 75, 77.

10. The Palladium, once known as the Academy of Music, opened in 1927, and was owned by William Fox, head of the Fox Film Corporation. It operated as a movie house through the early 1970s and, following the closing of Fillmore East, hosted rock concerts, beginning in 1971, and was renamed the Palladium in 1976. See John Rockwell, "Pop Music View" *New York Times*. December 26, 1976, http://query.nytimes.com/mem/archive/pdf?res=F00B16FE3E59137A93C4AB1789D95F428785F9, last accessed January 13, 2014; Robert Christgau, "Robert Christgau's Consumer Guide," *Village Voice*. September 3, 1979, 71; Robert Christgau, "Pazz & Jop Product Report," *Village Voice*. September 10, 1979, 63; Robert Christgau, "Voice Choices," *Village Voice*. September 24, 1979, 24.

11. Pat Hackett, ed., *The Andy Warhol Diaries* (New York: Warner, 1989), 243–44.

12. Harvey Leeds, interview by telephone, June 20, 2009. All Leeds quotes from this source unless indicated otherwise; Beck, e-mail correspondence, July 24, 2012.

13. Harron, "Clash in NYC"; Schwartz, in *New York Rocker*, also indicated dissatisfaction with the Thursday show; Barry "DJ Scratchy" Myers, interview by telephone, April 28, 2009.

14. Many thanks to Dave Marin, who helped me connect the audio transcription to this article.

15. Knowles, *Clash City Showdown*, 59.

16. Gray, *Return of the Last Gang in Town*, 280, 321, 345; see Gilbert, *Passion Is a Fashion*, 196, where Rhodes refers to Jones's cocaine habit; Valentine, *New York Rocker*, 264.

17. *Rolling Stone*, "Readers Poll: The Best Album Covers of All Time." June 15, 2011, http://www.rollingstone.com/music/pictures/readers-poll-the-best-album-covers-of-all-time-20110615/the-clash-london-calling-0390006#ixzz1x1fybmbt, last accessed June 6, 2012. Simonon later cited the influence of the bouncers, who kept the audience in their seats. Footage from that show, however, seems to indicate the audience is on their feet and enthusiastic.

18. Beck, e-mail correspondence, July 24, 2012.

19. Gray, *Route 19 Revisited*, 393.

20. Dave Marin, e-mail correspondence, April 12, 2012.

21. Simonon also claimed that he smashed his watch in his outburst and presented it later to Smith as a token of remembrance, frozen at 9:50 p.m. Gilbert, *Passion is a Fashion*, 251. Bollocks. On both nights, the start time was eight p.m., the opening acts included Sam & Dave and The Undertones, and The Clash's set on September 21 lasted close to ninety minutes. Simonon may have smashed his watch that night, but it was either still on central time on their fifth day in the eastern time zone, or the watch was already kaput.

22. Gray, *Return of the Last Gang in Town*, 321; Antonio D'Ambrosio. *Let Fury Have the Hour: The Punk Rock Politics of Joe Strummer* (New York: Nation Books, 2004), xxi; Gilmore, "Clash: Anger on the Left," 22.

23. Ron McCarrell, interview by telephone, June 25, 2012. All McCarrell quotes from this source unless indicated otherwise.

24. Dave DiMartino, "The Clash: Rash Clash Mash in Motor City Bash" (originally December 1979), in Robert Matheu and Brian J. Bowe, *Creem: America's Only Rock'n'Roll Magazine* (New York: Harper Collins, 2007), 156; Chris Salewicz, "The Clash Play Revolution

Rock," *Trouser Press*, March 1980, http://homepage.mac.com/blackmarketclash/Bands/ Clash/recordings/1980/80-00-00%20Tour%20Reviews/The%20Clash%20Play%20 Revolution%20Rock.html, last accessed June 5, 2012; Lester Bangs, "The Fire Next Time," *Soho Weekly News*, March 5, 1980, 53, http://londonsburning.org/art_soho_ weekly_05_80.html, last accessed February 27, 2010.

25. Gray, *Route 19*, 230. Gray, alas, does not indicate how he determined that Jones had full control over the sequencing of the albums. Baker found the claim incredible at best.

26. Mark Meyers, "The Sound of Going to Pieces: The Clash's Surviving Members Recount the Making of a Punk Anthem," *Wall Street Journal*, August 29, 2013, http://online.wsj. com/news/articles/SB10001424127887323407104579037083846165414, last accessed March 27, 2014.

27. "I would take Mick into Vanilla studio on Sundays. One Sunday he was trying out different guitar riffs and I was playing the backing track we had recorded and recording his new riffs. The studio was a haze of ganga-smoke as Mick was constantly rolling up while listening to each take. All of a sudden, a fully uniformed police officer walked straight through the door into the room. Both of us just stared in shock, our stomachs turning to water—it was a certain bust!

"After a few seconds the cop said he was looking for the studio owner. I rose from the mixing desk and guided him back down the stairs to the office. When I got back upstairs Mick had hidden all his grass and we both just sat in silence—too shocked to say a word. The cop HAD to have seen and smelt the clouds of smoke and how we didn't get busted was, and still is, a complete mystery.

"So that's how Jimmy Jazz got its theme (the band called grass 'Jazz')." Barry Auguste, e-mail correspondence, March 9, 2014.

28. Susan Whitall, "The Clash Clamp Down on Detroit," *Creem*, June 1980, 41.

29. Chris Knowles, author of *Clash City Showdown* (and Clash fan/critic *nonpareil*) makes an impressive argument about the virtues of *Rope*: see *Clash City Showdown*, 63–64; Gilbert, *Passion Is a Fashion*, 193.

30. Ibid., 194.

CHAPTER 7

1. Warren Kinsella, *Fury's Hour: A (Sort-of) Punk Manifesto* (Canada: Random House Canada), 121.

2. Frank Rose, "Is Real-Rock Radio Normal?" *New York*, February 4, 1980, 64.

3. Marc Kirkeby, "Will PIX Nix Hard Lix?," *Village Voice*, December 17, 1979, 108; "Tri-State Area's Top 12," WPIX Playlist, January 29, 1980, and "Tri-State Area's Top 12," WPIX Playlist, February 26, 1980.

4. Neer, *FM*, 183; Kirkeby, "Will PIX Nix Hard Lix?," 108.

5. In Stephen Holden's review of the album for *Rolling Stone*, he writes: "Elvis Costello's compositions are probably the worst casualties" among the covers on this LP. "Costello's songs boast some of the snappiest melodies in all of rock & roll [and] demand an unpretty voice like Costello's and fierce, clanging settings. By treating Costello's work as pop lieder, Linda Ronstadt and Peter Asher simply undermine its neurotic urgency." Will Keller interview

with Jane Hamburger, unpublished manuscript; Debra Rae Cohen, "WPIX: Sitting in Limbo," *Village Voice*, March 17, 1980, 72.

6. Neer, *FM*, 271.
7. Arnold, *Route 666*, 22.
8. "DVD Looks Back on The Clash's 'Revolution,'" *Billboard*. April 25, 2008, http://www.billboard.com/news/dvd-looks-back-on-the-clash-s-revolution-1003794881.story#/news/dvd-looks-back-on-the-clash-s-revolution-1003794881.story, last accessed June 26, 2012; see also Howard Bloom, "Breaking the Color Barrier," *Billboard*, August 8, 1981, 16.
9. Prior to the crackdown on peer-to-peer file-sharing sites, digital versions of this bootleg could be found with little difficulty.

AFTERWORD

1. Edward Gibbon, *The Decline and Fall of the Roman Empire, Volumes 1–3* (New York: Everyman's Library, 1993), 552.
2. For a loving tribute to that event, see Todd Inoue, "Modern Love," *Metro, Silicon Valley's Weekly Newspaper*, May 22–28, 2003, http://www.metroactive.com/papers/metro/05.22.03/dotg-0321.html, last accessed May 25, 2012.
3. Gray, *Return of the Last Gang in Town*, 494.
4. Sirius XM deejays provide the playlists, but not the segues, alas. The actual assembly of the playlist is designated either to a machine or less skilled laborers, according to my sources.
5. "XNAS:SIRI Sirius XM Radio Inc. Annual Report." *Morningstar*, December 31, 2011, http://doc.morningstar.com/doccenter.aspx?doccategory=equity&mode=normalview&companyid=0C0000092B&display=XNAS:SIRI&clientid=dotcom&key=9bc0dc0ff19106fc###, last accessed March 28, 2012; John C. Ogg. "Another Credit Rating Hike for SIRIUS XM (SIRI, P)," *24/7 Wall St. Wire*, October 26, 2011, http://247wallst.com/2011/10/26/another-credit-rating-hike-for-sirius-xm-siri-p/#ixzz1qROX9iJo, last accessed March 28, 2012; "Yahoo! Finance: Sirius XM Holdings Inc. (SIRI)," http://finance.yahoo.com/q/bs?s=SIRI+Balance+Sheet&annual, last accessed April 1, 2014.
6. E.P. Thompson, *The Making of the English Working Class* (New York: Vintage, 1966), 12.
7. E.P. Thompson, *Customs in Common* (New York: The New Press, 1993), 467–69, 69.
8. The degree to which McLaren and Rhodes successfully imparted lessons of philosophy and revolution is widely disputed. See, to begin, Greil Marcus, *Lipstick Traces: A Secret History of the Twentieth Century* (New York: Faber & Faber, 1989), and Heylin, *Babylon's Burning*. Still, Simonon embraces the Situationist sentiment when he notes, "The worst [of punk] was that the initial enthusiasm was watered down, which was a shame, as at the time everything seemed possible." Colegrave and Sullivan, *Punk*, 377; Thompson, *Making of the English Working Class*, 13.
9. Douglas, *Listening In*, 268.
10. Neer, *FM*, 273; Pete Fornatale agreed to be interviewed for this project but died before we could schedule an interview. He was a great deejay, a great writer, and a great friend to those who knew him.
11. Neer, *FM*, 183; Metromedia traded publicly from 1961 until 1984, when John Kluge led a group of investors to take Metromedia private in a $1.6 billion deal. See "Metromedia

Company," Funding Universe, http://www.fundinguniverse.com/company-histories/Metromedia-Company-Company-History1.html, last accessed June 5, 2012.

12. Eric W. Rothenbuhler, "Commercial Radio and Popular Music: Processes of Selection and Factors of Influence," *Popular Music and Communication*, edited by James Lull (Newbury Park, NJ: Sage, 1987), 83.

13. Krieger, *Hip Capitalism*, 197.

14. Neer, *FM*, 252–53.

15. "Vox Jox," *Billboard*. January 23, 1982, 35.

16. Christgau, "Avant-Punk," 74.

17. Sam Binkley, *Getting Loose: Lifestyle Consumption in the 1970s* (Durham, NC: Duke University Press, 2007); Jennifer Robison, "Decades of Drug Use: Data From the '60s and '70s," *Gallup*, http://www.gallup.com/poll/6331/decades-drug-use-data-from-60s-70s.aspx, last accessed May 28, 2012; Lana D. Harrison, Michael Backenheimer and James A. Inciardi. "Cannabis use in the United States: Implications for Policy," in Peter Cohen and Arjan Sas, editors, *Cannabisbeleid in Duitsland, Frankrijk en de Verenigde Staten.* (Amsterdam: Centrum voor Drugsonderzoek, Universiteit van Amsterdam, 1996), 206–30, http://www.cedro-uva.org/lib/harrison.cannabis.03.html, last accessed May 28, 2012; Andrew Kopkind, "The Dialectic of Disco," *Village Voice*, February 2, 1979, 11.

18. Roman Kozak, "Davis Hails, McLaren Rails As 1,200 Gather at New Music Meet," *Billboard*, July 31, 1982, 3.

19. John Seabrook, "The Song Machine," *The New Yorker*, March 26, 2012, 48.

20. Ibid., 50.

21. Josh Sanburn, "Advertising Killed the Radio Star: How Pop Music and TV Ads Became Inseparable," *Time*, February 3, 2012, http://business.time.com/2012/02/03/advertising-killed-the-radio-star-how-pop-music-and-tv-ads-became-inseparable/4/, last accessed May 28, 2012.

22. Reports of fisticuffs between Strummer and David Lee Roth seem to be exaggerated, although the pissing match in the press included a sodden Roth who noted—in regards to The Clash's performance the previous night—"The Clash did save the world for about half an hour last night, ladies and gentlemen." Steven Russell, "Sweaty & Filthy & Crazy & Drunk," *Spin*, May 2007, 78.

23. It's uncertain whether the source of this bootleg was the soundboard or a home recording.

24. Kent, *Apathy for the Devil*, 331.

Index

About the Authors

Randal Doane grew up in Northern California on a diet of casseroles, iceberg lettuce, and rockabilly, and currently works as an assistant dean at Oberlin College. Alongside his affinity for great bands from the punk and post-punk era, Randal maintains an affection for the edgier work of Donna Summer. He sends out dispatches on music and culture at stealingalltransmissions.wordpress.com and @stealingclash.

Barry "The Baker" Auguste served as backline roadie and drum tech for The Clash from 1976 to 1983. He lives outside of Philadelphia, blogs periodically at thebaker77.wordpress.com, and is holding out hope for humanity, for now.

About
PM Press

PM Press was founded at the end of 2007 by a small collection of folks with decades of publishing, media, and organizing experience. PM Press co-conspirators have published and distributed hundreds of books, pamphlets, CDs, and DVDs. Members of PM have founded enduring book fairs, spearheaded victorious tenant organizing campaigns, and worked closely with bookstores, academic conferences, and even rock bands to deliver political and challenging ideas to all walks of life. We're old enough to know what we're doing and young enough to know what's at stake.

We seek to create radical and stimulating fiction and nonfiction books, pamphlets, T-shirts, visual and audio materials to entertain, educate, and inspire you. We aim to distribute these through every available channel with every available technology, whether that means you are seeing anarchist classics at our bookfair stalls; reading our latest vegan cookbook at the café; downloading geeky fiction e-books; or digging new music and timely videos from our website.

Contact us for direct ordering and questions about all PM Press releases, as well as manuscript submissions, review copy requests, foreign rights sales, author interviews, to book an author for an event, and to have PM Press attend your bookfair:

PM Press ✦ PO Box 23912 ✦ Oakland, CA 94623
510-658-3906 ✦ info@pmpress.org

Buy books and stay on top of what we are doing at:

www.pmpress.org

MONTHLY SUBSCRIPTION PROGRAM

These are indisputably momentous times—the financial system is melting down globally and the Empire is stumbling. Now more than ever there is a vital need for radical ideas.

In the six years since its founding—and on a mere shoestring—PM Press has risen to the formidable challenge of publishing and distributing knowledge and entertainment for the struggles ahead. With over 250 releases to date, we have published an impressive and stimulating array of literature, art, music, politics, and culture. Using every available medium, we've succeeded in connecting those hungry for ideas and information to those putting them into practice.

Friends of PM allows you to directly help impact, amplify, and revitalize the discourse and actions of radical writers, filmmakers, and artists. It provides us with a stable foundation from which we can build upon our early successes and provides a much-needed subsidy for the materials that can't necessarily pay their own way. You can help make that happen—and receive every new title automatically delivered to your door once a month—by joining as a Friend of PM Press. And, we'll throw in a free T-Shirt when you sign up.

Here are your options:
+ $30 a month: Get all books and pamphlets plus 50% discount on all webstore purchases
+ $40 a month: Get all PM Press releases (including CDs and DVDs) plus 50% discount on all webstore purchases
+ $100 a month: Superstar—Everything plus PM merchandise, free downloads, and 50% discount on all webstore purchases

For those who can't afford $30 or more a month, we're introducing *Sustainer Rates* at $15, $10, and $5. Sustainers get a free PM Press T-shirt and a 50% discount on all purchases from our website.

Your Visa or Mastercard will be billed once a month, until you tell us to stop. Or until our efforts succeed in bringing the revolution around. Or the financial meltdown of Capital makes plastic redundant. Whichever comes first.

BARRED FOR LIFE
How Black Flag's Iconic Logo became Punk Rock's Secret Handshake
Stewart Dean Ebersole
Additional Photographs by Jared Castaldi
$24.95 • 10x8 • 328 pages

Barred for Life is a photo documentary cataloging the legacy of Punk Rock pioneers Black Flag, through stories, interviews, and photographs of diehard fans who wear their iconic logo, The Bars, conspicuously tattooed upon their skin. Author Stewart Ebersole provides a personal narrative describing what made the existence of Punk Rock such an important facet of his and many other people's lives, and the role that Black Flag's actions and music played in soundtracking the ups and downs of living as cultural outsiders.

Stark black-and-white portraits provide visual testimony to the thesis that Black Flag's factual Punk-pioneering role and their hyper-distilled mythology are now more prevalent worldwide then when the band was in service. An extensive tour of North America and Western Europe documents dedicated fans bearing Bars-on-skin and other Black Flag iconography. Nearly four hundred "Barred" fans lined up, smiled/ frowned for the camera, and issued their stories for the permanent record.

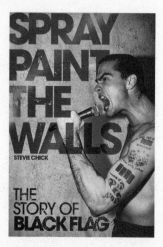

SPRAY PAINT THE WALLS
The Story of Black Flag
Stevie Chick
$19.95 • 9x6 • 432 pages

Spray Paint the Walls tells Black Flag's story from the inside, drawing on exclusive interviews with the group's members, their contemporaries, and the bands they inspired. It's the story of Henry Rollins, and his journey from fan to iconic frontman. And it's the story of Greg Ginn, who turned his electronics company into one of the world's most influential independent record labels while leading Black Flag from punk's three-chord frenzy into heavy metal and free-jazz. Featuring over 30 photos of the band from Glen E. Friedman, Edward Colver, and others.

Sober Living for the Revolution

Hardcore Punk, Straight Edge, and Radical Politics

Edited by Gabriel Kuhn

$22.95 • 9x6 • 304 pages

Since straight edge's origins in Washington, D.C., in the early 1980s, it has been linked to radical thought and action by countless individuals, bands, and entire scenes worldwide. *Sober Living for the Revolution* traces this history.

It includes contributions by numerous artists and activists connected to straight edge, from Ian MacKaye (Minor Threat/Fugazi) and Mark Andersen (Dance of Days/Positive Force DC) to Dennis Lyxzén (Refused/ The (International) Noise Conspiracy) and Andy Hurley (Racetraitor/Fall Out Boy), from bands such as ManLiftingBanner and Point of No Return to feminist and queer initiatives, from radical collectives like CrimethInc. and Alpine Anarchist Productions to the Emancypunx project and many others dedicated as much to sober living as to the fight for a better world.

Positive Force: More Than a Witness

30 Years of Punk Politics In Action

Directed by Robin Bell

$19.95 • DVD • 90 minutes

This feature-length film by Robin Bell skillfully mixes rare archival footage (including electrifying live performances from Fugazi, Bikini Kill, One Last Wish, Nation of Ulysses, Crispus Attucks, Anti-Flag, and more) with new interviews with key PF activists like co-founder Mark Andersen (co-author of Dance of Days) and supporters such as Ian MacKaye, Ted Leo, and Riot Grrrl co-founder Allison Wolfe. Covering a span of 30 years, *More Than A Witness* documents PF's Reagan-era origins, the creation of its communal house, FBI harassment, and the rise of a vibrant underground that burst into the mainstream amidst controversy over both the means and the ends of the movement.

LEFT OF THE DIAL
Conversations with Punk Icons
David Ensminger
$20.00 • 9x6 • 296 pages

Left of the Dial features interviews with leading figures of the punk underground: Ian MacKaye (Minor Threat/Fugazi), Jello Biafra (Dead Kennedys), Dave Dictor (MDC), and many more. Ensminger probes the legacy of punk's sometimes fuzzy political ideology, its DIY traditions, its rupture of cultural and social norms, its progressive media ecology, its transgenerational and transnational appeal, its pursuit of social justice, its hybrid musical nuances, and its sometimes ambivalent responses to queer identities, race relations, and its own history. Passionate, far-reaching, and fresh, these conversations illuminate punk's oral history with candor and humor.

In addition, Ensminger has culled key graphics from his massive punk flyer collection to celebrate the visual history of the bands represented. The book also features rare photographs shot by Houston-based photographer Ben DeSoto during the heyday of punk and hardcore, which capture the movement's raw gusto, gritty physicality, and resilient determination.

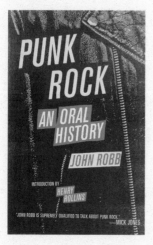

PUNK ROCK
An Oral History
John Robb • Introduction by Henry Rollins
$19.95 • 8.5x5.5 • 584 pages

Vibrant and volatile, the punk scene left an extraordinary legacy of music and cultural change. John Robb talks to many of those who cultivated the movement, such as John Lydon, Lemmy, Siouxsie Sioux, Mick Jones, Chrissie Hynde, Malcolm McLaren, Henry Rollins, and Glen Matlock, weaving together their accounts to create a raw and unprecedented oral history of UK punk. Over 150 interviews capture the excitement of the most thrilling wave of rock 'n' roll pop culture ever. Ranging from its widely debated roots in the late 1960s to its enduring influence on the bands, fashion, and culture of today, this history brings to life the energy and the anarchy as no other book has done.

THE STORY OF CRASS
George Berger
$20.00 • 9x6 • 304 pages

Crass was the anarcho-punk face of a revolutionary movement founded by radical thinkers and artists Penny Rimbaud, Gee Vaucher, and Steve Ignorant. When punk ruled the waves, Crass waived the rules and took it further, putting out their own records, films, and magazines and setting up a series of situationist pranks that were dutifully covered by the world's press. Not just another iconoclastic band, Crass was a musical, social, and political phenomenon.

Commune dwellers who were rarely photographed and remained contemptuous of conventional pop stardom; their members explored and finally exhausted the possibilities of punk-led anarchy. They have at last collaborated on telling the whole Crass story, giving access to many never-before-seen photos and interviews.

THE PRIMAL SCREAMER
Nick Blinko
$14.95 • 8.5x5.5 • 128 pages

A Gothic Horror novel about severe mental distress and punk rock. The novel is written in the form of a diary kept by a psychiatrist, Dr. Rodney H. Dweller, concerning his patient, Nathaniel Snoxell, brought to him in 1979 because of several attempted suicides. Snoxell gets involved in the nascent UK anarcho-punk scene, recording EPs and playing gigs in squatted Anarchy Centers. In 1985, the good doctor himself "goes insane" and disappears.

This semi-autobiographical novel from Rudimentary Peni singer, guitarist, lyricist, and illustrator Nick Blinko, plunges into the worlds of madness, suicide, and anarchist punk. Lovecraft meets Crass in the squats and psychiatric institutions of early '80s England. This new edition collects Blinko's long sought after artwork from the three previous incarnations.

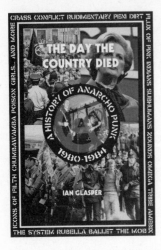

THE DAY THE COUNTRY DIED
A History of Anarcho Punk 1980–1984
Ian Glasper
$24.95 • 9x6 • 496 pages

The Day the Country Died features author, historian, and musician Ian Glasper exploring in minute detail the influential, esoteric UK anarcho punk scene of the early Eighties.

With Crass and Poison Girls opening the floodgates, the arrival of bands such as Zounds, Flux of Pink Indians, Conflict, Subhumans, Chumbawamba, Amebix, Rudimentary Peni, Antisect, Omega Tribe, and Icons of Filth heralded a brand new age of honesty and integrity in underground music. With a backdrop of Thatcher's Britain, punk music became self-sufficient and considerably more aggressive, blending a DIY ethos with activism to create the perfectly bleak soundtrack to the zeitgeist of a discontented British youth.

BURNING BRITAIN
The History of UK Punk 1980–1984
Ian Glasper
$24.95 • 9x6 • 456 pages

As the Seventies drew to a close and the media declared punk dead and buried, a whole new breed was emerging from the gutter. Harder and faster than their predecessors, not to mention more aggressive and political, the likes of Discharge, the Exploited, and G.B.H. were to prove not only more relevant but arguably just as influential.

Burning Britain is the true story of the UK punk scene from 1980 to 1984 told for the first time by the bands and record labels that created it. Covering the country region by region, author Ian Glasper profiles legendary bands like Vice Squad, Angelic Upstarts, Blitz, Anti-Nowhere League, Cockney Rejects, and the UK Subs as well as the more obscure groups like Xtract, The Skroteez, and Soldier Dolls.

DEAD KENNEDYS
Fresh Fruit for Rotting Vegetables, The Early Years
Alex Ogg • Illustrations by Winston Smith
Photographs by Ruby Ray
$17.95 • 9x6 • 224 pages

Dead Kennedys routinely top both critic and fan polls as the greatest punk band of their generation. Their debut full-length, *Fresh Fruit for Rotting Vegetables*, in particular, is regularly voted among the top albums in the genre. *Fresh Fruit* offered a perfect hybrid of humor and polemic strapped to a musical chassis that was as tetchy and inventive as Jello Biafra's withering broadsides. Those lyrics, cruel in their precision, were revelatory. But it wouldn't have worked if the underlying sonics were not such an uproarious rush, the paraffin to Biafra's naked flame.

The book uses dozens of first-hand interviews, photos, and original artwork to offer a new perspective on a group who would become mired in controversy almost from the get-go. It applauds the band's key role in transforming punk rhetoric, both polemical and musical, into something genuinely threatening—and enormously funny. The author offers context in terms of both the global and local trajectory of punk and, while not flinching from the wildly differing takes individual band members have on the evolution of the band, attempts to be celebratory—if not uncritical.

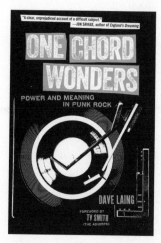

ONE CHORD WONDERS
Power and Meaning in Punk Rock
Dave Laing • Foreword by TV Smith
$17.95 • 9x6 • 224 pages

Originally published in 1985, *One Chord Wonders* was the first full-length study of the glory years of British punk rock. The book argues that one of punk's most significant political achievements was to expose the operations of power in the British entertainment industries as they were thrown into confusion by the sound and the fury of musicians and fans.

BURN COLLECTOR
Collected Stories from One through Nine
Al Burian
$16.00 • 8.5x5.5 • 312 pages

Burn Collector compiles the first nine issues of Al Burian's sporadically published and widely acclaimed personal zine. Beginning in the mid-nineties, Burian distributed his work through the tight-knit network of the DIY punk music scene. *Burn Collector* caught on because of its unusual content—in a scene rife with dogmatic political diatribes and bland record reviews, Burian presented his readers with humorous anecdotes, philosophical musings, and nuanced descriptions of odd locales and curious characters, taken mostly from outside of the punk milieu—and also because of the author's narrative voice, which reflected the literary influences of Celine, Henry Miller, or even David Sedaris more than the influence of his contemporaries in the zine world. The writing in *Burn Collector* blueprinted a post-punk persona that was smart, strange, political but not correct, attached to subculture, but striving also for a connection to the world at large, and to the greater themes of human existence.

A MIX OF BRICKS & VALENTINES
Lyrics 1979–2009
G.W. Sok • Foreword by John Robb
$20.00 • 7.5x5.25 • 384 pages

G.W. Sok co-founded the internationally acclaimed independent Dutch group The Ex in 1979. He became the singer and lyricist, more or less by coincidence, since he wrote the occasional poem and nobody else wanted to sing. At the same time he turned himself into a graphic designer of record sleeves, posters, and books.

A Mix of Bricks & Valentines showcases the lyrics Sok wrote during his three-decade period of Ex-istence. More than 250 songs of agitprop lyrics, poetry, and rantings are included along with an introduction by the author discussing his development as a writer. A foreword by English journalist, author, and musician John Robb (the Membranes, *Punk: An Oral History* and *Death to Trad Rock*) puts the work of Sok into perspective.